Learning and Collective Creativity

This book brings together leading representatives of activity-theoretically oriented and socioculturally oriented research around the world, to discuss creativity as a collective endeavor strongly related to learning to face the societal challenges of our world. As history shows, major accomplishments in arts and technological innovations have allowed us to see the world differently and to identify new learning perspectives for the future that were seldom limited to individual action or isolated activities. This book, although primarily focused on educational institutions, extends its examination of creativity and learning to include other settings (such as government agencies) beyond the limits of schooling.

Annalisa Sannino is academy research fellow at the Centre for Research on Activity, Development, and Learning at University of Helsinki. She is the leading editor of the volume *Learning and Expanding with Activity Theory* (coedited with Harry Daniels and Kris Gutierrez) published in 2009.

Viv Ellis is professor and head of education at Brunel University in London, UK and was until recently co-convener of the Oxford Centre for Sociocultural and Activity Theory Research. He is the lead editor of *Cultural-Historical Perspectives on Teacher Education and Development* (coedited with Anne Edwards and Peter Smagorinsky) published in 2010.

Routledge Research in Education

Learning and Collective Creativity

Activity-Theoretical and
Sociocultural Studies

**Edited by Annalisa Sannino
and Viv Ellis**

Routledge
Taylor & Francis Group
NEW YORK   LONDON

First published 2014
by Routledge
711 Third Avenue, New York, NY 10017

Simultaneously published in the UK
by Routledge
2 Park Square, Milton Park, Abingdon, Oxon OX14 4RN

*Routledge is an imprint of the Taylor & Francis Group,
an informa business*

Library of Congress Cataloging-in-Publication Data
Learning and collective creativity : activity-theoretical and sociocultural
studies / edited by Annalisa Sannino, Viv Ellis.
    pages cm.—(Routledge research in education)
    Includes bibliographical references and index.
1. Creative thinking—Social aspects.   2. Learning.   I. Sannino,
Annalisa, 1975–   II. Ellis, Viv, 1965–
    BF408.L39 2013
    370.15'7—dc23
    2013009106

ISBN13: 978-0-415-65710-5 (hbk)
ISBN13: 978-0-203-07735-1 (ebk)

Typeset in Sabon
by IBT Global.

Printed and bound in the United States of America
by IBT Global.

Contents

PART I
Creative Collective Endeavors as Pathbreakers of New Learning

PART II
Creative Production and Innovation as Collective Activities Crossing Epistemic Boundaries

PART III
Interventions Mobilizing Creative Efforts in Collective Problem Solving and Development of Activities

Figures

Tables

Activity-Theoretical and Sociocultural Approaches to Learning and Collective Creativity
An Introduction

Annalisa Sannino and Viv Ellis

In the social sciences, the topics of learning and creativity have been widely but separately explored. The relation between learning and creativity is still poorly understood, especially when creativity is taken in a collective sense. Creativity has been primarily conceptualized as the quality of an innovative individual or as a novel outcome of individual action. In both these cases, creativity exists as a mental property. Such a view disregards the collective processes of creation, the learning involved in those processes, and their foundational role in cultivating creative minds as well as in producing creative outcomes of societal relevance.

Historically, the domain of creativity research has emphasized the lives and achievements of remarkable individual human beings, leading to perspectives according to which "without the exceptional individual, there is no creative work" (Solomon, Powell, & Gardner, 1999, p. 282). Within such perspectives creativity is defined as

> cognitive processes and overt behaviors that result in new ideas, products or performances and that are judged by some audience to be new, original, useful and/or aesthetically pleasing. . . . Ultimately it is thinking that yields new ideas and new productions that come to be accepted by some audience or constituents. (Feldhusen, 1999, p. 777)

In recent years, however, some authors have focused attention on mundane, collective, and collaborative aspects of creativity (e.g., John-Steiner, 2000; Sawyer, 2012a, 2012b). More inquiries are needed to take into account the tremendous potential of the often unnoticed but continuous work of anonymous collectives, who on a daily basis build thick textures of innovation and change in many constantly transforming practices. When change or transformation are addressed in creativity research, they tend to be primarily conceived as something spectacular or even "legendary" (Kaufman & Beghetto, 2009), something that radically transforms an entire field of endeavor, that changes the world (Feldman, Csikszentmihalyi, & Gardner, 1994).

Predominant lines of research on learning do not include creativity as a central element of their research agendas. Those who have gone beyond the individualist paradigm of creativity have not focused on the relation between creativity and learning. Bringing creativity (as a collective and cultural phenomenon) and learning together opens up a dialogue between two fields of research that have remained separate, even though often tantalizingly close. Examples of such bridging attempts are the proposals for a "systems" or "field" view of creativity (Sternberg, 1988; Sternberg & Lubart, 1999) or for intermediate concepts such as "little c" and "Pro-c" creativity (Craft, 2005; Kaufman & Beghetto, 2009).

Over the last decade, especially, there has been increasing attention by researchers to learning and creativity in school settings (Craft, 2005; Loveless, 2003; Sawyer, 2011; Sefton-Green, Thomson, Jones, & Breslin, 2011), where learning is often bounded to relatively well-stabilized knowledge codified in a formal curriculum. This volume puts creativity and learning in the context of diverse human activities and innovations beyond the limits of schooling. Recently some similar initiatives have appeared, calling for studies of creativity in diverse social contexts. Rickards and De Cock (2009) and Littleton, Taylor, and Eteläpelto (2012), for instance, take a wide perspective on creativity and development within organizations and professional domains.

Activity theory and sociocultural studies can contribute to a novel conceptualization of learning and collective creativity along these lines by revitalizing the Vygotskian tradition on art and imagination. Connery, John-Steiner, and Marjanovic-Shane (2010) take a step in this direction, offering an interesting discussion of Vygotsky's ideas on creativity and imagination, particularly in relation to adolescent development. Although they discuss creativity mainly from the perspective of aesthetic education, with a special focus on school settings, Connery, John-Steiner, and Marjanovic-Shane's work makes an important contribution in identifying the affective and relational dimensions of creativity and its social organization.

This volume brings together leading representatives of activity-theoretically and socioculturally oriented research from different parts of the world, to discuss creativity as a collective endeavor strongly related to learning, poised to face the societal challenges of our world. A common inspirational source of the authors in this endeavor is the work of Lev Vygotsky on creativity, art, and imagination.

CREATIVITY: VYGOTSKY ON ART AND IMAGINATION

The Psychology of Art (1971) is one of Vygotsky's key texts on these themes, comprising the results of his early inquiries during the years from 1915 to 1922 (Leont'ev, 1971). Even though Vygotsky received a contract for the publication by the Leningrad State Editions in 1925 (Vygodskaia & Lifanova, 1996), the book remained unpublished during the author's lifetime.

In the introduction to *The Psychology of Art*, Leont'ev (1971) writes:

When he [Vygotsky] had finished his work on the manuscript [*The Psychology of Art*], he had already become aware of the potentialities of a new direction in the scene of psychology, to which he attributed a very great, even decisive, importance for understanding the mechanisms of artistic creativity and the specific functions of art. He was compelled to follow this direction in order to complete his work on the psychology of art and prove what still remained unproven. (pp. ix–x)

For Sobkin and Leontiev (1992), "Vygotsky's *Psychology of Art* is essential to an understanding of the evolution of his theoretical approach. It influenced profoundly not only his own research, but also that of his colleagues, disciples and present-day followers" (p. 190). Although Vygotsky never comprehensively returned to the thesis presented in *The Psychology of Art,* it is significant that the themes of creativity, imagination, and art consistently reappear throughout his writings in later years (Vygotsky, 1997a, 1998, 1999, 2004). It is the emphasis on these themes that makes Vygotsky's psychological project so distinctive.

For Vygotsky, creativity was a complex dialectical process of historical production and reproduction of artistic creation. From the very beginning, efforts to create and recreate have been made by human beings to keep their lives and societies functioning. Works of art are crystallizations of human creative activities into material objects and of new knowledge which becomes instrumental for future generations. Vygotsky (1971) saw art as "one of the vital functions of society, intimately connected with all the other spheres of social life in its material-historical state" (p.10). This view of art and creativity was to be taken up in the late twentieth century by cultural studies scholars who argued, like Vygotsky, that it was "the fact of creativity in all our living" that "ratified" intentionally aesthetic or artistic productions (Williams, 1965, p. 34).

The vital societal function of art was explicated by Vygotsky (1971) in connection to emotions: "Art systematizes a very special sphere in the psyche of social man—his emotions" (p. 13). According to Vygotsky (1997a), "Art does not just provide an outlet and expression for a particular emotion, it always resolves this emotion and liberates the psyche from its somber influence" (p. 267). Creative activities are therefore both liberating and empowering. Throughout creative production, human beings liberate themselves from *and* gain control of their straightforward reactions and emotions (for a discussion of *The Psychology of Art* with a special focus on emotions, see Smagorinsky, 2011).

Vygotsky's thesis in *The Psychology of Art* (1971) and in his other works on creativity (Vygotsky, 1997a, 1998, 1999, 2004) can today serve as a springboard for much needed discussions about and elaborations of the essence, processes, and potentials of creative production. The arts are the domain in which such creative production discloses itself with the most accentuated traits, but in fact to some degree, all domains of life are concerned with creative processes:

> Any human act that gives rise to something new is referred to as a creative act, regardless of whether what is created is a physical object or some mental or emotional construct that lives within the person who created it and is known only to him (Vygotsky, 2004, p. 7).

The dynamics of artistic creativity can therefore serve as a window to understand creativity at large. Testing the insights stemming from Vygotsky's *The Psychology of Art* (1971) and expressed in his works on creativity (1997a, 1998, 1999, 2004) in contexts of life outside the arts can be particularly fruitful in today's world in which

> creativity becomes a necessary tool for survival for contemporary workers, enabling them to be flexible and entrepreneurial, inside and outside organizations, to re-shape their work identities, negotiate uncertain career pathways and generally manage unpredictable situations, including the precarious circumstances of the knowledge economy. (Littleton, Taylor, & Eteläpelto, 2012, p. 1)

In the following extract from *Educational Psychology*, Vygotsky (1997a) elaborates a view of the centrality of creativity to human existence that echoes the early emphasis in Marx (1937) on the potential of creative human agency to disrupt oppressive social structures:

> Beauty has to be converted from a rare and festive thing into a demand of everyday existence—and creative effort has to nourish every movement, every utterance, every smile of the child's. Potebnya put it quite elegantly when he said that, just as electricity is present not only when there are thunderstorms, so is poetry present not only where there are works of art, but wherever man speaks. This is the poetry "of every moment", and it is this which is the most important of all the tasks of esthetic education. . . . The rule to follow here is not the embellishment of life, but the creative reworking of reality, a processing of things and the movements of things which will illuminate and elevate everyday experience to the level of the creative. (Vygotsky, 1997a, p. 261)

Vygotsky's conceptualization of creativity as a distinctively human capacity was developed in his later discussions of creativity in childhood, adolescence, and adulthood (Vygotsky, 1998, 2004). Collective creativity is presented in this extract from "Imagination and Creativity in Childhood" as the locus for just that distinctively human capacity:

When we consider the phenomenon of collective creativity, which combines all these drops of individual creativity that frequently are insignificant in themselves, we readily understand what an enormous percentage of what has been created by humanity is a product of the anonymous collective creative work of unknown inventors.... A scientific understanding of this phenomenon thus compels us to consider creativity as the rule rather than the exception. (Vygotsky, 2004, p. 10–11)

One of the key dynamics of artistic creation presented by Vygotsky in *The Psychology of Art* (1971) is catharsis—that is, the transfiguration of matter and emotions and their transcendence from the individual to the social. This process crystallizes in the materiality of the product of a creative effort. When the product of a creative effort becomes the object of an activity, it can cross the boundaries of the local circumstances in which it was created and can potentially acquire historical and societal relevance. The way in which the essence of creative activities crystallizes in the object of human work is of great importance also for understanding and promoting learning. "Creativity as a tool for survival" in today's world, to recall the expression used in the quotation above from Littleton, Taylor, and Eteläpelto (2012, p. 1), becomes a process in which individuals learn to face the conflicts in their lives and to deal with the historical contradictions of their time by focusing on their objects and on redesigning their futures.

Imagination plays a crucial role in creative activities that are seen as a means to shape human learning, to influence history, and to redesign the future. As Vygotsky pointed out, "absolutely everything around us that was created by the hand of man, the entire world of human culture, as distinct from the world of nature, all this is the product of human imagination and of creation based on this imagination" (Vygotsky, 2004, p. 9–10).

Vygotsky explicitly referred to imagination as the crucial function that turns creative activities into empowering history-making processes across the past, the present, and the future.

Vygotsky characterized the materialization of what has been imagined as an essential step for a creative effort to be able to have a concrete influence:

A construct of fantasy may represent something substantially new, never encountered before in human experience and without correspondence to any object that actually exists in reality; however, once it has been externally embodied, that is, has been given material form, this crystallized imagination that has become an object begins to actually exist in the real world, to affect other things. In this way imagination becomes reality. (Vygotsky, 2004, p. 21)

At the end of *The Psychology of Art,* Vygotsky strongly emphasizes the future-orientation of artistic creation:

The view that art returns us to atavism rather than projecting us into the future is erroneous. . . . Art is the organization of our future behavior. It is a requirement that may never be fulfilled but that forces us to strive beyond our life toward all that lies beyond it. (p. 253)

Future-orientation is a key element of recent developments of the Vygotskian legacy, in particular in activity-theoretical concepts related to the theory of expansive learning (Engeström, 1987). In the next section, we turn to some key concepts in sociocultural and activity-theoretical research that are taken up in the chapters that follow.

The continuity between *The Psychology of Art* and other more influential works by Vygotsky—and his followers—is particularly apparent in the emphasis on the need for new methodological instruments in psychology. In *The Psychology of Art*, Vygotsky refers to the necessity for the psychologist "of actually creating the object of his study by means of indirect, that is, analytic methods" (Vygotsky, 1971, p. 23). The indirect method is a key and foundational theme in Vygotsky's works, notably developed in *The Historical Meaning of the Crisis in Psychology* (Vygotsky, 1997b), completed in 1926, soon after *The Psychology of Art*.

In *The Historical Meaning of the Crisis in Psychology*, Vygotsky formulated a program for studying human practices that requires the application of an indirect method. The indirect method is a dialectical method of inquiry aimed at uncovering the complexity of reality, which is not immediately accessible with the help of traditional empirical methods. The indirect method proceeds by reconstructing or recreating the object of study through interpretation of its traces and influences (Vygotsky, 1997b, p. 272). In the past 20 years, a number of intervention methods to promote change in work and educational practices have been developed within activity theory inspired by this notion of indirect method (Sannino & Sutter, 2011). The intervention methods of the studies in this volume are examples of the application of this notion of indirect method.

LEARNING: SOME IMPORTANT SOCIOCULTURAL AND ACTIVITY-THEORETICAL CONCEPTS

The brief introductions to key concepts below are offered as a guide to readers of this volume who may not be familiar with the perspectives taken by the authors of the chapters that follow. These concepts potentially offer a vocabulary for expanding creativity research so as to disclose the relationship between collective creativity and learning.

Zone of Proximal Development

The zone of proximal development is one of the best known concepts derived from Vygotsky's work, usually referenced to the collection of papers published as *Mind in Society* in 1978 (Vygotsky, 1978). Vygotsky defines the zone of proximal development as:

> the distance between the actual developmental level as determined by problem solving and the level of potential development as determined through problem solving under adult guidance or in collaboration with more capable peers. (Vygotsky, 1978, p. 86)

From this definition, the distance between these levels is the "zone" or social space within which human development can be stimulated through collaboration. It was this distance that, for Vygotsky, constituted a more reliable and holistic assessment of the child's development than the single measurement of an outcome. Vygotsky pointed out also that "with collaboration, direction, or some kind of help the child is always able to do more and solve more difficult tasks than he can independently" (Vygotsky, 1978, p. 209). In these texts, Vygotsky's interest was in development (rather than in the learning of specific skills or concepts) and in collaboration within collective, social situations (rather than prioritizing the influence of an expert or instructor). But whereas Vygotsky's emphasis was on the development of the individual child in his or her social situation, more recent extensions of Vygotsky's ideas (Engeström, 1987) have emphasized the development of the collective and the role of education in leading that development. These recent advances in sociocultural and activity theory have led to methodological innovations discussed in the chapters of this volume that demonstrate the potential of educational or formative interventions in collective activities through the creation of zones of proximal development.

Object

A. N. Leont'ev, Vygotsky's student and colleague, shifted analytic focus in studying human development from the individual to the collective. Leont'ev distinguished between the automatic *operations* of the individual subject, the individual's or group's goal-oriented *actions,* and the level of *activity* that was given cultural and historical meaning and significance by a shared object—its object-orientedness. Leont'ev's interest was in human activity, and he was a major contributor to the Soviet line of activity theory, arguing that, as Stetsenko puts it, "human psychological processes . . . are object-related in opposition to conceptualizing them as a solipsistic mental realm" (Stetsenko, 2005, p. 75). For Leont'ev, the object of activity was actually its "object-motive," and he explained it as follows:

> The main thing which distinguishes one activity from another, however, is the difference in their objects. It is exactly the object of an activity that gives it a predetermined direction. According to the terminology I have proposed, the object of the activity is its true motive. (Leont'ev, 1978, p. 62)

The importance of the object in activity theory derives from the inter-relatedness of the two concepts, object and activity. Following Leont'ev, culturally or societally significant practices that have historically been undertaken by collectives and have a potentially shared object may be defined as activities. The object is both what engages and motivates the intentional participation of groups of people and what is fashioned and potentially transformed through their participation. As Kaptelinin points out, "the object of activity has a dual status; it is both a projection of the human mind onto the objective world and a projection of the world onto human mind" (Kaptelinin, 2005, p. 5). For researchers, as Kaptelinin also suggests, "the object of activity is a promising analytic tool providing the possibility of understanding not only what people are doing, but also why they are doing it" (Kaptelinin, 2005, p. 5).

This engagement of subjects by an object is what is referred to as object-orientation or object-relatedness. Object-orientation is a dialectical rela-tionship through which both the subjects and the activity change. Davydov, Zinchenko, and Talyzina (1983) point out that "human activity is always directed towards the transformation of an object that is able to satisfy some specific need" (p. 32).

Expansive Learning

Expansive learning is essentially learning something that is not yet there. This goes beyond the acquisition of already well-established sets of knowl-edge and the participation in relatively stable practices. This is a creative type of learning in which learners join their forces to literally create some-thing new. The metaphor of expansion depicts the multidirectional move-ment of learners constructing and implementing a new, wider, and more complex object for their activity. In expansive learning, the object of the activity is reconceptualized and transformed with the help of the mediating means employed and built throughout the process.

The theory of expansive learning is epistemologically grounded in the dialectics of ascending from the abstract to the concrete (Davydov, 1990; Il'enkov, 1977). At the beginning of a process of expansive learning, the object is only abstractly mastered as a partial entity, separated from the functionally interconnected system of the collective activity. By ascending to the concrete, an abstract object is progressively cultivated into concrete systemic manifestations and transformed into a material object that reso-nates with the needs of other human beings as well. These phases often require the subject to struggle and break out of previously acquired con-ceptions in conflict with new emerging ones (Sannino, 2010). This process opens up multiple possibilities for the learner to creatively experiment with new solutions and innovative ideas.

Expansive learning manifests itself in changes in the object of an activity. This can lead to qualitative transformations both at the level of individual actions and at the level of the collective activity and its broader context (Engeström & Sannino, 2010, p. 8). When human beings pursue and grasp the object of their activities, their long-term devoted engagement with the object can not only fulfill their lives, it can also have a significant societal impact.

Activity System

From the perspective of activity theory, the prime unit of analysis is the activity system. The model of an activity system is a representation of the social and historical organization of the concept of "object-orientated, collective, and culturally-mediated human activity" (Engeström & Miettinen, 1999, p. 9). "Culturally-mediated" refers to the role of artifacts—semiotic and material—in the participating subjects' joint work on the object of their activity. The basic components of an activity system, therefore, include the subject, the object, mediating artifacts, the rules of participation, the specific community, and the division of labor among participants (Engeström, 1987).

Modeling the activity system in interventionist efforts reveals the potential of the internal tensions and contradictions as motives for change and transformation. And, as participants are never in the subject position in only one activity system at any one time, their participation in multiple and intersecting activity systems increases the potential for generative contradictions to be experienced, surfaced, and examined both between and within activity systems. The relationship between multiple activity systems and their outcomes (and their multiple perspectives and voices) is presented as the foundation of what is known as the "third generation" of activity theory (Engeström, 1996).

Double Stimulation

Vygotsky's search for new methodological instruments led him to elaborate what he referred to as the principle of double stimulation (Vygotsky, 1987, 1997c). His aim in undertaking this approach to experimental methods in psychology was to challenge the researcher to see psychological processes as dynamic and historical, "undertaking changes right before one's eyes" (Vygotsky, 1978, p. 61). Appropriating the language of behaviorism, Vygotsky described the researcher-set problem as the "stimulus-end" and the potentially helpful tools as the "stimulus-means" or "auxiliary means." By studying the ways in which subjects appropriate these tools in their work on the problem— the object of their activity—Vygotsky argued that it was possible to reveal the ways in which those subjects made sense of the worlds they were acting in:

> We simultaneously offer a second series of stimuli that have a special function. In this way, we are able to study the process of accomplishing a task by aid of the specific auxiliary means: Thus we are able to discover the inner structure and development of higher mental processes. (Vygotsky, 1978, p. 74)

In recent activity-theoretical research, double stimulation is at the core of intervention methods such as the Change Laboratories (Engeström, 2007; Sannino, 2011). In a Change Laboratory intervention, the "auxiliary means" is often a model of the activity system, represented diagrammatically and used with participants in a joint analysis of data generated from the current practices.

Contradictions

In an activity-theoretical analysis of change, the concept of contradiction is of great importance. Although sometimes sociocultural and other analyses refer to "tensions" much more loosely, contradictions in activity-theoretical terms are not only personally experienced, ontological dilemmas but also systemic and structural constraints that need to be overcome and broken away from in order for human agency to be exercised and new forms of activity to emerge. The importance of contradiction as a concept reveals the influence of Marxian historical analysis in the elaboration of activity theory. Vygotsky's analysis of human development draws on Marx's (e.g., Marx & Engels, 1964) dialectical materialism and understanding of historical change as the sublation of simultaneously ideal and material oppositions by a synthesis that both supersedes and contains them.

Engeström's theory of expansive learning (1987) poses contradictions as the generators of change in the development of activity systems. Historically new forms of activity emerge when internal contradictions within the activity system are resolved. Participants in activity systems, upon recognizing the constraints of their situation (sometimes expressed as a "double-bind" or a situation characterized by conflicting demands), appropriate available cultural tools in order to break away from that situation and to transform it. Engeström (1987) identified four types of contradictions within activity systems beginning with the primary contradiction (under capitalist conditions) between use value and exchange value, most importantly with reference to the shared object. Secondary contradictions emerge between components of the activity system. Tertiary contradictions arise from the introduction of qualitatively new forms of the activity that are resisted by deep-seated old dynamics in the system. And quaternary contradictions emerge between interacting activity systems that need to reorganize their relations.

The Russian philosopher Il'enkov noted that historically new modes of action and production, "before becoming generally accepted and recognized, first emerge[s] as a certain deviation from previously accepted and codified norms" (Il'enkov, 1982, pp. 83–84). Such historically new forms of activity across various social worlds, emerging as Il'enkov suggested out of contradictions, as exceptions from the rule, may be regarded as history-making creative endeavors.

THE THEMATIC STRUCTURE AND CHAPTERS OF THE BOOK

This book proposes to see learning and collective creativity as foundationally intertwined processes. Such a view opens up new vistas for the study of cognition and human activity in the following three ways, which correspond to the three parts of the book.

Part 1: Creative collective endeavors are pathbreakers of new learning that involve clashes with historically stabilized knowledge and traditions.

Karin Johansson takes up the pressures in contemporary global societies that bring musicians to constantly face new learning challenges to develop the meaning of their music and ways to create favorable conditions to perform it. Professional music making is becoming an increasingly fragile domain due to pervasive insecurity and unpredictable economic developments. In these circumstances, creativity and learning become a necessity for reaching innovative outcomes. Yet the shaping and transformation of artistic musical activities is often constrained by the burden of centuries-old traditions and consolidated collective knowledge. Innovative initiatives in the domains of music usually clash with conservative institutional orientations worshiping cultural preservation and craftsmanship transmission.

The activity-theoretical analysis undertaken by Johansson articulates the historically layered complexity of learning and collective creativity in two empirical cases of instrumental tuition of vocal students and professional organ improvisation. The chapter illustrates how engagement with historical tensions shapes collective creativity and learning that challenge established norms and promote new modes of musical expression and the exploration of new ways of knowing.

Annalisa Sannino examines critical transitions toward creative production of culture as foundational steps in learning to create. The critical transition to creative writing in the biography of the French existentialist writer Simone de Beauvoir is used as an example to highlight the role of personal and societal struggles in processes of creation and learning. These struggles are undertaken because charting new terrains of knowledge requires positioning within an intellectual landscape in a given culture and in specific historical circumstances, often hostile toward the new.

De Beauvoir's transition from her successful years as a student to the difficult 10 years after her graduation, filled with unsuccessful attempts to publish her first book, illustrates how the process of creation and learning can take the shape of a prolonged struggle with and breaking away from oppressive boundaries of the dominant intellectual culture. The analysis shows how such struggles are essential aspects of transitions toward the creation of something genuinely novel. Such transitions are depicted as journeys along hostile, unpaved paths and toward directions that are only vaguely perceptible at the beginning.

Katsuhiro Yamazumi presents a case of intervention research in a Japanese school aimed at challenging the typical separation of educational institutions from direct societal influence and collaboration. In partnership with local farmers, experts, volunteering citizens, and a governmental agency, the school in the longitudinal intervention became involved in hybrid educational activities for the revitalization of a local plant, traditionally consumed as a vegetable, but brought to the verge of extinction with increasing urbanization. Collective learning and creative efforts by the multiple parties involved led to innovative outcomes of societal relevance for the local communities.

With the help of this example, the author emphasizes that learning and collective creativity in school settings require going beyond traditional methods of teaching and learning that primarily focus on cultural transmission and preservation. Instead, learning and collective creativity are at play when schools engage themselves in processes of cultural creation and transformation that transcend the school's institutional boundaries and respond to pressing societal needs.

Kai Hakkarainen, Kaisa Hytönen, Juho Makkonen, Pirita Seitamaa-Hakkarainen, and *Hal White* address the challenge of contemporary universities to educate doctoral students in knowledge-creating practices resulting in high-level academic productivity. The authors focus in particular on the collective creativity of academic research, using the case of the adoption by educational sciences of the article-based approach to doctoral education previously typical to natural sciences. Based on interviews with leading European scientists, the study highlights the role of cultures and communities as key factors contributing to creativity. Creativity is described as a systemic phenomenon emerging routinely in the shared knowledge practices of innovative research communities and their networks.

The authors point out that the scope of doctoral education is significantly broadened when students' work on their doctoral theses is supported by the collective practices of research teams and by coauthoring refereed journal articles. Collective creativity is at play when novices and experienced researchers share the scientific practices and knowledge accumulated over time by the research community to which they belong. Collective creativity understood in these terms is referred to as the foundation of practices of scientific excellence. Immediate immersion of doctoral students in these advanced research practices is possible and allows these students to avoid painful trial-and-error actions typical to those who are pursuing doctoral studies without the support of a research community.

Part 2: Creative production and innovation, commonly reduced to individual skills and expertise or individual genius, also materialize as collective activities that cross epistemic boundaries and work through their contradictions and historical transformations.

Anne Edwards and *Marc Thompson* focus on the learning and collective creativity involved in the formation of leaders' organizational narratives and reconfiguring of organizational practices. Their analysis highlights how leaders mobilize available human capital and emotional resources when taking forward changes in new multiprofessional configurations of services to support the well-being of vulnerable children and young people. The analysis shows how collective and creative envisioning of future practices takes shape among the leaders, creating a shared and contestable narrative that represents priorities of the multiple professionals involved.

The study is situated in the context of recent policy changes in the UK that have led to dramatic cuts of funding for welfare services and increasing loss of professional identity for the involved practitioners. In this context, leaders are faced with the challenge of realigning disrupted practices and working resourcefully with limited and damaged human capital. The study shows how the leaders developed future-oriented organizational narratives built on "what matters" to the parties involved, which reflected and sustained the practitioners' identities and supported their collective work. These narratives enabled the participants to agentively act together on demanding work problems and to shape future directions for the development of the practitioners and the practices.

Sten Ludvigsen and *Monika Nerland* focus on the development and use of standardized knowledge in the three professional and organizational settings of nursing, software development, and accountancy. Because of the introduction of new tools or requirements and increasingly constraining standards, in these three knowledge-intensive contexts, practitioners face the challenge of localizing and sharing scientific or standardized knowledge for achieving creative solutions to novel local tasks.

Learning and collective creativity involved in such contexts in the process of solving novel problems requires recontextualization, transformation, and expansion of universal knowledge, standards and procedures to local meaningful actions and circumstances. Learning and collective creativity are shown to materialize as processes of knowledge construction and knowledge sharing for the solution of new problems in social practices. Asymmetries of different positions, already established knowledge and institutional histories among the participants in the sharing process, are seen by the authors as factors enhancing learning and creativity.

Harry Daniels and *Peter Johnson* focus on the challenges of end-user services formed by assembling originally separate and independent agencies. The authors examine cases in which it is necessary to mobilize truly collective efforts to provide seamless and fit-for purpose services to users whose needs are increasingly specific and constantly evolving.

With the help of examples of children's services and disaster response emergency services, the authors discuss the learning and collective creativity at play in the sociocultural practices of such service providers. The examples illustrate situations in which the service agencies are confronted with problems for which there is not an appropriate answer available. The authors advocate the adoption of information-technology tools able to support creative interactions, collective awareness of new complex problems, and distributed attempts to solve them.

Reijo Miettinen focuses on creative encounters between experts representing different activities that lead to processes of important innovative product development. The collaborative agency and the creative interactions at play in such encounters are seen as deriving from the meeting of individuals' needs and a shared object of activity.

Two product development processes are used as examples to illustrate how the complementarity of historically formed knowledge and expert resources can mobilize collective creative endeavors leading to important new innovations and technologies. The study describes the creative encounter of a physicist and research manager of a small manufacturing enterprise of radioactivity measuring devices with a client and user of their products who was a university professor in a department of molecular endocrinology. The encounter led to the development of a new immunodiagnostic method. The second example concerns the creative encounter between the CEO of a biotechnology enterprise and the leader of a research group on hot-spring bacteria, which led to the study of thermo-stable enzymes. The chapter points to the crucial importance for collaborative learning and creativity of developing spaces that allow encounters across epistemic boundaries similar to those discussed in the examples.

Part 3: The study of collective creativity and learning will benefit from interventions aimed at mobilizing creative efforts of practitioners and communities in problem solving and development of activities.

Klaus-Peter Schulz and *Silke Geithner* address the challenge of fostering collective creativity and learning in organizational development. The authors discuss the use of play in corporate environments to support collective interactions to resolve emerging contradictions in the organization and to build new perspectives for the future.

An application of the "serious play" method using LEGO bricks is discussed to illustrate how such means allow practitioners to bridge their different perspectives to develop solutions based on an understanding of the contradictory forces at play in the organization. The authors reflect on the use of this method in a product development and design research institute that needed to develop a new vision for its future. The use of this method allowed the participants to adopt a systemic point of view on the research institute beyond the traditional disciplinary and intraorganizational boundaries.

Gerhard Fischer discusses learning and collective creativity as a necessity for addressing fundamental problems of today's world, problems that are increasingly systemic, ill-defined, and unique. The study brings attention to the shift from consumer cultures, based on production and passive consumption of finished goods, to cultures of participation, which allow people to actively contribute to creation processes and to the solution of personally meaningful problems. Cultures of participation are seen by the author as key new opportunities and challenges to foster learning and collective creativity.

The chapter presents four examples of sociotechnical environments that serve as effective support tools for cultures of participation, collective creativity, and learning. The examples show how these environments give space to diverse voices and perspectives, allow accessibility to the work and ideas of all users, and contribute to community development.

With a particular emphasis on the context of educational reforms in the UK, *Viv Ellis* discusses the current vulnerability of the teaching profession due to neoliberal pressures toward marketization of public services that often produces isolation among teachers within their schools and among schools themselves. Against this background, learning and collective creativity are conceptualized as essential, defining features of the professional cultures of teaching through which the actions of individual practitioners can gain meaning and societal significance.

The study brings attention to the need of community-based professional creativity developed through future-oriented intellectual interdependence where teaching practitioners jointly nourish the object of their activity. A way to foster professional creativity is presented with the help of the example of a three-year intervention effort involving English language and literature teachers in several schools, aimed at stimulating the relational development of collaborative and creative ties among them.

Yrjö Engeström examines learning and collective creativity as processes of formation of new concepts that guide and organize future work. An emergent concept is described as taking shape through multiple attempts at representing and stabilizing which, although never fully controllable or complete, crystallize collective learning potentials and creative novelty for transforming work.

The author offers as examples two interventionist projects that led to the formation of such concepts, one in a university library and another one in a home care service for the elderly. Concept formation transpires from these cases as a creative and collective process embedded in the space of the local material and social circumstances in which the practitioners examine, debate, and work out the contradictions in their work activities.

CONCLUDING REMARKS

Learning and collective creativity are reflected upon in these chapters with a particular emphasis on endeavors attempting to meet contemporary societal challenges. Such endeavors include various projects of design, innovation, and the arts and have indisputable learning and creative potentials. The analysis of such endeavors can significantly enrich our understanding of learning and collective creativity.

Art and innovation in these cases are hybridized with various kinds of practical activities, usually not conceived as settings of artistic or aesthetic production or innovation. In this volume, creativity is seen as permeating our daily activities. Whereas studies of situated learning in everyday contexts have mainly dealt with the acquisition of already existing expertise, in this book, the focus is on creation of new practices and new knowledge in contexts of everyday activity. Learning emerges as movement through historical transformations.

Collective creativity and learning are seen here as indispensable for facing the societal challenges of our time. The book as a whole is an argument for collective involvement in searches for creative solutions to the pressing societal problems of today's world. The case studies of interventionist attempts included in the book are examples of ways to mobilize collective efforts of professional practitioners and communities in creative societal problem solving and learning.

ACKNOWLEDGMENTS

The initial idea of this book originated during the International Workshop for Sociocultural and Activity-Theoretical Research Centers, held in Helsinki, on December 21–22, 2009. The workshop brought together leading representatives of socioculturally and activity-theoretically oriented research centers around the world, to discuss and shape an agenda for collaboration on issues of collective creativity and learning. The workshop was organized by the Center for Research on Activity, Development, and Learning (director Yrjö Engeström). Researchers from the following research centers from six countries joined the workshop at the Center for Research on Activity, Development, and Learning: Center for Lifelong Learning and Design, Boulder, Colorado (director Gerhard Fischer); Center for Human Activity Theory, Osaka, Japan (director Katsuhiro Yamazumi); Centre for Sociocultural and Activity Theory Research, Bath, UK (director Harry Daniels); Intermedia, Oslo, Norway (director Sten Ludvigsen); the Laboratory of Comparative Human Cognition, San Diego, California (director Michael Cole); the Linnaeus Centre for Research on Learning, Interaction, and Mediated Communication in Contemporary Society, Göteborg, Sweden (director Roger Säljö); and Oxford Centre for Sociocultural and Activity Theory Research, Oxford, UK (director Anne Edwards). The workshop initiated substantive discussion and generation of ideas that led to this volume.

Many colleagues contributed to the preparation of this volume with insightful comments and invaluable support. Our thanks go to the following colleagues for reviewing the chapters: Tony Burgess (University of London, UK); Chris Davies (University of Oxford, UK); Alaster Douglas (Roehampton University, UK); Valerie Farnsworth (University of Leeds, UK); Sten Ludvigsen (University of Oslo, Norway); David Guile (University of London, UK); Kai Hakkarainen (University of Turku, Finland); Ken Jones (University of London, UK); Anu Kajamaa (University of Helsinki, Finland); Monika Nerland (University of Oslo, Norway); Monica Nilsson (Stockholm University, Sweden); Sami Paavola (University of Helsinki, Finland); Klaus-Peter Schulz (ICN Business School Nancy-Metz, France); Berthel Sutter (Blekinge Institute of Technology, Sweden); and Katsuhiro Yamazumi (Kansai University, Japan). We want to express our big thanks to Hannele Kerosuo (University of Helsinki, Finland) for helping during the first steps in the conception of this book. Our deepest gratitude goes to Yrjö Engeström (University of Helsinki, Finland) in supporting and guiding us through challenging phases of this work.

The editing of this volume was supported in part by an Academy Research Fellowship granted to Annalisa Sannino (No. 264972) by the Academy of Finland, Research Council for Culture and Society.

REFERENCES

Connery, M. C., John-Steiner, V., & Marjanovic-Shane, A. (2010). *Vygotsky and creativity: A cultural-historical approach to play, meaning making, and the arts.* New York, NY: Peter Lang.

Craft, A. (2005). *Creativity in schools.* Abingdon, England: Routledge.

Davydov, V. V. (1990). *Types of generalization in instruction: Logical and psychological problems in the structuring of school curricula.* Reston, VA: National Council of Teachers of Mathematics.

Davydov, V. V., Zinchenko, V. P., & Talyzina, N. F. (1983). The problem of activity in the works of A. N. Leontiev. *Soviet Psychology, 21,* 31–42.

Engeström, Y. (1987). *Learning by expanding: An activity-theoretical approach to developmental research.* Helsinki, Finland: Orienta-Konsultit.

Engeström, Y. (1996). Developmental work research as educational research: Looking ten years back and into the zone of proximal development. *Nordisk Pedagogik: Journal of Nordic Educational Research, 16,* 131–143.

Engeström, Y. (2007). Putting activity theory to work: The change laboratory as an application of double stimulation. In H. Daniels, M. Cole, & J. V. Wertsch (Eds.), *The Cambridge companion to Vygotsky* (pp. 363–382). Cambridge, England: Cambridge University Press.

Engeström, Y., & Miettinen, R. (1999). Introduction. In Y. Engeström, R. Miettinen, & R-L. Punamaki (Eds.), *Perspectives on activity theory* (pp. 1–18). Cambridge, England: Cambridge University Press.

Engeström, Y., & Sannino, A. (2010). Studies of expansive learning: Foundations, findings and future challenges. *Educational Research Review, 5*, 1–24.

Feldman, D. H., Csikszentmihalyi, M., & Gardner, H. (1994). *Changing the world: A framework for the study of creativity*. Westport, CT: Praeger Publishers/Greenwood Publishing.

Feldhusen, J. F. (1999). Talent and creativity. In M. A. Runco & S. Pritzker (Eds.), *Encyclopedia of creativity* (Vol. 2, pp. 623–627). San Diego, CA: Academic Press.

Il'enkov, E. V. (1977). *Dialectical logic: Essays on its history and theory*. Moscow, Russia: Progress Publishers.

Il'enkov, E. V. (1982). *The dialectics of the abstract and the concrete in Marx's Capital*. Moscow, Russia: Progress Publishers.

John-Steiner, V. (2000). *Creative collaboration*. New York, NY: Oxford University Press.

Kaptelinin, V. (2005). The object of activity: Making sense of the sense-maker. *Mind, Culture and Activity, 12*(1), 4–18.

Kaufman, J. C., & Beghetto, R. A. (2009). Beyond big and little: The four C model of creativity. *Review of General Psychology, 13*, 1–12.

Leont'ev, A. N. (1971). Introduction. In L. S. Vygotsky (Ed.), *The psychology of art* (pp. v–xi). Cambridge, MA: MIT Press.

Leont'ev, A. N. (1978). *Activity, consciousness and personality*. Englewood Cliffs, NJ: Prentice Hall.

Littleton, K., Taylor, S., & Eteläpelto, A. (2012). Special issue introduction: Creativity and creative work in contemporary working contexts. *Vocations and Learning, 5*(1), 1–4.

Loveless, A. (2003). *Creativity, technology and learning: A review of recent literature*. Bristol, England: Futurelab.

Marx, K. (1937). *The eighteenth brumaire of Louis Bonaparte*. Moscow, Russia: Progress Publishers.

Marx, K., & Engels, F. (1964). *The German ideology in collected works volume 5: Marx and Engels: 1845–1847*. Moscow, Russia: Progress Publishers.

Rickards, T., & De Cock, C. (2009). Understanding organizational creativity: Toward a multiparadigmatic approach. In M. Runco (Ed.), *The creativity research handbook* (Vol. 2, pp. 1–31). Creskill, NJ: Hampton Press.

Sannino, A. (2010). Teachers' talk of experiencing: Conflict, resistance and agency. *Teaching and Teacher Education, 26*(4), 838–844.

Sannino, A. (2011). Activity theory as an activist and interventionist theory. *Theory & Psychology, 21*(5), 571–597.

Sannino, A., & Sutter, B. (2011). Special issue introduction. Cultural-historical activity theory and interventionist methodology: Classical legacy and contemporary developments. *Theory & Psychology, 21*(5), 557–570.

Sawyer, R. K. (Ed.). (2011). *Structure and improvisation in creative teaching*. New York, NY: Oxford University Press.

Sawyer, R. K. (2012a). *Explaining creativity: The science of human innovation*. Oxford, England: Oxford University Press.

Sawyer, R. K. (2012b). Extending sociocultural theory to group creativity. *Vocations and Learning, 5*(1), 59–75.

Sefton-Green, J., Thomson, P., Jones, K., & Breslin, L. (Eds.). (2011). *The Routledge international handbook of creative learning*. London, England: Routledge.

Smagorinsky, P. (2011). Vygotsky's stage theory: The psychology of art and the actor under the direction of perezhivanie. *Mind, Culture, and Activity, 18*, 319–341.

Sobkin, V. S., & Leontiev, D. A. (1992). The beginning of a new psychology: Vygotsky's psychology of art. In G. C. Cupchik & J. László (Eds.), *Emerging visions of the aesthetic process: Psychology, semiology, and philosophy* (pp. 185–193). Cambridge, England: Cambridge University Press.

Solomon, B., Powell, K., & Gardner, H. (1999). Multiple intelligences. In M. A. Runco & S. R. Pritzker (Eds.), *Encyclopedia of creativity* (Vol. 2, pp. 273–283). London, England: Academic Press.

Sternberg, R. J. (Ed.). (1988). *The nature of creativity: Contemporary psychological perspectives*. Cambridge, England: Cambridge University Press.

Sternberg, R. J., & Lubart, T. I. (1999). The concept of creativity: Prospects and paradigms. In R. J. Sternberg (Ed.), *Handbook of creativity* (pp. 5–15). Cambridge, England: Cambridge University Press.

Stetsenko, A. (2005). Activity as object-related: Resolving the dichotomy of individual and collective planes of activity. *Mind, Culture and Activity, 12*(1), 70–88.

Vygodskaia, G. L., & Lifanova, T. M. (1996). *Lev Semenovich Vygotskii: Zizn', dejatel'nost', strihi k portretu* [Lev Semenovich Vygotsky: Life, career, brushstrokes of a portrait]. Moscow, Russia: Smysl.

Vygotsky, L. S. (1971). *The psychology of art*. Cambridge, MA: MIT Press.

Vygotsky, L. S. (1978). *Mind in society: The development of higher psychological processes*. Translated by M. Lopez-Morillas. Edited by M. Cole, V. John-Steiner, S. Scribner, & E. Souberman. Cambridge, MA: Harvard University Press.

Vygotsky, L. S. (1987). Lectures on psychology. In *The collected works of L. S. Vygotsky: Problems of general psychology* (Vol. 1, pp. 289–373). New York, NY: Plenum.

Vygotsky, L. S. (1997a). *Educational psychology*. Boca Raton, FL: St. Lucie Press.

Vygotsky, L. S. (1997b). The historical meaning of the crisis in psychology: A methodological investigation. In *The collected works of L. S. Vygotsky: Problems of the theory and history of psychology* (Vol. 3, pp. 233–343). New York, NY: Plenum.

Vygotsky, L. S. (1997c). The instrumental method in psychology. In *The collected works of L. S. Vygotsky: Problems of the theory and history of psychology* (Vol. 3, pp. 85–89). New York, NY: Plenum.

Vygotsky, L. S. (1998). Imagination and creativity in the adolescent. In *The collected works of L. S. Vygotsky: Child psychology* (Vol. 5, pp. 151–166). New York, NY: Plenum.

Vygotsky, L. S. (1999). On the problem of the psychology of the actor. In *The collected works of L. S. Vygotsky: Scientific legacy* (Vol. 6, pp. 237–244). New York, NY: Plenum.

Vygotsky, L. S. (2004). Imagination and creativity in childhood. *Journal of Russian and East European Psychology, 42*(1), 7–97.

Williams, R. (1965). *The long revolution*. London, England: Pelican Books.

Part I

Creative Collective Endeavors as Pathbreakers of New Learning

1 Musical Creativity and Learning across the Individual and the Collective

Karin Johansson

From the perspective of Vygotsky's (2004) dialectical view on fantasy and imagination, creativity is a necessary part of development and maturation and, simultaneously, "always based on a lack of adaptation which gives rise to needs, motives and desires" (p. 29). It is thus always socially situated in a present-day situation that includes a conflict, a relationship to history, and a direction toward the future. May (1994), who emphasizes the importance of a spiritual creativity in art as a complement to technological innovative development sees creativity as the artist's "meeting with the world on a level where the split between the subject and the object is undone" (p. 49). Through art, the individual has an original and unique possibility to express, transform, and transcend the given limitations of social existence. This often implies an inherent challenging of status quo for which "divergence" or "divergent thinking" (Cropley, 2006) is needed. This might be the reason for both the fascination with creativity and the many attempts to define and regulate it as a phenomenon; it is a two-edged sword with possibly dark and destructive aspects (Cropley, 2010).

Sahlin (1997) argues that any organization can only take a limited amount of creative persons before it collapses and suggests that they have to develop "effective tools and methods to suppress creativity" (p. 65). In educational systems, this kind of suppression might be brought about both by the identification of creativity with adaptability and general flexibility. The still prevalent discourse on creativity as an entirely positive asset and a tool for self-fulfillment then "supports a liberal political position and the reading of economic, social and political issues as problems of personal growth" (Prichard, 2002, p. 271). A formation of the creative individual as a genial and bohemian outcast (Dawson, 1997) serves the function of placing social responsibility with the individual only and, furthermore, renders art socially harmless. In this context, the discipline of artistic research has much to add by shedding light on processes of artistic work from the inside.

A growing number of studies in the field of artistic research (e.g., Biggs & Karlsson, 2011), show that it is possible to investigate and describe processes of artistic expression, interpretation, and knowledge creation from insiders' perspectives. Even though processes of musical creativity and learning are still often described as "largely shrouded in mystery" (Juslin, 2001, p. 410) in scientific contexts, experiences from this young discipline (e.g., Frisk, 2008; Hultberg, 2005a; Östersjö, 2008) point to how all situations of tuition, performance, improvisation, composition, or listening involve aspects both of incorporating existing knowledge and imagining new musical dimensions (Hargreaves, Miell, & MacDonald, 2012; Johansson, 2012a).

Learning and creativity on individual and collective levels interact and form a dynamic situation where performers, teachers, and students as well as audiences and music institutions may experience tensions that relate to the interaction between receptivity, creativity, and change. In this chapter, I focus on collective musical creativity and learning from the perspective of cultural-historical activity theory (CHAT). In terms of CHAT, this can be formulated as a relationship between internalization, externalization, and transformation: "Internalization is related to reproduction of culture; externalization as creation of new artifacts makes possible its transformation" (Engeström, Miettinen, & Punamäki, 1999, p. 10). This relationship is clearly illustrated by musicians in the so-called classical tradition, which is what I deal with in this chapter.

Music institutions like orchestras, conservatoires, academies, and the Church usually hold a tension between tradition and innovation. Whereas knowledge of the tradition is a prerequisite for system-developing creativity, acquiring the basic skills needed for becoming an accepted expert is a time-consuming task that is often opposed to creative, experimental acting and thinking. On the one hand, "creativity, and more generally, skill in coping with novel environments, is more important than ever," and on the other hand, "schools around the world, today as in the past, on average, do little to develop creativity" (Sternberg & Kaufman, 2010, p. 475). As craftsmen, all musicians are trained to internalize and reproduce the musical culture and, as artists, to externalize and transform it. A successful musician must be able to balance craftsmanship and artistic initiative, which means that a clear division between "learning" on the one hand and "creativity" on the other hand is not possible or fruitful to uphold. In most musical practices, reproductive and innovative aspects coexist, and one of the aims of this chapter is to illustrate and discuss how creativity and learning are inextricably connected in the process of creating new knowledge and art works in music. Here, I see the formulation of creativity as "breaking the rules in acceptable ways" (Folkestad, 2012, p. 195) as productive, because it points to how transformation and development are situated in contexts where rules are established and upheld by a community.

Sahlin (2001) suggests that there are two types of creativity, rule creativity and concept creativity, where the former is not regarded as "true" creativity, because it does not represent a new system or introduce new concepts, whereas the latter is exemplified with John Cage's piano piece 4' 33' as breaking with conventions and traditions—thus, something new. Still, the ability to perceive that a piano piece consisting of silence represents something "new" requires a familiarity and identification with the established system, as well as a readiness to accept challenges to it. The ideal creative product can then be understood and categorized by the audience, at the same time as it is experienced as different and "new" enough to result in surprise. "Breaking the rules in acceptable ways" thus depends on and results in a negotiated agreement concerning how knowledge and creativity are defined at a certain moment in history.

MUSIC MAKING AS INDIVIDUAL AND COLLECTIVE CREATIVITY

In today's society, music plays an important part in many people's lives even if they do not perform or create music themselves. Music is simultaneously a product on the market as a commodity in the commercial creative industry and a verb (Small, 1998): To "music" is a natural part of human culture, and the way music is made in a society describes its history and its present but also foretells its future. Music stands at the crossroads of now and then: It is simultaneously reproductive *and* productive. Jacques Attali (2011) calls it prophetic, in the sense that "its styles and economic organization are ahead of the rest of society because it explores, much faster than material reality can, the entire range of possibilities in a given code" (Attali, 2011, p. 11). From this perspective, performers, composers, listeners, and consumers all take part in a global process of "musicking" regardless of on what level of musical action, initiative, and professionality they are. They are all constantly learning the meanings of music and creating the conditions for how to "music" in our society.

In the Vygotskian tradition, this anonymous, collective, and continuous creativity is considered a necessary condition for the emergence of ideas or products that become recognized as individual, surprising, new, and important by the society. It constitutes the horizon, or field, to which creative agents relate to make themselves understood and appreciated by the surrounding world. Speaking of Vygotsky's model of internalized interaction, Sawyer (2003) says: "Artist and scientists who do not internalize such a model are not likely to generate products judged as creative" (p. 133). Individual musicians are thus always integrated in an intertextual network where, as suggested by Folkestad (2012), music making involves a double dimension of collectivity:

> There are two levels of collective communication in the process of collective, creative music-making: (1) one interpersonal, or "interpsychological" functioning (Wertsch, 1997, p. 226), between the individuals of the working group of the collective activity, and also (2) one intrapersonal, or "intrapsychological" (p. 228), a dialogue with the collective experiences and knowledge of previous composers, mediated by

the tools in use. The latter also constitutes the collective dimension in "individual" activities. (p. 198)

This means that even when musicians practice or play in solitude, they are not alone—they conduct and take part in a dialogue with the collected experience of the musical culture. Situations of collective creativity and learning in music may be, for example, the (re)production of composed or improvised music that has or has not been heard before, the expansion and (re)construction of new formats for expression, or processes of (re)thinking in music making. These present the participants with what Krüger (1998) calls an epistemological space that "regulates what possibilities of experience the actors involved are offered" (p. 172) and which is hence also linked to their possible creative space. According to Vygotsky (2004), the range and strength of imagination is directly linked to experience and knowledge. The ability to be creative is a function of lived experience and always related to a need for social adaptation or change. What he calls "crystallization, or the transformation of imagination into reality" (p. 28) is the final point of a full creative circle, that, in order to be complete, ends with the implementation of new external images that have been constructed through processes of dissociation, association, and concept formation.

This transformative nature and power of creativity concerns both persons and cultural domains. When participants in a certain practice have "internalized all that the domain has to offer at the particular historical moment and must . . . try to make socially acceptable meaning out of vague sense of what s/he anticipates it to be" (Moran & John-Steiner, 2003, p. 27), it can result in extensions of the common domain, for example, as in artistic or pedagogical innovations. Hereby, individuals' epistemological agency (Smith, 2006) as well as the collective epistemological and creative space may be widened, in "innovative interaction" (Engeström, 2008, p. 169). This is the kind of collective creativity and learning that is focused in this chapter—expansive learning, that crystallizes experience and imagination in collective journeys through zones of proximal development (Del Rio & Álvarez, 2007; Engeström, 1987; Vygotsky, 1978). In this chapter, I attempt to show how agentive learning across the individual and the collective in music making may fruitfully be studied as expansive learning (Engeström, 1987) by drawing on empirical data from two cases: one of the instrumental tuition of vocal students and one of professional organ improvisation.

Collective Music Making as Expansive Learning

Forms of activity that have to be "learned as they are being created" (Engeström, 2005, p. 66) are common in today's society, when "people face not only the challenge of acquiring established culture; they also face situations in which they must formulate desirable culture" (Engeström et al., 1999, p. 35). Agency on all levels is needed and theories of learning that presuppose the learning content to be stable and bringing about changes only in individual learners are insufficient:

> Traditionally we expect that learning is manifested as changes in the subject, i.e., in the behavior and cognition of the learners. Expansive learning is manifested primarily as changes in the object of the collective activity. In successful expansive learning, this eventually leads to a qualitative transformation of all components of the activity system. (Engeström & Sannino, 2010, p. 8)

A methodology for studying expansive learning and development involves cooperation with the participants in activity systems and often result in the creation of new practices. Through expansive cycles, analyses of historical contradictions may result in agentive efforts to transform a certain activity as a whole. The cycle of expansive learning consists of a sequence of "epistemic actions" (Engeström, 2005, p. 322) that typically start with a questioning of the accepted practice, which does not necessarily come as a negative reaction to insufferable circumstances but might present itself in the form of constructive ideas. After an analysis of the situation, a model is created, examined, implemented, and evaluated, where after it might be applied and used in a new practice. A fundamental thought in activity theory is that historically generated contradictions provide the energy for innovations and development, and the articulation of contradictions in a system is an important part of expansive learning. For this purpose, analytical and reflective work in studies of expansive learning is made in collaboration between participants and researchers. This may encourage the agents to assume "responsibility of the advancement of their collaborative inquiry and shared knowledge rather than merely pursue their own learning agendas" (Paavola & Hakkarainen, 2005, p. 554).

From my horizon of music education and performance, there are many similarities between the expansive cycle and creative artistic work. It might be argued that artistic practice in itself presupposes and embodies the most important outcome of expansive learning, namely agency: "participants' ability and will to shape their activity systems" (Engeström & Sannino, 2010, p. 20). Constructing or performing works of art means stepping into or inventing a set of rules that guide the process, and learning to create therefore means learning to become aware of the system structure—on micro and macro levels—changing it, and using it for artistic purposes. Both in situations of education and performance, artistic work might be described as entering into a collective activity system, adapting to it, and transforming it by expanding it into new zones of proximal development. At the same time, artistic work is often, as for example in the area of classical music, heavenly burdened by tradition and an increasing amount of collective knowledge that constantly has to be taken into account.

Music institutions are commonly and by necessity conservative and tend to have a focus on transmission of craftsmanship and preservation of culture rather than on transformation. In contexts of music education and performance, the theory of expansive learning may therefore serve both to articulate the complex dimensions of artistic processes and to inspire and support the questioning of established norms, reaching out toward new modes of expression and examining alternative ways of knowing. There are as yet no examples of studies on creative processes in the arts as expansive learning apart from Johansson's study of organ improvisation (2008). In the field of music education, some applications of activity theory contribute to the understanding of the interaction between individual development and collective transformation in musical practice—for example, a study of the introduction of female choristers into a previously all-male choral tradition (Welch, 2007), a study of children's composition (Burnard & Younker, 2008), and a study of the intensity of interaction in one-to-one tuition (Heikinheimo, 2009).

In the following examples of two research projects on music education and performance formulated as expansive learning, I illustrate how collective creative processes and learning in contemporary music making are shaped by the engagement with historical tensions that are inherent in the practice, and which are in turn triggered by the interventionist involvement of the researcher.

Case 1: Obstacles and Options in Instrumental Tuition

Case 1 is set in the practice of higher music education in a music academy. The education of classical musicians carries an inherent tension between tradition and independence, craftsmanship and artistry, reproduction and innovation. In line with the Bologna process, students are increasingly expected to rephrase their definitions of what success as a musician means throughout their careers (Bennett, 2008) and to continuously identify their own needs for competence development (Smilde, 2008). The insecure and unpredictable future for professional music making in Western culture presents teachers, students, and institutions alike with the challenge to educate musicians who are both respectful carriers of craftsmanship and tradition and innovative creative agents in a complex cultural situation. Whereas instrumental teachers expect their students to be and become creative and independent, studies point to how the one-to-one teaching situation itself and the teaching strategies that are used may be counterproductive to the aim of developing agency (Gaunt, 2008; Johansson, 2012a).

In the conservatoire tradition, knowledge often remains on an individual level as personal assets of esteemed musicians and teachers and is thus not made attainable for the collective of practitioners. However, recent studies (e.g., Hultberg, 2005b) describe how researchers who are "insiders" may establish collaborative relationships with practitioners and access the personal and embodied knowledge of teachers and students. The epistemological space that is offered to instrumental students during lessons is related to, for example, the teacher's position as a professional (Nerland, 2007). As a consequence, the one-to-one lesson is not only a meeting between individuals but also an occasion where a novice interacts with agents in the field of music making, such as the symphony orchestra, the conservatoires, and the freelance market.

As a collective activity, higher music education has the object of producing competent musicians for society's musical life, whereas individual teacher or student actions may have goals that only partly coincide with this. For the sake of investigating musical learning and artistic knowledge development as related to individual goal-oriented action and collective object-oriented activity (Leont'ev, 1981), this study was carried out as a collaborative, longitudinal case study during one academic year of two undergraduate vocal students (Anne and Betty) and their teacher (Tessa). As part of the larger project Students' Ownership of Learning at the Royal Academy of Music in Stockholm, (Hultberg, 2010), it focused especially on uncovering and verbalizing obstacles for students' independent learning (Johansson, in press). The study evolved as a cycle of expansive learning in which the teacher and the students together questioned and investigated their own practice together with me, the researcher, in interviews, video-recorded musical performances, stimulated recall sessions, and focus group discussions. My role in Case 1 was that of an intervening, participating observer who could initiate probing questions based on my background—apart from being a researcher with a PhD in music education, I am also a conservatoire-trained organist, a professional musician, and previously an instrumental teacher in the academy.

In line with the Change Laboratory method (Engeström, 2005; Engeström & Sannino, 2010), collaborative and reflective work was initiated with the collective. As mentioned by Daniels (2008), asking fundamental and seemingly simple questions about the object of a certain activity constitutes "a very powerful first step in the identification of systemic contradictions" (p. 137) because it commonly reveals to the participants themselves as well as to researchers that they have not clarified what they are trying to achieve. This was confirmed in the present study, where it turned out that the teacher and the students had completely opposite views on goals, methods, and knowledge development, as illustrated below:

Tessa	Anne and Betty
The goal is to be a singer.	The goal is not to be a singer.
Singing is a craft and possible for everyone.	Singing is a gift and impossible for me.
As a consequence, we work hard.	As a consequence, I don't practice.

This was seen as a manifestation of fundamental contradictions in the activity (Engeström & Sannino, 2011; Il'enkov, 1977), and as an example of how the unique setup of inherent tensions in every practice—and in every person—can be investigated and interpreted as material for creative development rather than as problems that have to be removed. From this slightly difficult starting point, the sheer formulation of the contradictory object of their common activity provided Anne, Betty, and Tessa with energy for the extensive reflective work that was conducted in the study. In vocal lessons, performances, and exams, the students and the teacher verbalized and examined positive insights as well as experiences of tension, difficulties, and problems. The participants reflected upon their actions in stimulated recall sessions together with the researcher. Problems were unearthed and discussed but were *not solved* during the year. The study resulted in documented metalearning that enabled the students to transfer their experiences to professional situations, which in turn made it possible for them to utilize the knowledge offered to them by their teacher. Suggestions for changes in the practice of one-to-one vocal teaching were produced such as the introduction of video recording of all exams and part-time exams. These were implemented and are, at present, continuously evaluated.

In the course of the project, what Tessa called a "creative dialogue" was developed, that made it possible for all participants to verbalize their experiences and share inside perspectives on the learning process. For example, Tessa describes a turning point caused by the use of video recordings:

Tessa: Watching the video together gave me as a teacher the opportunity to take part in the students' self-confrontation. In fact, their reflections during these occasions were the most important triggers for development of our mutual process during the project.

R: Can you give a concrete example?

Tessa: The students had negative conceptions of their singing abilities, but watching the video they discovered qualities in their singing that they had not been aware of, even though I, as their teacher, had pointed them out. They were very surprised, and during their first confrontation with themselves, they asked several times "can I trust the sound?" They suddenly started to act as their own teachers and came up with suggestions for new exercises and practice routines. For example, Betty said that "I have to work more with my vowels!," and Anne pointed out that "maybe if I memorize the music I will be able to maintain the rich sound quality that I find in the exercises also when I sing repertoire." To me, this was a turning point in their work.

In the course of the study, this continuous creative dialogue opened up the space for new insights and for knowledge transfer. For example, in one stimulated-recall session we watched a lesson where Anne practiced one of the songs from Robert Schumann's cycle *Frauenliebe und leben*. She had performed the entire opus as a pianist and now wanted to explore what this knowledge could give her as a singer. Watching the video, Anne found that she made compensatory hand movements while singing, and she related this to her own sense of frustration—while performing the song, she noted that she lost some of the sound qualities that we had previously commented upon and that had pleasantly surprised her. Then she realized:

> This is similar to my own piano students' frustration. I used to think they were annoyed with me, but then I realized they were actually annoyed with themselves! It's exactly the same with me.

By verbalizing her realization and connecting it to her own teaching, Anne was able to use and transform this experience to other areas of work. The process of articulating obstacles, confronting obstacles, and transforming obstacles into options resulted in an expanded and shared object: At the end of the study, Anne and Betty were active as solo singers in professional contexts and described how they could see themselves as singers in ways that did not replicate Tessa's. From this perspective, the students' initial refusal to imitate and identify with the teacher may be seen as an aspect of agency; because they did not initially have the means for formulating alternative opinions on the activity, their only possible action was to resist. Their resistance functioned as an obstacle for the development of vocal and artistic skills but was transformed into a tool for metalearning, in that it shed light on crucial issues that otherwise would have remained unarticulated.

Case 2: Improvisation as Action and Activity

Case 2 concerns the practice of contemporary, professional organ improvisation in Scandinavia. Historically, organists have had, and still have, an important function as musical leaders in local communities, where their music making influences and interacts with local and national culture. An essential feature of this improvisatory practice is that it is not only aurally transmitted but characterized in all its aspects by relationships to scores and by intertextuality. Organists become musically literate through extensive knowledge of major parts of the written repertoire and move between playing from scores and the spontaneous, immediate production of new musical material. In their musical training, organists focus on learning the craft, skill, and techniques of the trade, and through their occupation with scores, they take part in and are influenced by the entire development of Western European musical history. At the same time, the instrument encourages the use of unconventional sound combinations and experimental playing, and their duties as professionals demand that they daily produce "new" music *ex tempore*. Through a balance between internalization and externalization, they are, at best, constantly transforming the musical culture of which they are part. This background formed the starting point for an expansive cycle, which as a whole can be outlined as below (Engeström & Sannino, 2010, p. 7).

Part I

Questioning the culturally established dichotomy between interpretation and improvisation as opposed and separate musical practices.

Analyzing organists' ways of making music historically and empirically.

Modeling the relationship between interpretation and improvisation based on the analysis (Johansson, 2008).

Part II

Examining the model and experimenting on it in a collaborative artistic research project.

Implementing the model in concerts and workshops.

Reflecting on and evaluating the process.

PART I

In interviews and observations of 10 professional organists (Johansson, 2008, 2012b), I studied the relationship between interpretation and improvisation against the setting of determining musical, social, and historical rules and structures—that is, as a discursive practice: "a body of anonymous, historical rules, always determined in the time and space, that has defined the conditions for discourse in a given social, economic, geographical or linguistic area" (Foucault, 2002, p. 145, my translation). The concept of discourse in music (Folkestad, 2012) was used for accessing the tacit knowledge that is embodied in musical practice on macro and micro levels.

With a macro perspective, the limits and regulations for action, knowledge, and creation set by the existing musical language are studied, whereas a micro perspective focuses on individual agency—how individuals draw upon and develop "interpretive repertoires" (Potter & Wetherell, 1987, p. 146). This corresponds to the distinction between action and activity developed by Leont'ev (1981) that provides the means to analyze a phenomenon as consisting of goals and motives on individual as well as collective levels. The individual object-oriented action mediated by tools and artifacts is then seen as "the tip of the iceberg" (Engeström, 2005, p. 61) of a collective activity system deeply rooted in structures of motives, rules, and organization. Solo improvisation, which at first glance may seem to embody the essence of individual invention, could then be studied from the perspective both of what regulates the scope for individual musical action and as instances of using and developing the discourse in music within the framework of a collective activity.

Based on the results, I argued that organists have an "expansive approach" to music making that deconstructs the opposition between interpretation and improvisation that has been common in classical musical culture since the end of the nineteenth century. This is due to the fact that their music making takes place in two activity systems—the liturgy and the concert, with differing historical backgrounds, differing definitions of improvisation, and differing ways of learning and creating music, as suggested below:

The liturgy	*The concert*
Premodern origin	Romantic origin
The musician carries and develops traditional	The musician creates something "new" knowledge
No ownership	Copyright
Relating to the world of texts	Relating to the inner personal musical library

The activity systems of the liturgy and the concert also represent two differing economic cultures: The liturgy, with its situation in the institution of the church, might be seen as a remnant of a feudal society and is not only premodern but also precapitalistic in nature. Concert improvisation draws on bourgeois, romantic tradition with its closer connections to the commercial musical arena. This suggests an explanation to the differing views on creativity: premodern musicians are not dependent on individual originality, and their main focus is to adopt the given system, adapt to it, and perhaps develop it. Notions of copyright or musical ownership do not exist. Musicians in precapitalistic times did not own their compositions and musical works had no legal identities. When demonstrating strategies for learning and creating liturgical music, the musicians describe how they acquire the musical language in use—the discourse in music—and participate in maintaining and developing it. Their inspiration for improvising is seen as coming from the outside, from the world of texts (Fairclough, 2001). "Romantic" musicians aim at producing new and original products owned by the creator and, as concert improvisers, seldom make style studies of older or modern music. This can be interpreted as a sign of respect for the ownership and copyright of the composers. The musicians find their most important source of inspiration inside themselves, in the "inner personal musical library" (Folkestad, 2012).

For every individual organist-to-be, entering into the musical practice of organ improvisation also means entering into this complex picture, which can be described as a result of the meeting, or contradiction, between premodern and Romantic ways of making music, between oral and written musical culture, between informal and formal learning structures, and between collective and individualistic views of musicianship.

PART II

The collaborative, longitudinal case study *Rethinking Organ Improvisation* (Hannula, Suoranta, & Vadén, 2005) included five participants from the Part I and myself as performers. With inspiration from the Change Laboratory method, results from Part I were used as "mirror material" (Engeström & Sannino, 2010, p. 15). The study included six sets of workshops and concerts in Sweden, Denmark, and Norway in 2010 and 2011, and aimed at investigating how our individual musical language(s) and creative strategies relate to sociohistorical and musical structures in differing performance contexts. In a rethinking of our—mostly soloist—ways of making music, the purpose was to create collaborative performances where neither the format nor the content was preplanned.

As a first stimuli, I used a model of the expansive approach (Johansson, 2012b) that describes organists' improvisation in relation to the interpretation of scores (i.e., as being more or less close to notated music). This caused questions such as: Where do we position ourselves? Why? How do we relate to the activity systems of the liturgy and the concert? What do we learn and what are our creative strategies? How will we develop our playing and the collective practice in the future?

In Case 2, my role varied from that of a privileged observer or interviewer in Part I to a performing participant or researcher in Part II. As a consequence, I was studying the activity both from the outside and from my own perspective as a performer. Projects where artists cooperate with a researcher are not yet common in artistic research (Arlander, 2011), and my position in this study can be seen as an attempt to combine these two roles.

As a whole, this collaborative artistic research project consisted in a journey that made the experience of a collective dwelling in insecurity and involved several ruptures and, in some cases, expansive transitions (Engeström, 2008). The intention was to make visible and share our individual improvisatory practices but also to avoid producing a row of conventional and confirmatory self-presentations—we wished to create frameworks for alternative modes of listening. With inspiration from the Change Laboratory method (Engeström, 2005), our concerts and workshops were conceived as an experimental space. Initially, we worked with detailed plans for questioning familiar conventions and encouraging new ways of listening. For example, we used a strategy that can be described as a decontextualization and opening up of traditional formats for performance. In a three-hour night concert, we divided the time into five long sections according to the Ordinary of the Mass, which were thus detached from the function they normally have in a liturgy and through which we played in a rotating order. We could investigate in depth what happens when improvisation for the individual musician is dissociated from the normal rules and regulating structures. In our evaluation, we found that these initial contexts produced good music, but that our listening and interaction was not much developed and no great risks were taken.

As the project evolved, the intention was to maintain openness by not deciding concert formats or content in advance. This resulted in situations of collective insecurity, which were experienced as unpleasant in actual performance but that opened up for disturbances and boundary crossing (Engeström, 2008). For example, during a concert when we all—or so we believed—tacitly agreed that the final group improvisation now had come to an end, one player suddenly started over again several times, which forced us all to break our supposedly common structure. This event was not immediately discussable afterward. All except for the "disturbing" player later described the experience as difficult, until listening to the recording. Then, surprisingly, all participants revised their impressions and found that this group improvisation was one of the best ones so far. It would have remained only a memory of an unpleasant failure had we not all made the commitment to stick to the design of the study by listening, analyzing, and sharing our experiences of being in this kind of boundary zone, where the common direction became unclear and communication seemed to falter.

Our common analysis of this and similar situations showed that moments of insecurity were often accompanied by feelings of boredom, futility, and even despair, and that the musical process then was often interrupted too soon. As a consequence, musical ideas that were evaluated as especially good in the analysis were never developed, due to the fact that feelings of anxiety and loss of control were evaded, both in the group and individually. As a whole, the six performances display a process that can be described as a widening of both the epistemological and the creative space for the individual musicians as well as the group as a whole. Two conclusions from the study are that (a) negative feelings may be used as signposts on the road to artistic expansive learning and (b) resting assured in the unknown territory of the boundary zone requires discipline, endurance, and a willingness to risk individual and collective prestige.

Collective Creativity and Learning as Innovative Interaction

Above I have given brief examples of how musical practice may be studied as instances of expansive learning, where collective knowledge creation is made possible by the interventionist role of the researcher in combination with the active contribution of all participants. At best, this may result in innovative interaction and widen the epistemic and creative agency on individual and collective levels through a "creative reconstruction" (Engeström, 2008, p. 168) of the object of the activity. The research focus in both the described cases was on contradictions in the system, represented by individ-ual experiences of tensions and problems (Engeström & Sannino, 2011).

In Case 1, contradictions were not solved or investigated in depth, but articulating and discussing the contradictory object of this activity resulted in a radical development of the epistemological space for all participants. The conflicting views on singing demonstrate personal ways of handling problematic issues but also illustrate the systemic and primary contradic-tion between use value and exchange value: singing for fun in private situa-tions versus professional singing as a wage earner. Anne and Betty initially defended the former position whereas Tessa was strongly committed to the latter, and the development in the study may also be described as an ongoing debate about the role of music and of musicians, in a professional musical context. The *creative resistance* put up by the students toward imitation of and identification with their teacher was in this process transformed into a tool for metalearning, and the object was expanded to include a more com-plex picture of what it means to be a professional singer. In addition, the study led to a reformulation and restructuring of the formats for evaluation and examination of vocal students at the institution's bachelor program.

In Case 2, the process of rethinking improvisation expanded the object and hereby the participants' creative space, from an emphasis on individual, impressive self-presentations to collective risk-taking and reflective listening. An important experience was that individually experienced tensions (e.g., feelings of insecurity and vulnerability)—when articulated—can be used con-sciously as tools for artistic expansion and increased agency, individually as well as in the group. As professional musicians with long-term experience, we could smoothly produce concerts of improvisation that, so to speak, represent the essence of creativity. But could it be considered creative to continue doing what we had always done? This project showed that it was the disruptions and setbacks that made collective creative breakthroughs and new learning possible. The *creative disturbance* represented by, for example, the player who failed to comply with the rules that we all tacitly adhered to, was an individual action that caused collective insecurity. Simultaneously though, and through our common commitment to reflective and analytical procedure, it led to a creative expansion and showed that discipline, rules, and planning are impor-tant conditions for innovative interaction.

The production of art, such as music making, has historically been seen as an example of "positive creativity" (James & Taylor, 2010), but as sug-gested by these examples, its "dark" and troublesome aspects might be needed for development to take place. Resistance and disturbance are not commonly thought to promote creativity and learning, but when interpreted and treated as manifestations of inherent, systematic contradictions, they energize the sys-tem: "Disturbances and ruptures involving negation, rejection and destruction are often the first decisive indications of significant developmental processes" (Engeström, 2005, p. 195). Hypothetically, both these cases involved a risk of escalating conflict. In Case 1, the risk was the emergence of a conflict between the teacher and the students concerning content and meaning of the tuition. In Case 2, we potentially put the artistic quality of the concert at risk and also risked a conflict around musical aesthetics. However, in this respect, the study's framework and the researcher's role as both an insider and an outsider provided a protective structure. As mentioned, collaborative studies in music making are not yet common, but these studies suggest that the use of theoretical tools by researchers and practitioners in interaction may give the courage and endurance to approach and investigate problematic situations in both educational and performance contexts.

Finally, not only teams but also institutions today need to practice expansive learning to be able to provide tomorrow's musicians with space for knowledge creation and avoid an excessive focus on the reproduction of culture. With a widened perspective toward other disciplines, artistic practice and research in the arts may contribute to academia and to the development of theories on learning and creativity through the increasing publication and sharing of experience and knowledge about artistic procedures, processes, and products.

REFERENCES

Arlander, A. (2011). Characteristics of visual and performing arts. In M. Biggs & H. Karlsson (Eds.), *The Routledge companion to research in the arts* (pp. 315–332). London, England: Routledge.

Attali, J. (2011). *Noise: The political economy of music*. Minneapolis: University of Minnesota Press.

Bennett, D. (2008). *Understanding the classical music profession: The past, the present and strategies for the future*. Farnham, England: Ashgate.

Biggs, M., & Karlsson, H. (Eds.). (2011). *The Routledge companion to research in the arts*. London, England: Routledge.

Burnard, P., & Younker, B. A. (2008). Investigating childrens' musical interactions within the activities systems of group composing and arranging: An application of Engestrom's activity theory. *International Journal of Educational Research, 47*(1), 60–74.

Cropley, A. J. (2006). In praise of convergent thinking. *Creativity Research Journal, 18*(3), 391–404.

Cropley, A. J. (2010). The dark side of creativity: What is it? In D. H. Cropley, A. J. Cropley, J. C. Kaufman, & M. A. Runco (Eds.), *The dark side of creativity* (pp. 1–14). Cambridge, England: Cambridge University Press.

Daniels, H. (2008). *Vygotsky and research*. London, England: Routledge.

Dawson, V. L. (1997). In search of the wild bohemian: Challenges in the identification of the creatively gifted. *Roeper Review, 19*(3), 148–152.

Del Rio, P., & Álvarez, A. (2007). Inside and outside the zone of proximal development: An ecofunctional reading of Vygotsky. In H. Daniels, M. Cole, & J. Wertsch (Eds.), *The Cambridge companion to Vygotsky* (pp. 276–306). Cambridge, England: Cambridge University Press.

Engeström, Y. (1987). *Learning by expanding*. Helsinki, Finland: Orienta-Konsultit Oy.

Engeström, Y. (2005). *Developmental work research: Expanding activity theory in practice*. Berlin, Germany: Lehmanns Media.

Engeström, Y. (2008). From teams to knots: Activity-theoretical studies of collaboration and learning at work. Cambridge, England: Cambridge University Press.

Engeström, Y., Miettinen, R., & Punamäki, R. L. (Eds.). (1999). *Perspectives on activity theory*. Cambridge, England: Cambridge University Press.

Engeström, Y., & Sannino, A. (2010). Studies of expansive learning: Foundations, findings and future challenges. *Educational Research Review, 5,* 1–24.

Engeström, Y., & Sannino, A. (2011). Discursive manifestations of contradictions in organizational change efforts: A methodological framework. *Journal of Organizational Change Management, 24*(3), 368–387.

Fairclough, N. (2001). *Language and power*. London, England: Longman.

Folkestad, G. (2012). Digital tools and discourse in music: The ecology of composition. In D. J. Hargreaves, D. E. Miell, & R. A. R. MacDonald (Eds.), *Musical imaginations: Multidisciplinary perspectives on creativity, performance, and perception* (pp. 193–205). Oxford, England: Oxford University Press.

Foucault, M. (2002). *Vetandets arkeologi* [The archaeology of knowledge]. Lund, Sweden: Arkiv Förlag.

Frisk, H. (2008). *Improvisation, computers, and interaction: Rethinking human-computer interaction through music*. Malmö, Sweden: Malmö Academy of Music, Lund University.

Gaunt, H. (2008). One-to-one tuition in a conservatoire: The perceptions of instrumental and vocal teachers. *Psychology of Music, 36*(2), 215–245.

Hannula, M., Suoranta, J., & Vadén, T. (2005). *Artistic research: Theories, methods and practices*. Espoo, Finland: Cosmoprint Oy.

Hargreaves, D., Miell, D. E., & MacDonald, R. A. R. (Eds.). (2012). *Music imaginations: Multidisciplinary perspectives on creativity, performance, and perception*. Oxford, England: Oxford University Press.

Heikinheimo, T. (2009). *Intensity of interaction in instrumental music lessons*. Helsinki, Finland: Sibelius Academy.

Hultberg, C. (2005a). Musicians' interpretation-finding. In T. Lind & J. Wadensjö (Eds.), *Art, knowledge, insight: Texts on research and developmental work in the artistic area* (pp. 110–125). Stockholm, Sweden: The Swedish Research Council.

Hultberg, C. (2005b). Practitioners and researchers in cooperation: Method development for qualitative practice-related studies. *Music Education Research, 7*(2), 211–224.

Hultberg, C. (2010). *Vem äger lärandet?* [Students ownership of learning]. Stockholm, Sweden: Myndigheten för nätverk och samarbete inom högre utbildning.

Il'enkov, E. V. (1977). *Dialectical logic: Essays on its history and theory*. Moscow, Russia: Progress Publishers.

James, K., & Taylor, A. (2010). Positive creativity and negative creativity. In D. H. Cropley, A. J. Cropley, J. C. Kaufman, & M. Runco (Eds.), *The dark side of creativity* (pp. 33–56). Cambridge, England: Cambridge University Press.

Johansson, K. (2008). *Organ improvisation: Activity, action and rhetorical practice*. Malmö, Sweden: Malmö Academy of Music, Lund University.

Johansson, K. (2012a). Experts, entrepreneurs and competence nomads: The skills paradox in higher music education. *Music Education Research, 14*(1), 47–64.

Johansson, K. (2012b). Organ improvisation: Edition, extemporization, expansion, and instant composition. In D. J. Hargreaves, D. E. Miell, & R. A. R. MacDonald (Eds.), *Musical imaginations: Multidisciplinary perspectives on creativity, performance, and perception* (pp. 220–232). Oxford, England: Oxford University Press.

Johansson, K. (in press). Undergraduate students' ownership of musical learning: Obstacles and options in one-to-one teaching. *British Journal of Music Education.*

Juslin, P. (2001). Communicating emotion in music performance: A review and a theoretical framework. In P. Juslin & J. Sloboda (Eds.), *Music and emotion* (pp. 309–340). Oxford, England: Oxford University Press.

Krüger, T. (1998). *Teacher practice, pedagogical discourse and the construction of knowledge: Two case studies of teachers at work.* Bergen, Norway: Bergen University.

Leont'ev, A. N. (1981). *Problems of the development of the mind.* Moscow, Russia: Progress Publishers.

May, R. (1994). *The courage to create.* New York, NY: Norton.

Moran, S., & John-Steiner, V. (2003). Creativity in the making: Vygotsky's contemporary contribution to the dialectic of development and creativity. In R. K. Sawyer (Ed.), *Creativity and development* (pp. 61–90). Oxford, England: Oxford University Press.

Nerland, M. (2007). One-to-one teaching as cultural practice: Two case studies from an academy of music. *Music Education Research, 9*(3), 399–416.

Östersjö, S. (2008). *Shut up 'n' play! Negotiating the musical work.* Malmö, Sweden: Malmö Academy of Music, Lund University.

Paavola, S., & Hakkarainen, K. (2005). The knowledge creation metaphor—An emergent epistemological approach to learning. *Science & Education, 14,* 535–557.

Potter, J., & Wetherell, M. (1987). *Discourse and social psychology.* London, England: Sage.

Prichard, C. (2002). Creative selves? Critically reading "creativity" in management discourse. *Creativity and Innovation Management, 11*(4), 265–276.

Sahlin, N. E. (1997). Value-change and creativity. In Å. E. Andersson & N. E. Sahlin (Eds.), *The complexity of creativity* (pp. 59–66). Berlin, Germany: Springer.

Sahlin, N. E. (2001). *Kreativitetens filosofi* [The philosophy of creativity]. Nora, Sweden: Nya Doxa.

Sawyer, R. K. (2003). *Group creativity: Music, theater, collaboration.* New York, NY: Psychology Press.

Small, C. (1998). *Musicking: The meanings of performing and listening.* Hanover, PA: Wesleyan University Press.

Smilde, R. (2008). Lifelong learners in music: Research into musicians' biographical learning. *International Journal of Community Music, 1*(2), 243–252.

Smith, R. (2006). Epistemological agency in the workplace. *Journal of Workplace Learning, 18*(3), 157–170.

Sternberg, R. J., & Kaufman, J. C. (2010). Constraints on creativity: Obvious and not so obvious. In J. C. Kaufman & R. J. Sternberg (Eds.), *The Cambridge handbook of creativity* (pp. 467–482). Cambridge, England: Cambridge University Press.

Vygotsky, L. (1978). *Mind in society.* Cambridge, MA: Harvard University Press.

Vygotsky, L. (2004). Imagination and creativity in childhood. *Journal of Russian and East European Psychology, 42,* 7–97.

Welch, G. (2007). Addressing the multifaceted nature of music education: An activity theory research perspective. *Research Studies in Music Education, 28,* 23–37.

Wertsch, J. (1997). Collective memory: Issues from a sociohistorical perspective. In M. Cole, Y. Engeström, & O. Vasquez (Eds.), *Mind, culture and activity* (pp. 226–232). Cambridge, England: Cambridge University Press.

2 Critical Transitions in the Pursuit of a Professional Object

Simone de Beauvoir's Expansive Journey to Become a Writer

Annalisa Sannino

Transitions are an important aspect of creativity and learning. The concept of transitions appears in different ways in numerous works in the social sciences (e.g., Goodwin & O'Connor, 2009). Among these works, the literature that deals with transitions from formal education to work focuses on various ways to organize school to work transitions in different societies. In the case of this chapter, transitions are rather analyzed in terms of the intertwined personal and historical struggles involved in the pursuit of a creative endeavor. Longitudinal studies of creativity within Howard Gruber's tradition demonstrate the crucial importance of sequences of efforts to move from one stage or one activity to another (Gruber & Bödeker, 2005). Creativity within this tradition is not the outcome of a moment of extraordinary insight, but the laborious search for and creative production of a new activity. Also within this tradition, creative minds are referred to as "breakaway minds" (Gruber, 1981) who have the courage to say things against the conformist ideas of their times. Because of both this long-term and gradual shaping of creative production and this breakaway aspect, transitions toward creative production can easily turn into difficult and critical movements. This chapter examines the journey toward creative production in terms of "critical transitions." The chapter analyzes the nature of such transitions and the way to understand them as a central aspect of creativity and learning. In particular, the chapter aims at shedding light on the transition from being a traditional learner, who reproduces culture, to becoming a learner who is also a creative producer of culture.

The chapter includes as an example the critical transition to creative writing in the biography of the French existentialist writer Simone de Beauvoir (1908–1986), from her successful years as a student to the difficult 10 years after her graduation, when she was struggling to publish her first book. The chapter questions what might explain this kind of transition from the great promise of a top student to a long painful period, before the beginning of a steady, creative, and productive career as writer. Although this is an example of the extraordinary journey of one person, the learning and creative efforts generated in the course of this journey go beyond this individual case only, by expanding to meet the concerns of many in the specific historical circumstances and afterward. This difficult journey is not unique to this author. Beauvoir is, however, a rare case in that the transition is very well documented in her extensive autobiographical writings and in an authoritative biography (Bair, 1990), based on tape-recorded interviews. Direct quotes from these sources allow building the theoretical argument of this chapter on vivid empirical material.

Activity-theoretical concepts are used as lenses to conceptualize critical transitions toward creative production. In this framework, transitions are seen also as processes of learning, although not in the traditional sense of learning by acquiring something culturally already given. These are processes of learning in which a person together with others discovers and pursues something radically new. The view presented here on transition, creative production, and learning is based on my bridging of views from different authors in cultural-historical activity-theory. I rely on direct quotes from Vygotsky and other selected activity-theoretical sources in the attempt to build up connections between the different authors.

Beauvoir created a pioneering literary production focused on an existentialist view of women's condition. The new activity was her creative writing career. Her journey was not a lonely one. The close relationship and collaboration with the writer and philosopher Jean-Paul Sartre played a crucial role in shaping her journey. Creativity and learning transpire from the example as strongly collaborative and collective phenomena. The example and the theoretical tools from activity theory serve the purpose of opening up the concept of critical transitions and a way of studying them as an important aspect of creative production and learning.

I will begin with a biographical description of Beauvoir's journey toward productive creative writing. A discussion of different conceptualizations of transitions follows in the section titled "Temporal and Spatial Dimensions of Critical Transitions." The chapter continues with a description of critical transitions as intertwined with struggles, essential to genuine creative production and learning. A section follows that characterizes critical transitions as movements from an objectless need state to the discovery of an object, progressively expanding beyond the individual toward societally relevant endeavors. The last two sections conclude the chapter with a discussion of the driven nature of creative production through critical transitions, characterizing the type of learning involved in such transitions as expansive learning.

BEAUVOIR'S JOURNEY

Since childhood, Simone de Beauvoir was oriented toward having to train for a profession. The impoverished economical situation of the family prevented her parents to provide her with a dowry, and she and her sister were told by their father: "You girls must study hard to prepare yourselves to work all your lives, and so you must train for a profession" (Bair, 1990, p. 57). In Beauvoir's biography, Bair (1990) points out that both Simone and her sister referred to this dirge by their father in every interview, and this led the biographer to affirm that "it made a powerful impression upon them from a very young age, one which lasts until the present time" (p. 622).

The years of Simone's childhood and adolescence were a turning point in the history of bourgeois women's education in France. Up to the Great War, French education for bourgeois women was dominated by the orientation to prepare future wives and mothers to appropriate conduct and morals. Times were, however, changing. France's slow recovery from the industrial and general economic decline at the end of the nineteenth century translated into radical birthrate drops and decrease of marriages. The main concern of Simone's father was that she could work while still adhering to the prevailing standards of her social class (Bair, 1990, p. 89). Highly educated women at the time were, however, still very few, and the prejudice against women who could not marry was rather strong. Beauvoir's biographer comments on "the irony . . . that all the while he (Simone's father) was exhorting her to prepare herself to work, he was setting obstacles in her way" (Bair, 1990, p. 89).

Strongly encouraged by her father, Simone became an avid reader and soon started writing her own stories. Yet for her early education, Simone was enrolled in 1914 in the private *Institut Adeline Désir,* a snobbish institution devoted to piety, devotion to duty, and deportment—the bourgeois ideal of womanhood (Bair, 1990, p. 64). This choice was guided by the family's intention to keep "some social standards" (p. 65).

In 1924 Simone graduated from the *Institut Désir* and obtained her first *baccalauréat*—this was merely a school-leaving certificate traditionally meant for bourgeois girls before they would marry. The same year, French educational reforms granted women access to the *baccalauréat* academic qualification at the end of the secondary education. This was the necessary step to take for entering university studies and thus for qualifying for professional employment. The second *baccalauréat* examination required courses in classical languages and philosophy. This subject became available also for women only in 1924 in selected private schools such as the *Institut Désir*. With this qualification, good students like Simone could embark on a career as a teacher

and insure that although their status in life was lesser than their married classmates, it was still high enough to keep them on the fringes of the petty bourgeois class of their birth and education. For Georges de Beauvoir (Simone's father), this was the best to which his daughter could aspire. (Bair, 1990, p. 90)

Simone stayed at the *Institut Désir* to prepare for the *baccalauréat* examinations. Although philosophy was added there to the curriculum, none of the teachers in the school could teach this subject, and the task was given to the local priest.

> The abbé's method of teaching was to read an enlightening text aloud, then dictate passages from it, or else to have the students copy essays from the text into their notebooks, which he then corrected for spelling and penmanship rather than content. Everything began with piety and ended with "the truth according to Saint Thomas Aquinas." . . . The inadequacy of the teaching showed when she took the examinations: she barely passed philosophy. (Bair, 1990, p. 91)

In spite of the weakness of the teaching and the poor results in her first philosophy examination, Simone became very interested in philosophy. Before enrolling in a university, Simone had to first attend a regular secondary school—the *Institut Désir* from which she graduated had the actual status of a primary school. In these years, she was increasingly oriented toward philosophy, which was still a subject considered inappropriate for women. She had to meet the strong opposition by her parents, her father considering this subject "so much gibberish" and her mother fearing that by studying this subject she "will become immoral" (quotes from Beauvoir's interviews; Bair, 1990, p. 91). The clash between the parties was becoming critical in a way which threatened to shame them publicly (Bair, 1990, p. 92).

Finally Simone was allowed to attend the *Institut Sainte-Marie* in Neuilly, one of the most reputed secondary schools among those complying with both a more modern education for young women and the traditional Catholic doctrine. There she studied philosophy as well. The school proved to be very demanding and confirmed once more the poor preparation she had received in the previous years. She managed to catch up with the new demands, but the new environment did not match her expectations. Simone commented on this period in the following way, as reported by her biographer:

> Up to now, I had made the best of living in a cage, for I knew that one day—and each day brought it nearer—the door of the cage would open; now I had got out of the cage and I was still inside. What a letdown. (Bair, 1990, p. 97)

In the years of her higher education, she did not find the fulfillment she expected. She felt powerless and impatient with her progress. Simone decided that the only way off the treadmill was to shorten her program by one full year (Bair, 1990, p. 121).

In 1928 she passed philosophy exams with excellent grades, and she placed herself second in her class in two courses, after Simone Weil and before Maurice Merleau-Ponty. In 1929 Beauvoir was placed second after Jean-Paul Sartre in the highly competitive postgraduate examination in philosophy (the *agrégation*). She prepared for the exam by attending courses at the Sorbonne and by getting involved in a study group with three students coming from the prestigious *Ecole Normale Supérieure*. One of the students in this group was to become her lifetime companion and working partner, Jean-Paul Sartre. In her autobiography, Beauvoir (1965) comments on the experience of getting acquainted with the group of the three *normalians* by referring to the blow which this encounter had inflicted on her: "In order to recover my self-esteem"—she wrote—"I should have had to *do* something, and do it well" (p. 61). She felt she did not have the right mindset for becoming a philosopher and opted for her longtime interest to become a writer.

For 10 years after graduation, she was very troubled without being able to accomplish the goal she had set for herself since childhood. In these years, Beauvoir was not only struggling to find the topic and the tools of an independent writer but, at the same time, struggling to break through the dominant mold and boundaries in the intellectual landscape of her culture. In French intellectual circles at the beginning of the past century, a woman philosopher, representing very untraditional views, was most likely marginalized. Moreover, her school and university training were not meant to serve the undertaking of creative efforts in her work as a writer.

Breaking out of this mold in which she was constrained since her early years served her creative efforts to become a published writer. Another key factor in the critical transition toward her creative work as a writer was the historical turmoil of the years preceding World War II. The dramatic events of this period brought her to realize that her work could make a difference. From this period on, she was not anymore unsure about her position in the intellectual landscape in which she was moving. Her existentialist work on women's conditions originated in this period. This was not solely the outcome of the selection of a right topic and narrative medium. In activity-theoretical terms, this can be referred to as the discovery of "the object" of her writing. It is of significance to point out that this was the outcome of struggles against historically rooted oppositions, which tended to marginalize intellectual women.

Shedding light on this dimension of transitions can be very significant for the understanding of learning mechanisms that lead to a driven pursuit of creative production and that can make a difference societally. The struggles involved in transitions, such as those manifest in Beauvoir's case, are very weakly discussed in literature on transitions. These aspects point to a novel dimension in the conceptualization of transitions, the dimension of the societally engaged individual whose learning breaks out of normative boundaries and leads to genuine creative production.

Traditional learning theories have seen learning as a transmission process, which preserves culture. A challenge for today's learning theories consists in developing our understanding of learning as a process that creatively transforms culture, in the literal sense of *creating* culture. This is by nature a collective process in which human beings rely on each other and on the work of previous generations. At the same time, this is a process, which requires finding one's own object and breaking away from constraining aspects of the past to invest in the future.

TEMPORAL AND SPATIAL DIMENSIONS OF CRITICAL TRANSITIONS

In the conceptualizations of transitions, there seem to be two main orientations. One orientation primarily emphasizes a temporal dimension of transitions. Within this perspective, creativity is characterized in terms of temporal stepwise transitions (Kaufman & Beghetto, 2009). Rank, Pace, and Frese (2004) define creativity as the psychological phenomenon that facilitates "transitions into future states" (p. 519). In activity theory, this temporal dimension is strongly emphasized in the works of Bratus and Lishin (1983), El'konin (1977), and Leont'ev (1978, 1981). The second orientation primarily emphasizes the spatial dimension of transitions. This is evident in the community of practice tradition (Lave & Wenger, 1991) and in more recent work on boundary crossings (Akkerman & Bakker, 2011). This chapter attempts to bridge these two ways of conceptualizing transitions with the help of an additional transversal dimension (i.e., the dimension of personal and societal struggles—see Figure 2.1).

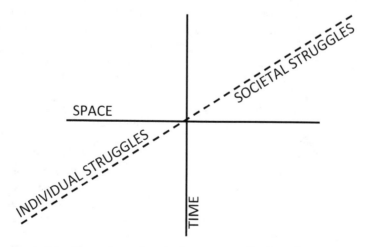

Figure 2.1   Three dimensions in the conceptualization of transitions.

Transitions conceived as in the representation in Figure 2.1 are not solely movements in time and in the space between activities. They are also movements in one's positioning within the intellectual landscape in a given culture and in specific historical circumstances. This positional aspect of transition is often neglected in conceptualizations of transitions, also in activity theory.

The temporal dimension in the conceptualization of transitions in activity theory is primarily historical. This is history understood as new productive forces struggling against and breaking through the constraints of existing relations of production. Entirely new forms of production are creative outcomes that emerge from this process. In El'konin's (1977) conceptualization, however, transitions lead to new activities that already exist culturally. El'konin represents development as on a timeline of activities that advance from early infancy to late adolescence. The timeline evokes biologically and culturally built-in teleological expectations of how human beings develop from play to school learning to adolescent peer interaction and work. El'konin indicates a sort of alignment of these activities with or against each other in a process that alters the status of previously existing activities and tends toward the primacy of one single activity, which he calls dominant activity.

El'konin's conceptualization of dominant activity aligns with Leont'ev's (1981) notion of the leading role of an activity in the early phases of human life: "Each stage of psychic development is characterized by . . . a definite, leading type . . . of activity" (p. 395). Leont'ev (1981) defines a leading activity as "the activity whose development governs the chief changes in the psychic processes and psychological features of the child's personality at a given stage of development" (p. 396). He also points out that leading activity "is the activity in whose form other, new types of activity arise, and within which they are differentiated" (p. 396).

El'konin (1977) and Leont'ev (1981) refer to shifts from one dominant leading activity to another as transitions. Transitions are gradual replacements of a leading activity with another in the progression from one stage of relational and intellectual development to the next: "The activity that used to play the leading role begins to be shed and pushed into the background. A new leading activity arises, and with it a new stage of development also begins" (Leont'ev, 1981, p. 416).

In El'konin's and Leont'ev's conceptualization of transitions, the new activities are already there; they are new only for the individual who moves from one activity to another in historically well-established sequences. When a child moves from play to school, the child enters a new world of extraordinary creative possibilities. However, to understand creative production, we need to understand also the creation of entirely new activities that are not pregiven. Creative formation of a new activity that is not yet culturally there requires breaking out from the timeline of already existing activities. A spatial dimension becomes, therefore, necessary to conceptualize transitions toward truly novel activities.

The community of practice tradition (Lave & Wenger, 1991) conceptualizes transitions as movements from the periphery to the center. This is a useful spatial metaphor as the orientation toward a genuinely new activity does require starting from the periphery. This is a place far away from accepted ideas and already tested procedures. Transitions in the legitimate peripheral participation approach are, however, primarily depicted as smooth and gradual movement from the periphery to the center. A primarily spatial conceptualization of transition can be traced also in recent discussions on boundary crossing between activities and institutional contexts (Akkerman & Bakker, 2011; Tanggaard, 2007).

The transition in Beauvoir's case is a long struggle with and a breaking away from oppressive boundaries of the dominant intellectual culture. Struggles against and breaking through marginalizing boundaries are essential aspects of transitions toward the creation of something genuinely novel. In such cases, the transitions take place along hostile unpaved paths and toward directions that are only vaguely perceptible at the beginning.

STRUGGLES IN TRANSITIONS

In an interesting study of creativity, Lovitts (2005) identifies facilitating and impeding factors in the transitions of doctoral students to independent research. The author sees the unequal distribution of individual, material, and social resources as factors affecting students' trajectories through their programs as well as their socialization into the selected field and the contribution they make to it. In order to positively affect these transitions, the author suggests changes in the social constellation that generates the impeding factors. In the perspective on transitions presented here, such impeding factors can play a crucial role in creative production if one struggles against and breaks through them. Simone de Beauvoir reflects on the crucial importance of these struggles in her autobiography: "Such culture as I had acquired, inadequate though it might be, was essential . . . The very confusion against which I struggled goaded me on irresistibly towards the goal I had long since set myself: the writing of books" (Beauvoir, 1965, p. 364).

In the activity-theoretical tradition, the already mentioned works by El'konin (1977) and Leont'ev (1978, 1981) on dominant and leading activities do not elaborate on the struggles involved in transitions. They depict transitions primarily as positive and successful moves. This optimistic view of normative stepwise development minimizes gaps, divergences, and conflicts that may be necessary for the new to emerge (Engeström, 1996a; Griffin & Cole, 1984).

Particularly in adult work, transitions do not easily follow institutionally predetermined paths in which changes coincide with individual needs. Also, leading activities can direct human actions to the point of becoming dysfunctionally constraining enclosures. In such cases, leading activities can literally dominate development to the point of stagnation. Although leading activities such as schooling come to an end, the long-term involvement in such activities has a lasting influence on activities in which we get involved later on in our lives. Leading activities carve our personality. In order to free oneself from the heritage of long-term involvement in leading activities, one has to break out of this constraining past without the support of a predetermined institutional frame.

Beach's (1999) concept of consequential transition is similar to Leont'ev's and El'konin's notion of transitions in that it emphasizes continuity rather than obstacles in the transitional movement. The activity-theoretical perspective on transition developed in this chapter aims at highlighting challenging discontinuity as an intrinsic and productive feature of transitions. In this respect, my conceptualization of transitions aligns more closely with Bronfenbrenner's (1979) definition of ecological transitions. According to Bronfenbrenner, the position of a person in environmental circumstances is altered when the person's role and/or the setting change. However, Bronfenbrenner, too, ultimately depicts transitions as positive processes of mutual accommodation of the organism and its surroundings.

Learning to pursue new activities is demanding because the individual has to *build up* continuity between the new and what already exists. Also, the emerging motive of an envisioned activity often contradict the motive of previous leading activities. The transition toward a new leading activity can, therefore, be a critical and conflictual experience. Vasilyuk (1988) characterizes these situations as critical conflicts in which inner doubts paralyze the individual who faces contradictory motives. Commonly, an individual without external support surrenders in front of the conflict and searches for easy ways out. Critical conflicts may prevent individuals from engaging in collective creative redesign of their material circumstances if collective resources are not mobilized for facing the conflicts.

The hard work and numerous difficulties involved in transitions toward creative pursuits have been in the focus of authoritative creativity studies (Csikszentmihalyi, 1996; Gruber & Bödeker, 2005; Sawyer, 2012). Yet shedding light on the nature of the struggles involved in transitions toward creative endeavors can be beneficial for understanding and supporting the kind of learning needed in such transitions. Vygotsky's works on creativity offer useful ideas in this direction, ideas which have not been fully discussed in contemporary creativity studies. New developments in the Vygotskian tradition should lead to further elaborations that Vygotsky himself did not have a chance to accomplish (Leont'ev, 1971).

The act of creation, its genesis, and nature are discussed in several texts of Vygotsky (1971, 1997, 1998, 1999, 2004). These texts consistently refer to the struggles with which the creator is confronted. Vygotsky (2004) refers to the creator's experiences of these struggles in terms of agonies of creation. The example of Beauvoir illustrates this type of struggle:

From the beginning she had problems with narrative voice, or "how to distinguish the observer from the one she observes." But the one insurmountable problem was of organization and structure, of not knowing how to tell an anecdote succinctly or how to arrange transitions such as the passage of time and the movement of a character from one place to another. "The mechanics of fiction totally eluded me. It was very frustrating."[1] (Bair, 1990, p. 175)

Prior to these struggles, however, there are other more significant struggles from which the drive to create originates. These are the struggles between the individual and the challenging world:

If life surrounding him does not present challenges to an individual, if his usual and inherent reactions are in complete equilibrium with the world around him, then there will be no basis for him to exercise creativity. A creature that is perfectly adapted to its environment would not want anything, would not have anything to strive for, and, of course, would not be able to create anything. Thus, creation is always based on lack of adaptation, which gives rise to needs, motives, and desires. (Vygotsky, 2004, pp. 28–29)

Creativity in this perspective becomes the precious link that pushes human beings to learn how to achieve what they strive for and at the same time to make the world a better place. For Vygotsky, creative production serves the purpose of transcending and triumphing over constraining aspects of the circumstances we live in. Vygotsky uses the example of writing poems to depict this essentially transformative function of creative production:

If the ultimate goal of a poem about melancholy was only to tell us about melancholy, this would be a rather sad state of affairs for art. Obviously, in this case the goal of lyric poetry is not just to afflict us, as Leo Tolstoy puts it, with someone else's feelings, in this case, someone else's melancholy, but to be victorious over it, to transcend melancholy. (Vygotsky, 1997, p. 252)

Vygotsky's reference to the classic notion of catharsis from the ancient Greek tradition is crucial to grasp his conception of the act of creation as freeing human beings from their limitations and constraints. Catharsis is "a liberation and resolution of the spirit from the passions which torment it" (Vygotsky, 1997, p. 253). Leont'ev (1971) comments on this notion of catharsis by linking it to the intrapersonal conflicts experienced in the act of creation and to the broader relation between the individual and the world: "To Vygotsky, catharsis is not simply the release of overwhelming affective attraction . . . It is rather the resolution of a certain, merely personal conflict, the revelation of a higher, more general, human truth in the phenomena of life" (p. ix).

In a text not yet available in English, Leont'ev (1983)[2] describes how the act of creation can arise from the above-mentioned struggles. Creativity involved in the creation of novel aesthetic activities is, according to Leont'ev, "a problem of sense" (p. 237):

> *Art is that only activity which meets the aim of discovery, expression and communication of the personal sense of reality.* . . . The content of aesthetic activity is always a process of penetration beyond meaning. We need to free ourselves from the indifference of meaning, we need to go beyond it; in that case, of course, activity assumes a character of fight, clash, demolition of one and establishing of the other (p. 237, italics in the original).

The act of creation is the triumph of human beings' willed quest to establish their personal sense of a problematic reality. This act transcends the limits of already existing and well-stabilized meanings. In the same text, Leont'ev takes up the example of the literary act of creation with a reference to the struggles involved in it. The example nicely resonates with the example of Beauvoir:

> In aesthetic activity a constant struggle with the material takes place, the overcoming of material and removal of its' sluggishness. How does this struggle go? The most difficult case is a struggle with the material in literature. Language is a world of meanings, linguistic works of art carry all these meanings. And the most difficult in the art of words is to go beyond the meaning in the material of meanings. It seems to be easier in poetry: Perhaps, the form helps; in prose it is harder, and a lot of issues of aesthetics arise, which I am able only to mention: the issue of the style of artwork, linguistics expressive means and many others. (Leont'ev, 1983, p. 238)

In the following excerpt from her biography, Beauvoir explicitly refers to the struggles she experienced together with Sartre, facing the challenging world without appropriate tools. The excerpt also points to their persistent orientation toward what they sensed to be "their own path":

> We were lost in a world the complexities of which lay far beyond our understanding, and we possessed only the most rudimentary instruments to guide us through it. But at least we persisted in hacking out our own path. Every step we took brought fresh conflicts, and moved us to yet further difficulties; and so during the years that followed we found ourselves swept far away from these first beginnings. (Beauvoir, 1965, p. 44)

FROM OBJECTLESS NEED STATE TO THE
DISCOVERY OF THE OBJECT

Bratus and Lishin's work (1983) on the development of activities helps us to elaborate further on the nature of the struggles involved in transition toward acts of creation. When the drive to create originates, due to disequilibrium between the individual and the environment, the actual act of creation has not been initiated yet. Bratus and Lishin (1983) examine how such an act emerges. The drive to create generates new needs, which must be satisfied for the individual to be able to engage in the act of creation. We are here confronted with similar circumstances as those described by Vygotsky (2004) with the expression "agonies of creation" when the drive to create does not coincide with the capacity to create (p. 40). According to Bratus and Lishin (1983):

> a changing need requires ever newer means and operational and technical possibilities for an activity to satisfy it, and finally a moment may occur when the means necessary to carry out an activity are not accessible to a person, and this sometimes subjectively may be acutely experienced as a state of dissatisfaction with the existing situation, a state of indeterminacy, even distraughtness, arrest, a crisis. (Bratus & Lishin, 1983, p. 42)

This is a situation in which a need cannot be satisfied by the previous set of means of activities (Bratus & Lishin, 1983, p. 43). In this situation,

> some special state of indeterminacy may arise in which desires, as it were, lose their object, and one may say that a person desires (sometimes very passionately) something he himself does not know and cannot clearly describe. This peculiar state of indeterminant, temporarily objectless desire may be called a need state, to use Leont'ev's term. (Bratus & Lishin, 1983, p. 43)

In contrast to needs as such, which have a relatively clear-cut object reference, need states have only potential, possible, hypothetical, but by no means fully fixed objects. The situation in which Beauvoir found herself after graduating is an example of such state of objectless indeterminacy. She had desired to become a writer since childhood, and she had been successful in building a solid educational basis for her future. Sartre was encouraging her to realize her potential. She was, however, in a state of paralysis (Bair, 1990, pp. 165–166).

Although in a situation such as this, nothing seems to happen in terms of creative production, and the individual appears as if paralyzed between wanting to create something and not knowing how to do it, this need state is also productive:

Sooner or later an encounter with, discovery, or active testing action of some object occurs; this object fits the particular need state, which places it in a qualitatively different rank, the rank of an objectified need, i.e., a need that has found its object or motive. Then, through the discovered motive, the need stimulates activity, during the course of which the need is reproduced and . . . is somewhat modified, impelling it on to a new cycle of activity that is different compared with the previous one, etc., i.e., a sequence of transformations emerges. (Bratus & Lishin, 1983, p. 43–44)

In Beauvoir's case, this state of paralysis went on for several years. During these years, Sartre kept encouraging her as she was dealing with the heavily constraining heritage from her past.

My work lacked all real conviction. Sometimes I felt I was doing a school assignment, sometimes that I had lapsed into parody. . . . I wrote in the spring of 1930, and a little later in June: "I have lost my pride—that means I have lost everything" . . . I learned that one's real and imagined desires may be very different—and learned, too, something of the malaise which such uncertainty can engender. . . . I was well on the road to self-betrayal and self-destruction. I regarded this conflict—at least, there were moments when I did—as a tragedy. (Beauvoir, 1965, p. 60)

The sequence of transformation for Beauvoir started when, after a conversation with Sartre, she realized she could convey in her writing her own personal sense of the world:

Themes had been going around my head for a long time now, but I had no idea how to tackle them. One evening . . . Satre and I were sitting inside the Dôme, discussing my work, and he criticized me for my timidity. . . . "Look," he said, with sudden vehemence, "why don't you put *yourself* into your writing?" . . . During the days that followed I thought over Sartre's advice. He gave me courage to devote myself seriously to a theme which I had been considering, in brief spasms, for at least three years. (Beauvoir, 1965, pp. 315–316)

She actively started writing what became her first book, and throughout the process, the object of her work started opening up to her. Retrospectively, it is possible to see the strong connection between this first work and the core of what became her contribution to literature, namely revealing the forces that determine women's lives.

In spite of this first accomplishment and this early exposure to her professional object, Beauvoir's transition toward creative production was still under way. Numerous struggles were still to be met in the process. The first book she finally managed to write underwent two painful rejections by leading publishers.

> The rejection stung, so much that she refused all Sartre's entreaties to allow him to submit it to another publisher. In 1982, shortly before the English-language publication of the stories, Beauvoir described her feelings: "Two rejections were enough insult, enough humiliation. I was so naïve then! If I had only known how many great writers are hurt by repeated rejection of their work, then I might have had the courage to try again with another publisher, but at the time I only believed that my work was inferior, undeserving public attention. I saw myself as a failure and for a long time viewed myself as unworthy." (Bair, 1990, p. 209)

The first book she wrote was published by Gallimard, 42 years after its completion and a few years before her death.

A further step in the sequence of transformation discussed by Bratus and Lishin (1983) consists of a "movement from a narrowly personal, individualistic standpoint to a collectivist and social one" (p. 49). The authors specify that by social collectivist motives they mean motives based on the need to do something useful for unknown, distant people (Bratus & Lishin, 1983, p. 46). Here the cycle, which started with disequilibrium with the environment, closes itself by returning to the environment with an empowered act of creation aimed at affecting the status quo. Also Vygotsky refers to this idea of completion of a full cycle when the ideal materializes in the act of creation:

> Every product of the imagination, stemming from reality, attempts to complete a full circle and to be embodied in reality. A product of the imagination, which has arisen in response to our drive and inspiration, shows a tendency to be embodied in real life. . . . The product of creative imagination is an ideal that is only manifest with true and living force when it guides human actions and activities in its drive to be realized or embodied. (Vygotsky, 2004, p. 41)

Such materialization is however not only the concretizing of an ideal form. It is a vision of a contribution to the societal, which materializes itself. With the act of creation, the creator transcends the individual to reach the societal (Leont'ev, 1971). This step in the sequence of transformation and in the transition toward creative production is vividly reported by Beauvoir in her autobiography: "In order to write . . . the first essential condition is that *reality should no longer be taken for granted*; only then can one both perceive it, and make others do so" (Beauvoir, 1965, p. 365; italics in the original).

Life could not anymore be taken for granted in the perspective of another World War. These historical circumstances became the catalyst of her actual creative production. Through her writing, she felt now part of a broader collective and social endeavor:

> I began *She Came to Stay* in October, 1938, and ended it in the late spring
> of 1941 . . . Suddenly, History burst over me . . . I woke to find myself
> scattered over the four quarters of the globe, linked by every nerve in me
> to each and every other individual. (Beauvoir, 1965, p. 369)

From that point on, she produced a steady and self-ensured body of
creative work.

> After the declaration of war, things finally ceased to be a matter of
> course. Misfortune and misery had erupted into the world, and lit-
> erature had become as essential to me as the very air I breathed. . . .
> Conscious of the gulf that lay between my impressions and the factual
> truth, I felt the need to write, in order to do justice to a truth with
> which all my emotional impulses were out of step. A writer's business is
> . . . to point out those horizons which we never reach and scarcely per-
> ceive, but which nevertheless are there. (Beauvoir, 1965, p. 606–607)

DRIVING OBJECTS

As Beauvoir's example shows, cultural-historical circumstances powerfully
shape our lives. At the same time, human beings themselves continuously
reshape cultural-historical circumstances, when they find objects that drive
them allowing them to push forward their learning and to creatively model
their future. As Vygotsky points out:

> If human activity were limited to reproduction of the old, then the
> human being would be a creature oriented only to the past and would
> only be able to adapt to the future to the extent that it reproduced
> the past. It is precisely human creative activity that makes the human
> being a creature oriented toward the future, creating the future and
> thus altering his own present. (Vgotsky, 2004, p. 9)

The concept of object is central in cultural-historical activity theory. Within
this approach "an object is not . . . understood as a thing that exists in itself
and acts upon the subject" (Davydov, Zinchenko, & Talyzina, 1983, p. 31).
An object is "that toward which an act is directed, i.e., something to which
a living being relates, as the object of his activity" (Leont'ev, 1981, p. 49).
Relationality is an essential quality of the object. The subject develops a
very personal, almost intimate relationship with the object. At the same
time, the object connects the subject to other human beings who are or
have been involved in the pursuit of the same or similar object. The pursuit
of an object is, therefore, both an individual and a collective journey.

Subject and object are intertwined: "Subject and object become constitu-
ents of an integral system, within which they acquire the systemic qualities

inherent in them. . . . In the activity approach the subject actively interacts with the object; it 'meets' the object with partiality and selectivity" (Davydov, Zinchenko, & Talyzina, 1983, p. 33). An activity is shaped by the subjects' practical and physical engagement with their object: "Activity in its original and fundamental form is sensuous, practical activity in which people enter into practical contact with the objects of the world around them, experience their opposition, and act upon them, subordinating themselves to their objective properties" (Leont'ev, 1978, p. 20). The engagement of the subject in the activity is also referred to as object-orientation. Object-orientation is a dialectical relationship through which both the activity and the subject change. Interactions between the subject and the object are of great significance for understanding activities and their transformation: "Human activity is characterized not only by its objectiveness but also by its subjectiveness: The activity of the subject is always directed toward the transformation of an object that is able to satisfy some specific need" (Davydov, Zinchenko, & Talyzina, 1983, p. 32).

Within activity theory, a vision is understood as materializing in creative investigation and transformation: "An important aspect of this process of orientation is exploratory processes" (Davydov, 1981, p. 18). The subject's concrete experimentation with his or her envisioned object can itself transform an activity. Davydov refers to "the plasticity and assimilability of activity and its primary forms, manifested in exploratory and testing movements" (Davydov, 1981, p. 16). In these terms, the object is an invitation to interpretation, personal sense making, and societal transformation (Engeström & Sannino, 2010).

In an object-oriented relationship, the subject appears as driven by the object. Drivenness is understood here as a movement of attraction that mobilizes the subject in the pursuit of an object that can satisfy his or her need and can at the same time support the development of an activity: "Taken from this point of view, activity appears as a process in which mutual transfers between the poles 'subject-object' are accomplished. 'In production the personality is objectivized; in need the thing is subjectivized,' noted Marx" (Leont'ev, 1978, p. 50). The concept of object is also at the core of the work of Knorr-Cetina. There are interesting differences and similarities between Knorr-Cetina's concept of object and the concept of object within the activity-theoretical tradition. Knorr-Cetina refers to a structure of wanting to characterize the subject's desire to grasp the object. In Knorr-Cetina's conceptualization, however, the structure of wanting seems to reside primarily in the subject, whereas in activity theory the dynamics of objects themselves draw the subject.

Knorr-Cetina discusses the features of the object in terms of "sociality with objects" (Knorr-Cetina, 1997, p. 1), whereas Engeström talks about "sociality of things" (Engeström, 1996b, p. 263). Sociality with objects is a relationship, which binds, situates, and stabilizes subjects. The sociality of things, on the other hand, may be characterized as object-driven sociality (i.e., a relationship of opposite forces which at the same time gives freedom and creates binds, positions and displaces, stabilizes, and destabilizes. The power of the mutuality between the object and the subject lies in its potential to transcend exclusive "subjective fusion with the object" (Knorr-Cetina, 1997, p. 18). Interactions between the driven subject and his or her object imply also an envisioning of and striving for unity and sharing with larger and more comprehensive entities beyond the immediately given object and beyond the individual subject. Within an activity-theoretical perspective, objects have also desituating and destabilizing power. In addition to having a centering function, they have also conflictual and expansive driving potentials.

THE EXPANSIVE PURSUIT OF THE OBJECT

In schools, learners are traditionally confronted with tasks involving contents well known ahead of time. In the transition toward work, as in the case of Beauvoir, learners have to redefine the object of their activity, and traditional modes of learning become insufficient. In this transition, learners face the challenge of creatively designing a new activity for themselves and at the same time acquiring knowledge and skills required by the new activity. This type of challenge requires learners to engage in an expansive and practical quest to grasp the object of their activity. This is at the core of the theory of expansive learning.

Expansive learning (Engeström, 1987) is a form of learning that transcends linear and sociospatial dimensions of the learner's individual and short-lived actions. Within the expansive approach, learning is understood in the broader and temporally much longer perspective of a third dimension (i.e., the dimension of the development of the activity). This dimension coincides with the third dimension introduced in this chapter to conceptualize critical transitions (i.e., the dimension or struggles against and breaking through marginalizing boundaries, Figure 2.1).

Expansion is the result of a critical transition from actions currently performed by individuals to a new activity. In such a transition, learners become aware of the contradictions in their current activity and engage in creative, transformative actions in the perspective of a new form of activity. In the example of Beauvoir, the critical transition leads to the realization of the contradictory forces that emancipate and marginalize women. Her tentative writing actions in the book *When Things of the Spirit Came First* progressively expanded in the new activity of her creative writing career.

Contradictions are historically accumulated tensions that represent a key factor leading to expansive learning. Contradictions alone, however, cannot automatically generate this type of learning. Expansive learning is tied to both historical forces and collective human agency and engagement. Whereas historical forces influence human life and choices, individuals are not necessarily aware of them. Human actions and needs as such cannot affect the development of entire activities. Creative potentials become apparent when human needs meet an object that answers them (Leont'ev, 1978, p. 54). Leont'ev (1978) refers to this as an "extraordinary act" (p. 54). In these circumstances, individuals join their forces and invest focused, long-term efforts to pursue their object. The strong interest in philosophy and in the writing profession brought Beauvoir very close to Sartre in what became a lifelong journey. Beauvoir's pursuit of her object was a shared endeavor in which Sartre played the persistent role of an encouraging pair and a constructive critique. Beside Sartre, Beauvoir's journey involved also several other contemporary intellectuals.

At the level of daily human actions, contradictions manifest themselves as problems, conflicts, and dilemmas, such as those reported in the quotes by Beauvoir in this chapter during the years of paralysis. Contradictions mobilize expansive learning when individuals deal with them as being the roots of their problems and conflicts, and by newly appropriating the object of their activity. Forming a new, expanded object of activity requires "questioning and breaking away from the constraints of the existing activity and embarking on a journey across the uncharted terrain" (Engeström & Sannino, 2010, p. 7). Yet, "expansion does not imply an abrupt break with the past or a once-and-for all replacement of the existing object with a totally new one. Expansion both transcends and retains previous layers of the object" (Engeström, Puonti, & Seppänen, 2003, p. 181–183).

The expansive and creative potential of critical transitions resides in this engagement with intertwined personal and historical struggles. Expansive learning and creative production in the case of Beauvoir stem from her struggles with and breaking away from oppressive constraints in her personal life, which reflected the historical circumstances of her time and lead to changes in the lives of many other women. The extraordinary nature of the encounter between a human being and his or her object lies in the collective and creative potentials of such an encounter. Human beings in these circumstances can become capable of shaping cultural landscapes and in some cases even write new pages of history. Beauvoir's book, *The Second Sex,* marked a turning point in women's history and inspired the activist Women's Liberation Movement of the late 1960s and 1970s. This is the essence of the collective nature of creativity in the case of Simone de Beauvoir.

CONCLUDING REMARKS

Supporting the finding and the pursuit of an object should be the key contribution of educational activities to the students' learning and creative potentials. In the case of Beauvoir, the object existed as a distant vision since her childhood, when she dreamed to become a writer. The path to materialize this vision was still to be made, and her years as a student did not directly serve this purpose. In Beauvoir's example, the transition from the leading activity of schooling to the leading activity of work was a critical one. Theories of creativity and learning seldom address the obstacles in transitions between dominant activities from the point of view of the object pursued by the learner and the creative person. This chapter attempted to start addressing this issue with the help of the notion of critical transitions.

When the object comes into the picture, the type of learning involved becomes both expansive and creative in that one must learn and create "something which is not yet there" (Engeström, 1991, p. 270). Critical transitions toward this type of learning and creativity remind us of the collective nature of these two. Collective learning and creativity occur not only when human beings join forces that have strong generative and innovative potentials. Creativity is collective because the driven act of creation connects individuals with broader collective and societal causes. This coincides with the attracting power of driving objects that bring together people sharing the same ideals and visions of a better world, as in the example of Beauvoir. Genuine collective learning and creative endeavors are these types of spontaneous formations of human beings going through deep personal and societal struggles, attracted and seduced by objects that drive them.

ACKNOWLEDGMENTS

The research on which this chapter is based was supported in part by an Academy Research Fellowship granted to Annalisa Sannino (No. 264972) by the Academy of Finland, Research Council for Culture and Society. I am grateful to Liubov Vetoshkina for her precious support with the translation from Russian of a text by Leont'ev not yet available in English. I warmly thank Anne Laitinen, Jenny Vainio, and the three anonymous reviewers for their invaluable comments on an earlier version of this chapter. The statements of this chapter are, however, solely my responsibility.

NOTES

1. Beauvoir's own words, as recorded in an interview to her biographer.
2. Translation from Russian by Liubov Vetoshkina, CRADLE, University of Helsinki.

REFERENCES

Akkerman, S. F., & Bakker, A. (2011). Boundary crossing and boundary objects. *Review of Educational Research, 81*, 132–169.

Bair, D. (1990). *Simone de Beauvoir: A biography.* London, England: Jonathan Cape.

Beach, K. D. (1999). Consequential transitions: A sociocultural expedition beyond transfer in education. *Review of Research in Education, 24,* 101–139.

Beauvoir, S. (1965). *The prime of life.* Harmondsworth, England: Penguin.

Bratus, B. S., & Lishin, O. V. (1983). Laws of the development of activity and problems in the psychological and pedagogical shaping of the personality. *Soviet Psychology, XXI,* 38–50.

Bronfenbrenner, U. (1979). *The ecology of human development.* Cambridge, MA: Harvard University Press.

Csikszentmihalyi, M. (1996). *Creativity: Flow and the psychology of discovery and invention.* New York, NY: HarperCollins.

Davydov, V. (1981). The category of activity and mental reflection in the theory of A. N. Leontiev. *Soviet Psychology, 19,* 3–29.

Davydov, V. V., Zinchenko, V. P., & Talyzina, N. F. (1983). The problem of activity in the works of A. N. Leontiev. *Soviet Psychology, 21,* 31–42.

El'konin, D. B. (1977). Toward the problem of stages in the mental development of the child. In M. Cole (Ed.), *Soviet developmental psychology* (pp. 85–93). White Plains, NY: M. E. Sharpe.

Engeström, Y. (1987). *Learning by expanding: An activity-theoretical approach to developmental research.* Helsinki, Finland: Orienta-Konsultit.

Engeström, Y. (1991). Developmental work research: Reconstructing expertise through expansive learning. In M. Nurminen & G. Weir (Eds.), *Human jobs and computer interfaces* (pp. 265–290). Amsterdam, The Netherlands: Elsevier.

Engeström, Y. (1996a). Developmental work research as educational research: Looking ten years back and into the zone of proximal development. *Nordisk Pedagogik: Journal of Nordic Educational Research, 16,* 131–143.

Engeström, Y. (1996b). Interobjectivity, ideality, and dialectics. *Mind, Culture, and Activity, 3*(4), 259–265.

Engeström, Y., Puonti, A., & Seppänen, L. (2003). Spatial and temporal expansion of the object as a challenge for reorganizing work. In D. Nicolini, S. Gherardi, & D. Yanow (Eds.), *Knowing in organizations: A practice-based approach* (pp. 151–186). Armonk, NY: M. E. Sharpe.

Engeström, Y., & Sannino, A. (2010). Studies of expansive learning: Foundations, findings and future challenges. *Educational Research Review, 5,* 1–24.

Goodwin, J., & O'Connor, H. (Eds.). (2009). Special issue: Continuity and change in 40 years of school to work transitions. *Journal of Education and Work, 5*(22), 341–342.

Griffin, P., & Cole, M. (1984). Current activity for the future: The zo-ped. In B. Rogoff & J. Wertsch (Eds.), *Children's learning in the "zone of proximal development"* (pp. 4–64). San Francisco, CA: Jossey-Bass.

Gruber, H. (1981). Breakaway minds (Interview with Howard Gardner). *Psychology Today,* 68–73.

Gruber, H. E., & Bödeker, K. (Eds.). (2005). *Creativity, psychology and the history of science.* Dordrecht, The Netherlands: Springer.

Kaufman, J. C., & Beghetto, R. A. (2009). Beyond big and little: The four C model of creativity. *Review of General Psychology, 13*(1), 1–12.

Knorr-Cetina, K. (1997). Sociality with objects: Social relations in postsocial knowledge societies. *Theory, Culture & Society, 14*(4), 1–30.

Lave, J., & Wenger, E. (1991). *Situated learning: Legitimate peripheral participation.* Cambridge, England: Cambridge University Press.

Leont'ev, A. N. (1971). Introduction. In L. S. Vygotsky, *The psychology of art* (pp. v–xi). Cambridge, MA: MIT Press.

Leont'ev, A. N. (1978). *Activity, consciousness, and personality.* Englewood Cliffs, NJ: Prentice Hall.

Leont'ev, A. N. (1981). *Problems of the development of the mind.* Moscow, Russia: Progress Publishers.

Leont'ev, A. N. (1983). *Izbrannie psihologicheskie proizvedeniya [Collected psychological works],* Vol. 2. Moscow, Russia: Pedagogika.

Lovitts, B. (2005). Being a good course-taker is not enough: A theoretical perspective on the transition to independent research. *Studies in Higher Education,* 30(2), 137–154.

Rank, J., Pace, V. L., & Frese, M. (2004). Three avenues for future research on creativity, innovation, and initiative. *Applied Psychology: An International Review, 53,* 518–528.

Sawyer, R. K. (2012). *Explaining creativity: The science of human innovation.* New York, NY: Oxford University Press.

Tanggaard, L. (2007). Learning at trade vocational school and learning at work: Boundary crossing in apprentices' everyday life. *Journal of Education and Work, 20*(5), 453–466.

Vasilyuk, F. (1988). *The psychology of experiencing.* Moscow, Russia: Progress Publishers.

Vygotsky, L. S. (1971). *The psychology of art.* Cambridge, MA: MIT Press.

Vygotsky, L. S. (1997). *Educational psychology.* Boca Raton, FL: St. Lucie Press.

Vygotsky, L. S. (1998). Imagination and creativity in the adolescent. In *The collected works of L. S. Vygotsky, Vol. 5: Child psychology* (pp. 151–166). New York, NY: Plenum.

Vygotsky, L. S. (1999). On the problem of the psychology of the actor. In *The collected works of L. S. Vygotsky, Vol. 6: Scientific legacy* (pp. 237–244). New York, NY: Plenum.

Vygotsky, L. S. (2004). Imagination and creativity in childhood. *Journal of Russian and East European Psychology, 42*(1), 7–97.

3 Beyond Traditional School Learning
Fostering Agency and Collective Creativity in Hybrid Educational Activities

Katsuhiro Yamazumi

Today, educational reform in several settings is increasingly concerned with how to shift school practices to foster greater agency—the intellect and energy to act—and creativity among various actors, especially children, which has tended in the context of traditional schooling to be poorly prompted and supported. One approach to bringing about agency and creativity in teaching and learning is the effort to achieve a transition from methods of teaching and learning that just transmit and preserve cultural forms to those that actually transform and create culture.

In traditional schooling, the core activity is classroom-based teaching that is intended simply to transfer the content of the textbook to children. Educational institutions are typically tightly closed activity systems that have little direct impact on society. Children's learning, as Cole (2005) puts it, is typically confined to "standard classroom environments, with strict teacher control and one-to-many forms of discourse associated with transmission forms of education" (p. 10). Similarly, Rose (2009) makes a radical critique of today's narrow focus on high-stakes testing and economic competition as the goals of education: "We've reduced our definition of human development and achievement—that miraculous growth of intelligence, sensibility, and the discovery of the world—to a test score" (p. x). We need to go beyond this narrow idea of schooling and expand learning activities in schools especially at the K–12 stage to evoke and support the development of agency and creativity among children.

This chapter examines a new landscape of collaborative learning in schools, one that is fostering the agency and collective creativity of children. The discussion presented here is based on an analysis of findings from longitudinal intervention research on children's educational activities in Osaka. In alliance with local municipal elementary schools, this research project focuses on *hybrid educational innovation,* a process intended to create advanced networks of learning based on the principle of collaboration among a variety of participants both inside and outside a school, gradually transcending the school's institutional boundaries (Yamazumi, 2010a, 2010b).

With the increasing importance of networking and partnering among diverse cultural organizations, we need to call attention to the need for school practices to promote children's agency and collective creativity and to develop partnerships with community organizations, businesses, experts, and other relevant actors outside the school. Although such practices are rapidly becoming more widespread, there is little detailed empirical research on their form, content, strengths, and limitations (e.g., Burnard, 2011; Daniels, Leadbetter, Soares, & MacNab, 2006). These new forms of activity related to the education of children can be analyzed with the help of *cultural-historical activity theory* (Engeström, 1987, 2008; Leont'ev, 1978; Sannino, Daniels, & Gutiérrez, 2009).

Activity theory offers a conceptual framework that views the object-oriented collective activity system as the basic unit of analysis of human practices and development and as a rich source of ideas and tools for modeling future innovative activities. Within the general framework of activity theory, the concept of *knotworking* is particularly promising as a tool for analyzing newly emerging practices of collaboration between schools and the outside community. Knotworking refers to partially improvised but intense forms of collaboration between partners that, despite being otherwise only loosely connected, engage in solving problems and designing solutions rapidly when their common object so requires (Engeström, 2008; Engeström, Engeström, & Vähäaho, 1999). Applying this concept to hybrid learning activities, it should be possible to reconceptualize more familiar but yet theoretically weak notions of creative collaboration and partnership between multiple activity systems.

In the following sections, I first discuss the interrelation of learning, agency, and collective creativity in schooling. Second, to go beyond conceptualizations of pedagogical activity prevalent in the traditional school, I discuss collective educational innovation to construct hybrid and symbiotic forms of school activity. Hybrid educational innovation of this sort has the potential to stimulate participating organizations and actors to share a new, expanded sense of the sites, objects, and scope of educational work. Third, I analyze some findings from an intervention study on a hybrid educational project taking place in Osaka, with the help of the conceptual framework of activity theory and the concept of knotworking. Finally, I discuss knotworking-type of hybrid learning activities, looking at how emerging collaborative and creative learning activities expand into the surrounding communities and society and change them for the better.

EXPANSIVE LEARNING, AGENCY, AND COLLECTIVE CREATIVITY IN SCHOOLING

As Engeström (2000) points out, one lesson we can draw from intervention research is that change and development fail when they are imported from outside or implemented from above. From the perspective of cultural-historical activity theory, the process of putting an intervention into practice must in turn facilitate the process of "expansive learning" (Engeström, 1987). "In expansive learning, learners learn something that is not yet there. In other words, the learners construct a new object and concept for their collective activity, and implement this new object and concept in practice" (Engeström & Sannino, 2010, p. 2). In other words, practitioners involved in and affected by the learning that is taking place take the initiative to reforge the objects of their own current work—that is, reforging their practices, goals, and understanding of *why* they do things the way they do. Even more than observation or analysis, intervention needs to take account of the "human potential for agency, for intentional collective and individual actions aimed at transforming the activity" (Engeström, 2006, p. 4). This *agentive layer* focuses on the potential for agents to create intellectual, emotional, and moral judgments in their own names that function as intentional transformative actions.

Agentive action is a central thesis of Vygotsky's cultural-historical approach to human development, a key source in the development of activity theory (Lektorsky, 2009, pp. 76–77). A central theme of Vygotsky's approach is that there is "a new problem associated with volition or freedom in human activity and consciousness" (Vygotsky, 1987, p. 349): The problem of agency as the genesis of voluntary actions, that is, the potential of free will in agentive human activity and consciousness.

Vygotsky-inspired activity theory is a developmental theory distinguished by its concern with qualitative transformations in human practice over time. Its central concern is that human beings can become agents who can change themselves by changing their own institutions and practices in a way that mobilizes their collaborative agency. Making changes in our own real-life worlds is an endeavor at the heart of activity theory. From this perspective, agency is seen as the expression of the subject-potentialities and positions connected to the externalized creation of new tools and forms of activity with which humans transform both their outer and inner worlds and thus master their own social conditions (Engeström, 1991, 2006).

Thus, agency will help people gradually transform their own lives and futures. This is why learning, agency, and collective creativity are intertwined. They can be characterized as collective, future-making, and transformative processes, and agency and collective creativity are generated through "learning to create collectively imagined worlds," turning the imagined world into a living instrument of people's life-activities (Engeström & Kallinen, 1988, p. 67).

For Vygotsky, every form of creativity is based on *creative imagination*. Following Ribot (1906), he divides human behavior into two basic types: "reproductive activity" and "combinatorial or creative activity" (Vygotsky, 2004, pp. 7–9). The former is very closely linked to memory and results in the reproduction of previously experienced impressions or actions; in contrast, the latter drives the creation of new images or actions by combining and creatively reworking elements of our previous experience and using them to generate new propositions and new behavior (p. 9). Additionally, going beyond an individualist view, Vygotsky recognized the importance of the development of creativity in the process of constructing a human collective. Creativity is deeply related to this "collective subject" in Lektorsky's (1984) terms. Therefore, as Vygotsky wrote, creativity must be recognized as essentially collective:

> When we consider the phenomenon of collective creativity, which combines all these drops of individual creativity that frequently are insignificant in themselves, we readily understand what an enormous percentage of what has been created by humanity is a product of the anonymous collective creative work of unknown inventors. (Vygotsky, 2004, p. 11)

Vygotsky strongly advocates and asserts the importance of cultivating creativity through schooling on the basis that the main educational objective of learning in schools should be the guidance of children's agentive actions in such a way as to prepare them for the future: "The entire future of humanity will be attained through the creative imagination; orientation to the future, behavior based on the future, is the most important function of the imagination" (Vygotsky, 2004, pp. 87–88). Another reason is related to his conception of schooling: "School is an organization where children participate in the life which surrounds them" (Vygotsky, 1994, p. 24). This fundamentally Vygotskian view of school is closely related to his understanding of the plasticity of the life and social environment that children collectively create by and for themselves: "Ultimately, only life educates, and the deeper that life, the real world, burrows into the school, the more dynamic and the more robust will be the educational process" (Vygotsky, 1997, p. 345). As a consequence, he points out that the school as a collective activity system will provide children the "best stimulus of creativity" if it can collectively "organize their life and environment so that it leads to the need and ability to create" (Vygotsky, 2004, p. 66). As an example of what this would look like, Vygotsky uses the "widespread form of the children's magazine or newspaper" in schools, seeing it as an opportunity for children to pursue a deeper collective life and social environment.

> Virtually the greatest value of the magazine is that it brings children's creative writing closer to children's life. The children begin to understand why a person would want to write. Writing becomes a meaningful and necessary task for them. School and class newspapers have the same if not greater importance because they also make it possible to involve children who have the most diverse interests and talents in a joint group effort, as do creative evenings, and similar activities that stimulate children's creativity. (Vygotsky, 2004, pp. 66–67)

Here, it is obvious that Vygotsky is redefining the goal of the teacher from producing immediate effects in the children to (instead) indirectly affecting them through the social environment (Vygotsky, 1997, p. 49). As Davydov (1995) recalled, Vygotsky acutely points out that "a teacher can intentionally bring up and teach children only through continual collaboration with them and with their social milieu, with their desires and readiness to act together with the teacher" (p. 17). Thus, for Vygotsky, pedagogical practice amounts simply to *collective activity* or *collaboration*.

In the next section, I discuss intervention research with the potential to promote children's learning activities so as to evoke and generate the collective and creative agency that can "transcend the institutional boundaries of the school and turn the school into a collective instrument" (Engeström, 1991, p. 257) for transforming related activities, the surrounding community, and the real world at large.

HYBRID EDUCATIONAL INNOVATION AND EXPANSIVE DEVELOPMENT IN SCHOOLS

The intervention research discussed in this chapter proposes a concept of *hybrid educational innovation* (Yamazumi, 2008) for the expansive development of curriculum, instruction, and learning in schools. Hybrid educational innovation is based on collaboration with various sites of learning outside the K–12 school system (e.g., universities, experts, workplaces, community organizations) that offer different learning trajectories to teachers and children and are characterized by different rules and patterns of instruction and learning from those in classroom-based teaching. "Third-generation activity theory" (Engeström, 1996, pp. 132–133) exceeds the limits of a single activity system and adopts as its unit of analysis multiple activity systems that mutually interact, promoting empirical intervention research to design and implement networks, dialogues, and other mechanisms of collaboration between these systems. Applying this framework to school innovation, the idea behind this kind of intervention is that expanding school activity and learning are best carried out not from the inside alone but by creating hybrid and symbiotic activities in the real-life world (Yamazumi, 2009). In this context, hybrid educational innovation as an intervention in school learning constitutes part of a network of learning intended to try something new with children as learners.

As shown in Figure 3.1, hybrid educational innovation is envisaged as expanding along two dimensions with intersecting trajectories. The vertical dimension depicts the *objects* of learning (types of problems) children are working on. This dimension identifies a developmental trend from learning by acquiring correct answers as responses to given tasks, to learning by questioning and defining a problem in relation to real life and society. Alongside this, the horizontal dimension describes types of school *organizations* and their relation to outside communities and organizations, tracing the movement from an isolated school to a networked and hybridized school.

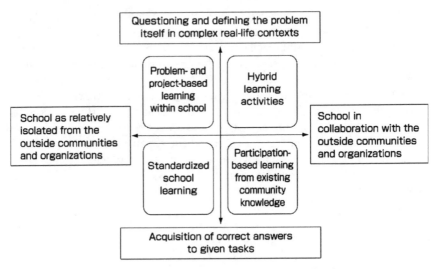

Figure 3.1   Two dimensions of expansive development in schools.

These two crossing dimensions are key features for the expansion of school activity to transcend both an encapsulated concept of school learning and the institutional boundaries of school organizations. In the pedagogical transformation that results from the combination of the two dimensions of expansion, learning is largely carried out in the new form of emerging hybrid learning activities in which various partners inside and outside the school collaborate. The following question becomes the center of inquiry: "What could replace the text as the object of schoolwork?" (Engeström, 2008, p. 90). Here, I present findings on the implementation of a project called the "New School" (NS). The aim of this project, conducted in Osaka, is to develop a hybrid activity system that attempts to transform the pedagogical activity of traditional schooling (Yamazumi, 2008, 2009, 2010a, 2010b).

NS is an after-school project intended to help children create advanced networks of learning based on cooperation among the following partners: a university, local elementary schools, families, experts, and community organizations outside the school. Since 2005, all these parties have been involved in designing and implementing mixed-grade group- and project-based learning and developing networks of learning, supported by our research group at Kansai University. Essentially, the project has seen elementary school children, with the support of university students studying to become elementary school teachers, engaged in fun, creative, and collaborative learning processes. Inspired by their own lives and practices, the children worked on themes such as food, eating, cooking, gardening, farming, and personal well-being with a focus on ecological awareness, responsibility for the environment, and a sustainable future. The NS activities develop the children's agentive, critical, and creative learning abilities. NS seeks to create project-based collaborative learning activities, not only for the children but also for the other participants, on the topic of sustainable living. The project discussed in this chapter is called *From Seed to Table* and involves participants in the experience of growing organic food, learning about ecology, and taking part in "slow food" cooking lessons.

As part of their NS activity, the children and university students engaged in project-based learning related to *suita kuwai*, the aquatic Japanese Arrowhead plant, *Sagittaria japonica*. *Suita kuwai* is a traditionally consumed vegetable native to the city of Suita in Osaka Prefecture, where the children involved in the project live and has been well-known for generations as a soft, sweet, distinctive-tasting vegetable. Being only partially domesticated, however, it was quickly extirpated amidst a wave of urbanization, and at one point was even on the verge of extinction. Thus, in recent years, local farmers, experts, citizens, and government agencies have established a network to revive *suita kuwai,* protect it and promote its proliferation, and ensure that it is passed onto future generations.

The activities and learning units developed by the NS project have been incorporated into instruction in some schools in the area, especially as curriculum units in "Period for Integrated Study." This period looks at interdisciplinary and cross-curricular themes for third-grade and older children, in addition to regular school subjects; content is not prescribed *per se* in the national curriculum standards, but schools are expected to make efforts to develop and conduct distinctive project-based learning activities. As part of this expansion, two regional elementary schools, the Suita Municipal Yamate Elementary School and the Suita Municipal Kita-Yamada Elementary School, have conducted *kuwai*-themed units. The children and their teachers of both these schools created each irrigated *kuwai* fields in the schoolyard with the support of a local farmer, experts, and regional government agencies. The children planted the seedlings themselves in June and then cultivated them and observed their growth. In December, the children harvested the vegetables and cooked and ate them—for example, they made *kuwai* bread, called *suita kuwai* rolls, with the help of the owner and baker at a nearby bakery. In addition, they prepared the vegetables for sale at their school festival.

Based on the model of hybrid educational innovation represented in Figure 3.1, the development of the NS project is envisaged to expand progressively through both the vertical and the horizontal dimensions in a synergetic manner (between the *object* and *organization*). NS has gradually expanded the object of its learning activities as well as its ties with cooperating organizations. In this expansion, children and teachers' investigations and collaborative learning related to *kuwai* have been supported and encouraged by many groups and individuals in a process transcending the boundaries of the school, including a partnership that has been established between our research group at Kansai University and local elementary schools.

Other individuals and organizations taking part include Mr. Koichi Hirano, a community-oriented farmer who produces *kuwai* and other traditional Osaka-area vegetables using only organic cultivation and natural agriculture methods; the *Suita Kuwai* Conservation Society, which has conducted its own volunteer activities over many years aimed at the proliferation of *kuwai* and its bequest to future citizens; regional government agencies such as the Suita City Office's Industrial Labor Section and the Osaka Prefectural Government's North Division Office for Agriculture–Forestry Promotion and Nature Conservation; and the Suita City Board of Education. This collaboration has created a network of learning for the children, tied into their real lives and social activities. This is an example of how hybrid educational innovation uses as its source of learning a network of volunteer activities conducted by people attempting to bring *suita kuwai* back into modern life in the region.

In our intervention research on hybrid educational innovation, creative collaboration of this kind is not operated by a network in the sense of a set of relatively stable, closed connections between organization units with a fixed framework and membership. This means that a central function or agent that controls learning activities does not hold. Learning is instead facilitated by a wide range of individuals and organizations, including producers, experts, volunteer organizations, and government agencies. The school provides initiative and oversees the periodic changes and rotation of these facilitators.

Engeström's notion of "negotiated knotworking" (Engeström, 2008; Engeström, Engeström, & Vähäaho, 1999) is useful for analyzing the creation of these flexible, fluid, and impromptu collaborations. The image of a *knot* refers to partially improvised forms of intense collaboration between otherwise loosely connected actors and activity systems engaging in problem solving and rapidly designing hybrid solutions as required by a common object. Drawing on the idea of knotworking, the goal in building hybrid activity systems as a form of intervention research is to have no fixed center of authority or control. By utilizing a knotworking-type formation for collaborative practice, the university research group avoids being cast as the authorities in the project.

A Period for Integrated Study in which an irrigated field was created in the schoolyard to cultivate *suita kuwai* took place at Yamate Elementary School during the 2008 school year. This was a first for an elementary school in Suita. The starting point for these activities was knotworking among diverse partners in a wide range of fields, beginning as part of assistance for agricultural education activities provided through a local agricultural cooperative. A research coordinator who was a member of our Kansai University research group became an intermediary, acting as a liaison to form *knots* between a diverse range of partners including the Suita

City Office, the Suita City Board of Education, organic vegetable farmers, and the elementary school staff, including the principal, vice principal, and homeroom teachers. These knots gave rise to Integrated Study Periods with a focus on irrigated *kuwai* fields. This type of collaboration among partners transcends the limits of closed organizations, where the frameworks and members are often fixed; by doing so, it enables flexible, fluid, and partially improvised activities. It is based on the principle of "distributed leadership" (Spillane, 2006), in which members play leadership roles on a rotating basis, taking the initiative in the face of situations and issues that emerge related to their respective areas of specialization. In this way, knotworking-type collaboration took shape to produce learning activity "without strong predetermined rules or central authority" (Engeström, 2008, p. 208) on the theme of irrigated *kuwai* fields in the schoolyard.

Hybrid activity and knotworking require and generate new types of agency that engage with the objects shared by activity networks. That is, knotworking-type hybrid learning activities evoke distributed and emergent agency in multiple dialogic, boundary-crossing, and hybridized activity systems. In the next section, I analyze the emergence of agency distributed in the knotworking engagements related to *suita kuwai* as the shared object of integrated learning activities.

LEARNING AND COLLECTIVE CREATIVITY DISTRIBUTED IN THE KNOTS

The intention of designing and implementing knotworking-type hybrid learning activities is to help to collectively generate complex, multiple learning trajectories of individuals, collectives, and the whole organization. In knotworking, in other words, participants connect and reciprocally share resources potentially related to these learning trajectories. For example, a participating fourth-grade homeroom teacher at Yamate Elementary School replied to our research group's question, "What are your views on conducting the Period for Integrated Study for *suita kuwai*?" as follows:

Excerpt 1

> I was one of those who learned about *suita kuwai* for the first time when I came to this school. Before that, I had heard of *kuwai*, but all I knew was that it is used in traditional Japanese New Year's meals. When I came here, I heard for the first time that people were involved in activities to promote *suita kuwai* because it was on the verge of extinction. I thought it would be really good if the fourth-grade children at Yamate Elementary School could participate in activities [related to *suita kuwai*] each year, so we started using the Period for Integrated Study for these activities (part of an interview on June 2, 2011).

This teacher expressed her hope that "the fourth-grade children at Yamate Elementary School could participate . . ." in *suita kuwai*–themed activities. This utterance indicates that her agency for integrated learning units at the school emerged from her encounter with *suita kuwai*. Specifically, her agency was generated in a knot configuration based on a shared object (*suita kuwai*) between partners who are otherwise loosely connected. This learning practice was also implemented benefiting from the knowledge gained from previous successful experiences from the previous year. The following excerpt is from the same interview with the fourth-grade homeroom teacher, in reply to the question, "What do you think the children will be able to learn from this class?"

Excerpt 2

The children really look forward to it, because they have a strong awareness that they are cultivating these vegetables themselves. They have developed an interest in observing nature as they watch the vegetables grow; for example, seeing that the leaves have gotten bigger, or insects are crawling on the plants. They're particularly thrilled when it comes time to harvest the vegetables. Last year, the children helped to prepare the vegetables for sale, washing them and putting them in bags, so that they could be sold at the school festival. We never told the children that they had to show up on Sunday; we just said, "If you want to come," and lots of children showed up. They sold the vegetables themselves, and they used that income to buy sheets and fertilizer to use for the soil this year. That's how we're using the money (part of an interview on June 2, 2011).

These agentive actions on the part of the children were generated in and through their own collective activities of harvesting and selling the *kuwai*. The activity the year before must have convinced the teacher herself of the significance of integrated learning on the theme of *kuwai*. The children's learning activities can be seen as demonstrating participation in and commitment to the knots of diverse individuals, organizations, and groups that are collectively created when boundaries are transcended by different people sharing a common object—namely, in this case, *kuwai*. Hence, it is obvious that the relevance of agency goes beyond the children's agency alone. The teacher's agency is also crucial, as is the agency of other "knot" partners.

Furthermore, we can see that this agency is generated and distributed among various providers of learning outside schools. For example, on January 13, 2012, the local farmer Mr. Hirano, who had supported the children cultivating the *kuwai* seedlings in the schoolyards, came to Kita-Yamada Elementary School to join the children in harvesting the vegetables. At that time, he had a conversation with the third graders about their harvest. The following is an excerpt:

Excerpt 3

Child: Mr. Hirano said that he couldn't grow many vegetables in his garden this year, but we grew a lot at Kita-Yamada Elementary School, so I was very happy.

Mr. Hirano: That's because the teachers and the children at Kita-Yamada Elementary School all worked so hard. This year was a really poor harvest year for suita kuwai in all parts of the Suita region. The harvest volumes were low for all of the farmers. . . . The kuwai that you grew here at the school were big, though, and round; they were the picture of health for a kuwai. . . . When I plant them, I always thought that I should leave about 35 cm between the plants. This was a poor harvest year, and the plants didn't grow very well at all. So, this year, it really would have been better to plant them closer together, maybe about 10 or 20 cm apart. At this school, all of the children wanted so much to plant one more, and then one more, that we ended up using those shorter distances. I think that's one of the reasons why you had such a great harvest. I ended up learning a lot. For me, as a farmer, I realized that it's much better to plant the kuwai plants at about half of the interval that I have used in the past. You gave me a lot to think about. So, this time, you kids are the ones who taught me. It was a very valuable lesson, so I'll have to pass this on to all of the farmers in Suita City planting kuwai next spring. . . . This year, Kita-Yamada Elementary School is the champion for growing suita kuwai.

All: Yay! (everyone applauds)

This type of agency generated through the *suita kuwai* project is engaged with a common object and distributed via knotworking. Similarly, learning and collective creativity are strongly distributed in this partially improvised knot, which connects and coordinates different actors, activity systems, and potential resources. Mr. Hirano said that he as a farmer ended up learning a lot from this experience with the children, to the extent that he realized there was a much better way to plant *kuwai* in his own operations. For the farmer, the irrigated fields in the schoolyards might become a kind of laboratory, helping give rise to better agricultural methods for the future. In this kind of partnership, teachers and children also get the chance to tackle authentic—and interesting—themes and problems, performing investigations to seek realistic solutions. This way, the reciprocal links between schools and communities are the site of the collective creation and sharing of the knowledge and practices acquired by all parties through their commitment to acting together.

Creativity or creation was, in this case, not limited to the production of subjectively new experiences and knowledge in the children; moreover, objectively, culturally new knowledge was produced through the work of the children. From the activity-theoretical perspectives discussed in the beginning of this chapter, creativity in the children here is understood as involvement in collective and externalized creation of new tools and forms of activity. As such, the children's engagement in a deeper collective life and social environment provided them with the "best stimulus of creativity," which leads to the need and ability to create, as Vygotsky (2004, pp. 66–67) illuminated well with the above-mentioned example of "widespread form of the children's magazine or newspaper" in schools.

The children in these knots may come to meet people involved in social activism to promote and support the cultivation and creative use of local and organic food products and nutritional practices (including "slow food") in collaboration with local farmers and others. Social movements of this sort try to change regional practices and everyday life for the better. Thus, knotworking-type hybrid learning activities have great potential to facilitate agentive learning on the part of children and collective creativity among all parties, aligned with and leading to active contribution to real collaborative activities outside the school. For example, in 2010, the group-based learning activities children participated in as part of the NS project included the creation of original scripts on the theme of Osaka's traditional vegetables and then performing these dramas for the public at a city museum. Here is a short excerpt from the children's original drama "News Flash! *Suita Kuwai* News":

Excerpt 4

Reporter Y: Do you all know about kuwai?
Everyone: No-o-o!
Reporter R: You've all said that you don't know, so I would like to explain a little bit about kuwai here.
　　　. . .
Reporter Y: Do you all understand?
　　　. . .
Reporter R: It looked like you were having fun. I would like you all to try growing kuwai yourselves. Suita kuwai is a traditional vegetable; so I hope you will all help to protect it.

Through such activities the children progressively expand the object-world of which they are aware, as Leont'ev (1981, p. 367) states in his analysis of the development of children's play. This expansion of the world via play includes "not only the objects that constitute the child's immediate environment, objects with which it can act and does act itself, but also objects with which adults act, with which the child is not yet able actually to operate, which are still beyond its physical capacity" (p. 367). In performing their own drama, the children became news reporters in the object-world of their creative imagination, beyond the learning that had taken place with regard to their relation to the actual object. With the help of these theatrical performances, the children could represent themselves as adult citizens, entreating the public to "help to protect" *suita kuwai.*

The division of labor in schools is largely compartmentalized, segregated, and individualized: "teachers teach and control, students study" (Engeström, 1991, p. 248). However, as illustrated above, the *kuwai*-themed NS activity and Period for Integrated Study in the schools was able to break through the institutionalized encapsulation characteristic of traditional school learning. To do so, hybrid educational innovations must be represented as emerging interinstitutional activity systems in which the object of the learning children are grappling with expands into the collaborative creation of living life activities and transforms the surrounding world, leading to community revitalization.

CONCLUSION

As described above, in various investigative and collaborative learning activities surrounding *suita kuwai,* different providers of learning and educational services outside the classroom have helped children and teachers embark upon expansive and powerful learning trajectories. The power of agency demonstrated in these hybrid learning activities is effectively distributed via knotworking so as to connect and reciprocally share potential resources for those learning trajectories. The learning and collective creativity of the children, the teachers, and the outside partners are generated and distributed in this fuzzy boundary zone as well, where multiple activity systems come into contact, cross, and interact with each other.

In the boundary zones between these hybrid, symbiotic activities, learning of a qualitatively different nature is emerging that (re)combines the motives and goals of all involved partners and institutions and "engenders more meaning for students long subjected to decontextualized lectures" (Lee, 2011, p. 409). Not only did the children use books, the Internet, and other materials to investigate the *kuwai,* but they also heard directly from people involved in protection and proliferation activities. In this way, the prevalent modes of participation in hybrid educational activities become "more 'horizontally' organized to encourage active student participation" (Cole, 2005, p. 10).

Knotworking-type hybrid integrated learning, which is created with assistance from cooperating members of the community, expands school activity along both the object and organization dimensions. This expansion breaks through the confines of textbooks and 45-minute single lessons in classrooms and providing children with the opportunity to encounter a different social world, for example through meetings with diverse individuals outside of the school (Yamazumi, 2005). This form of learning stimulates the diversity of the children's interests, exposing them to a wide range of interactions and relationships with people of different backgrounds. This in turn gives rise to fruitful opportunities for the children. Through these knots, the children can experience a type of learning that changes their own understanding of themselves. By collaborating with and harnessing the energy of transformative social movements, hybrid learning activities enable children and various partners in and out of the school to imagine better lives and futures for themselves and their societies.

The learning activities analyzed in this chapter are instances of expansive learning in which "human beings and their collectives, regardless of age, are creators of new culture. Although children's potential to create is commonly disregarded as disobedience, or mere play and fantasy, it does occasionally break through and become visible" (Engeström & Sannino, 2012, p. 51). Hybrid and symbiotic forms of children's learning activity that makes use of the power of activist attempts can potentially generate the development of greater agency and collective creativity in schools, via the learning of some specific content to expand the "range of human objects" (Leont'ev, 1981, p. 367) for the learners' own lives and for the future.

REFERENCES

Burnard, P. (2011). Creativity, pedagogic partnerships, and improvisatory space of teaching. In R. K. Sawyer (Ed.), *Structure and improvisation in creative teaching* (pp. 51–72). New York, NY: Cambridge University Press.

Cole, M. (2005). Foreword: Why a fifth dimension? In M. Nilsson & H. Nocon (Eds.), *School of tomorrow: Teaching and technology in local and global communities* (pp. 9–12). Bern, Switzerland: Peter Lang.

Daniels, H., Leadbetter, J., Soares, A., & MacNab, N. (2006). Learning in and for cross-school working. In K. Yamazumi (Ed.), *Building activity theory in practice: Toward the next generation* (pp. 45–72). Osaka, Japan: Center for Human Activity Theory, Kansai University.

Davydov, V. V. (1995). The influence of L. S. Vygotsky on education theory, research, and practice. *Educational Researcher, 24*(3), 12–21.

Engeström, Y. (1987). *Learning by expanding: An activity-theoretical approach to developmental research*. Helsinki, Finland: Orienta-Konsultit.

Engeström, Y. (1991). Non scolae sed vitae discimus: Toward overcoming the encapsulation of school learning. *Learning and Instruction: An International Journal, 1*, 243–259.

Engeström, Y. (1996). Developmental work research as educational research: Looking ten years back and into the zone of proximal development. *Nordisk Pedagogik [Journal of Nordic Educational Research], 16*, 131–143.

Engeström, Y. (2000). From individual action to collective activity and back: Developmental work research as an interventionist methodology. In P. Luff, J. Hindmarsh, & C. Heath (Eds.), *Workplace studies: Recovering work practice and informing system design* (pp. 150–166). Cambridge, England: Cambridge University Press.

Engeström, Y. (2006). Development, movement and agency: Breaking away into mycorrhizae activities. In K. Yamazumi (Ed.), *Building activity theory in practice: Toward the next generation* (pp. 1–43). Osaka, Japan: Center for Human Activity Theory, Kansai University.

Engeström, Y. (2008). *From teams to knots: Activity-theoretical studies of collaboration and learning at work.* Cambridge, England: Cambridge University Press.

Engeström, Y., Engeström, R., & Vähäaho, T. (1999). When the center does not hold: The importance of knotworking. In S. Chaiklin, M. Hedegaard, & U. J. Jensen (Eds.), *Activity theory and social practice: Cultural-historical approaches* (pp. 345–374). Aarhus, Denmark: Aarhus University Press.

Engeström, Y., & Kallinen, T. (1988). Theatre as a model system for learning to create. *The Quarterly Newsletter of the Laboratory of Comparative Human Cognition, 10*(2), 54–67.

Engeström, Y., & Sannino, A. (2010). Studies of expansive learning: Foundations, findings and future challenges. *Educational Research Review, 5,* 1–24.

Engeström, Y., & Sannino, A. (2012). Whatever happened to process theories of learning? *Journal of Learning, Culture and Social Interaction, 1,* 45–56.

Lee, Y.-J. (2011). More than just story-telling: Cultural-historical activity theory as an under-utilized methodology for educational change research. *Journal of Curriculum Studies, 43*(3), 403–424.

Lektorsky, V. A. (1984). *Subject, object, cognition.* Moscow, Russia: Progress Publishers.

Lektorsky, V. A. (2009). Mediation as a means of collective activity. In A. Sannino, H. Daniels, & K. D. Gutiérrez (Eds.), *Learning and expanding with activity theory* (pp. 75–87). Cambridge, England: Cambridge University Press.

Leont'ev, A. N. (1978). *Activity, consciousness, and personality.* Englewood Cliffs, NJ: Prentice Hall.

Leont'ev, A. N. (1981). *Problems of the development of the mind.* Moscow, Russia: Progress Publishers.

Ribot, T. (1906). *Essay on the creative imagination.* Chicago, IL: Open Court Publishing.

Rose, M. (2009). *Why school? Reclaiming education for all of us.* New York, NY: The New Press.

Sannino, A., Daniels, H., & Gutiérrez, K. D. (Eds.). (2009). *Learning and expanding with activity theory.* Cambridge, England: Cambridge University Press.

Spillane, J. P. (2006). *Distributed leadership.* San Francisco, CA: Jossey-Bass.

Vygotsky, L. S. (1987). Lectures on psychology. In *The collected works of L. S. Vygotsky. Problems of general psychology* (Vol. 1, pp. 287–358). New York, NY: Plenum.

Vygotsky, L. S. (1994). Principles of social education for deaf and dumb children in Russia. In R. Van der Veer & J. Valsiner (Eds.), *The Vygotsky reader* (pp. 19–26). Oxford, England: Blackwell.

Vygotsky, L. S. (1997). *Educational psychology.* Boca Raton, FL: St. Lucie Press.

Vygotsky, L. S. (2004). Imagination and creativity in childhood. *Journal of Russian and East European Psychology, 42*(1), 7–97.

Yamazumi, K. (2005). Do nexuses bring tolerance for diversity? Tolerance as a result of social development in school. In K. Yamazumi, Y. Engeström, & H. Daniels (Eds.), *New learning challenges: Going beyond the industrial age system of school and work* (pp. 243–266). Osaka, Japan: Kansai University Press.

Yamazumi, K. (2008). A hybrid activity system as educational innovation. *Journal of Educational Change, 9*(4), 365–373.

Yamazumi, K. (2009). Expansive agency in multi-activity collaboration. In A. Sannino, H. Daniels, & K. Gutiérrez (Eds.), *Learning and expanding with activity theory* (pp. 212–227). Cambridge, England: Cambridge University Press.

Yamazumi, K. (2010a). Schools that contribute to community revitalization. In K. Yamazumi (Ed.), *Activity theory and fostering learning: Developmental interventions in education and work* (pp. 133–160). Osaka, Japan: Center for Human Activity Theory, Kansai University.

Yamazumi, K. (2010b). Toward an expansion of science education through real-life activities in Japan. In Y.-J. Lee (Ed.), *The world of science education: Handbook of research in Asia* (pp. 187–202). Rotterdam, The Netherlands: Sense Publishers.

4 Interagency, Collective Creativity, and Academic Knowledge Practices

Kai Hakkarainen, Kaisa Hytönen, Juho Makkonen, Pirita Seitamaa-Hakkarainen, and Hal White

Completion of a doctoral dissertation may be regarded as an academic achievement that clearly involves some level of creativity attainable to hardworking university students. One may propose the analogy of creating a novel trail for exploring an at least partially unknown mountainous territory during which "one proceeds step by step, each step guided by those taken previously and by uncertain intimations about what lies ahead" (Holmes, 2004, p. xvi). Such an intellectually as well as socioemotionally demanding pursuit creates an extremely challenging double-bind situation (Engeström, 1987) in which the doctoral student has to jump into the unknown to create new capabilities required for the doctorate, but exercising competencies that have not yet been developed. Investigators have identified two prototypical approaches to undertaking the doctoral transformation, that is, the individual and the collective model (Becher & Trowler, 2001; Delamont, Atkinson, & Odette, 2000). One acknowledges, of course, hybrid cases and fuzzy boundaries of these models; nor is it our intention to depict a fundamental divide between them. The contrasting depictions just below are for analytical purposes.

The traditional *individual model of doctoral education* is well established in many social sciences in Europe and elsewhere. It involves a formative experience of personally constructing an extensive and well-argued monograph. Supervision takes place through personal meetings and research seminars that typically allow doctoral students to meet their supervisors two or three times a year for planning and discussing their investigations. To pursue the analogy, doctoral students may be seen to engage in a risky effort of trying individually to climb the mountain. Many students experience that they are not given sufficient guidance or supporting ropes. Collective sharing of the process is constrained by students pursuing personal study projects that are usually not related to their supervisors' research objects. Although many supervisors provide intensive academic guidance, some have difficulty providing proficient supervision for diverse personal dissertation projects that go into territories unknown to the supervisor. Because the monograph is considered to represent a student's personal academic contribution, supervisors sometimes intentionally leave students to manage doing it alone. Independent working is expected because the monograph and associated publications are considered to provide indications of the student's academic capabilities and personal achievements relevant for an academic career.

There appear also to be certain disciplinary and national differences in the nature of doctoral education, so that a student's capability to make contributions independent from the supervisor's personal support is more strongly emphasized in some countries (e.g., United Kingdom) than in others. The individual model is an established social system that has functioned adequately across many decades, in thousands of cases. It allows doctoral students to search for productive lines of inquiry in various unexplored territories. Nevertheless, the highest peaks of knowledge creation are, in practice, seldom reached when one relies mainly on personal and local experiences instead of taking part in and extending an already started "long march" (Holmes, 2004) of academic research. The vast majority of monograph dissertations in the social sciences are not, afterward ever referred to, and are rarely built upon, by subsequent investigators.

The *collective model of doctoral education* has been perfected by natural sciences across many decades and increasingly appropriated also by many social scientific research communities in Scandinavia and Europe. It involves socializing doctoral students to academic practices by providing them early opportunities to apprentice in research communities and, through intensive participation in solving collectively shared problems embedded in the supervisor's research projects (Gruber, 1974), grow up to become members of a scholarly community. A well-established collective approach to doctoral education involves pursuing article-based theses consisting of a summary and three to five articles coauthored with the supervisor and other senior researchers and published in internationally refereed journals (Green & Powell, 2005). These students, in their production, act within the milieu of a strong research community, which provides access to sophisticated academic practices, the appropriation of which assists in reaching at least some peaks of knowledge creation. They are, in the analogy, taking part in an organized mountain hike with experienced guides who have already mapped parts of the targeted territory and marked difficult parts of the trail. The whole group is guided toward mountain peaks, whose heights are approximately known, by relying on collectively accumulated expertise that helps overcoming obstacles.

Although pursuit of academic research is always risky and success is not guaranteed, joint efforts are likely to help attaining at least some lesser, though significant, mountain peaks as defined by the more senior researchers of the team. It is to be noted, however, that individually approached dissertations have occasionally attained extraordinary heights, and we are not suggesting such heights are necessarily more common with a collective approach. Learning valuable academic skills and competencies from peers provides novel socially distributed resources for guiding investigations. Certain processes are in place; procedures are imbued in the participants, but success, and any extraordinary merit of a given product, is not guaranteed.

The collective model, even as it is routinely successful for many who continue to engage it, is not without its own challenges. Pursuing investigations under a strict division of collective labor may reduce autonomy of doctoral students, lower their hierarchical position, and reduce possibilities of learning through personal explorations. Nevertheless, in producing coauthored articles, doctoral students undertake epistemic practices that put them into the very heart of the academic knowledge creation process of their communities. In order to cope with increasingly complex research objects and multidisciplinary projects, many social scientific research communities are appropriating the collective model from natural sciences and developing practices that involve giving students more intensive guidance and publication support than the individual model entails.

The purpose of this chapter is to analyze collective creativity of academic research by examining how the collective, article-based approach to doctoral education cultivated by natural sciences is productively extended to the field of education. We use the term *creativity* in a "bare bones" sense, to indicate what is expected of our participants, well-performing doctoral students in the programs under investigation, programs we believe to be among the best. Their *creativity*, for us, is demonstrated in their articles being of sufficient substance and novelty to achieve publication in reputable, refereed journals in the relevant field. There are some examples of truly notable excellence, as shown in articles that become widely cited and built upon, but such extraordinary contribution is not required for creativity as investigated in accord with the main focus of the present report.

In investigating the proposed extension, Hakkarainen, Hytönen, Makkonen, and Lehtinen (2012a) interviewed approximately 30 research leaders from well-known Finnish and European universities. The interviewees represented (a) professors of education engaged in individual doctoral training that involves supervising personal monographs (M1-M9), as well as two sets of professors engaged in collective practices of supervising dissertations based on journal articles coauthored with the supervisors; (b) professors of education (A1-A12); and (c) leaders of Finnish national centers of excellence (medicine, physics, neuroscience, N1-N9). We have also completed analyzing interviews of 13 doctoral students (medicine, science, S1-S13) to study their experiences of pursuing article-based theses in two cutting-edge Finnish research communities (Hakkarainen et al., 2012b). A corresponding interview study is going on with doctoral students who are pursuing either monograph or article-based dissertations in education.

We are reporting our empirical data in detail elsewhere but will utilize some excerpts from the interview transcripts, in the present article, in a manner we will now set out. These selected data are offered by way of illustration of our concepts and approach, not as proof of any hypotheses about collective approaches. The present interview data represent the participants' personal experiences of their communities. Extensive further ethnographic investigations should be carried out to examine actual, enacted practices prevailing in the communities in question. We have structured this article in the following way. First, we examine the role of collective practices in pursuit of academic research; second, we address the role of coauthoring in socializing doctoral students to knowledge creation; third, we examine various aspects of agency critical for knowledge creation; and finally, we address challenges of expansive transformation of academic knowledge practices. In each section, we briefly set out the relevant concepts of a collective approach, from both others' and our own writings. Next we present a few excerpts from our data, the reports of professors and students, followed with our concluding thoughts.

THE ROLE OF COLLECTIVE KNOWLEDGE PRACTICES IN PURSUIT OF ACADEMIC RESEARCH

Cultivation of a more collective approach on doctoral education appears to require problematizing prevailing individualist conceptions of creativity as a unique individual capacity to produce truly original ideas. In accordance with psychometric approaches, creative achievements are often considered to represent unique personal insights and, at their highest, exceptional, groundbreaking productions of eminent investigators (e.g., Simonton, 2010). By comparatively examining investigators with varying creative contribution, researchers with this approach have attempted to explain how those investigators who are able to make truly remarkable achievement differ from the mediocre ones. Although we are not focused on the remarkable— but upon the efforts of well-performing in an *ordinary* sense—students in a sample of the best doctoral programs, we believe similar principles apply. Beyond the qualities of creative persons, these investigators also examined other *P* variables of creativity, such as Process, Product, and Place (Kozbelt, Beghetto, & Runko, 2010), without, however, very much attention to the fourth, Place, variable. Although cultures and communities are acknowledged to have some contribution to creativity, those are often considered to represent mere background variables (e.g., organizational climate, openness to innovation, external pressure, or *spirit of time*).

Together with pioneering investigations of social aspect of creativity (Csikszentmihalyi, 1999; Miettinen, 2006; Sawyer, 2005), the present investigators examine creativity as a systemic phenomenon that takes place routinely within the chosen academic communities representing the designated research fields and academic domains. We argue that when examining doctoral education as carried out in leading-edge research communities, we are not, in fact, dealing with accidental or secondary environmental influences, but with communities that are deliberately created for facilitating pursuit of novelty and innovation in their standard practices. Such novelty, which we also term *creativity* (and the degree of which we are speaking), is evidenced by publication in the better refereed journals in the field and, generally, by recognition of other professionals in the field.

As summarized by Nersessian (2006), modern academic research takes place in laboratories or communities or research; these may be seen as purposefully created, complex *cognitive-cultural systems* that consist of integrated arrays of senior and junior investigators. They employ and produce tools and instruments, methods and procedures, research materials and databases, and systems and artifacts of knowledge, which we designate, later on, in our terms, as *objects*; further, those of particular concern here, have sufficient novelty and substance to be recognized by those outside a given project and institution. Such facts, we argue, have typically received less than proper attention from individually oriented researchers.

What appears, further, to have been missing from the conventional psychological accounts of creativity is the fifth *P*, Practice, cultivated by creative communities and their networks (Lee & Boud, 2009). The rationale of the collective approach is that creativity does not lie merely within the human mind but is embedded in shared knowledge practices cultivated by innovative knowledge communities and their networks (Paavola, Lipponen, & Hakkarainen, 2004). By *knowledge practices*, in turn, we refer to personal and social practices related to working with knowledge and carrying out academic inquiries (Hakkarainen, 2009; Ritella & Hakkarainen, 2012). The term *knowledge* is used in the broadest sense, to include what is explicit or stated in official discourse (e.g., approved texts), to what is implicit, informing one's habits (perhaps prereflectively) of expert working and further yet to that which underlies the competencies of experts, for example, so-called procedural knowledge.

Elaborating Knorr-Cetina's (2001) concepts, it may be argued that research communities rely on uncertainly determined, dynamically developing, exploration-oriented, and problem-laden practices that are occasionally innovative. Knowledge practices, although sometimes just supporting routine learning (transmission), at their creative edge, diverge from other routine social practices in that they take place in specific purposefully dynamic and fluid settings designed for the furtherance of innovation and knowledge (Knorr-Cetina, 1999). Rather than relying only on mere mundane habits or repeated routines (that may also be needed), such practices are aimed at solving emergent problems and constantly pursuing novelty and innovation. These problems and solutions, being refined, are in our terms, *objects*.

It may be argued that in the case of communities that follow such practices, "innovation and pursuit of novelty are themselves transformed to shared social practices" through the cultivation of corresponding personal and collective competencies and patterns of shared activity (Knorr-Cetina, 1999, 2001; Simon, 2002). A central characteristic of such activity is the deliberate reinvention of prevailing practices—for instance, developing instruments and methods with higher and higher resolution—so as to elicit pursuit of novelty (Knorr-Cetina, 2001). Reinvention and refinement treat practices, and component procedures, as objects. One expects that the model just outlined will be reflected in properly gathered data on participants' experiences in such undertakings, which we call *creative*, within research communities.

In our data, all of the interviewed research leaders committed to the collective approach highlighted the critical importance of research community in academic knowledge creation. Tackling ever more complex problems is possible by capitalizing on knowledge and competence of organized research communities and their networks in which doctoral students play an important role. The collectivization of academic research requires that investigators share all aspects of investigative pursuits from research problems to publications. Pursuit of academic research would not be possible without such a socially distributed system:

> Modern research is like that; you have a group which specializes in something that belongs to the specific research object, it's represented by an expert in the group, so if somebody knows about IT [information technology], then another one knows about genetics, a third knows about experimental techniques, and a fourth one knows about writing. So it's like, this expertise is divided (N5).

Research communities are needed because an individual cannot master all the complexities of research, and it is much more efficient and faster to rely on distributed expertise. The crucial role of community in research was beautifully expressed by a prominent medical researcher: "I've always, even as a young researcher, realized it pretty clearly that in this line of work you can't cope, if you're what they call a lone wolf or if you try to do something alone" (N3). Modern academic research takes place, she said, in "massive, knowledge producing and processing centers" that interlink globally distributed different research. Truly significant academic achievements are always made in research communities; "one person can never be the best in the world but a group can be the best" (N3).

The research community also plays a crucial role in the collective doctoral students' own accounts of their experiences. As elaborated later when we address agency in knowledge creation, two-thirds of the doctoral students' talk, during the interviews, addressed the issue of support and facilitation for knowledge creation provided by their research community. Doctoral students become acculturated to the laboratory practices through an apprenticeship process that engages them in working with collectively shared research objects. Novel cohorts of students come to the laboratory, each of them having unique knowledge, experience, and interests that affect the collective research agenda (Nersessian, 2006). Their challenge is to identify problems that promise to advance the shared inquiry—to refine its objects—and open up fresh lines of investigation.

Although research groups of social sciences may not rely on experimental systems that are as focused and constrained as those in natural sciences, they share conceptual and methodological instruments and practices and socialize doctoral students to use the collectively cultivated investigative repertoire for pursuing shared research objects: "If you are not able to establish the common research object that you share over a certain period of time, you will not be able to keep the group together, you will not be able to accumulate knowledge" (A2), and you will not be able to efficiently advance your research trail. Emergence of externally funded research projects in social sciences has made feasible collective investigative pursuits organized around a broader research theme.

SOCIALIZING DOCTORAL STUDENTS TO KNOWLEDGE CREATION THROUGH COAUTHORING

Scientific journal articles may be considered as principal creative products of academic research (Simonton, 2004). Creativity is involved, as we have proposed, because writing is not just mechanical reporting of investigations carried out, but a principal vehicle of scientific thought. Writing may be seen as a process of deepening inquiry by the creation of external epistemic artifacts that crystallize and promote evolving understanding, and provide stepping stones for directing and guiding further personal or collective inquiry efforts (Ritella & Hakkarainen, 2012). It is critical that epistemic artifacts involve, as they necessarily do, pointers (hints, guidelines, directions) implying what is missing from the picture and, thereby, guiding further inquiries (Knorr-Cetina, 2001). Epistemic artifacts can endlessly be reinterpreted and their evolving network used as a starting point of articulating and iteratively improving other such artifacts that are novel, though derived (Bereiter, 2002; Paavola et al., 2004).

The challenge of doctoral students is to go beyond acquiring and reproducing scientific knowledge and to learn to use knowledge as a tool to extend thinking and deliberately generate new ideas and conceptions. The traditional approach to doctoral education was based on the assumption that a scientific mind may be shaped through constructing independently, in a long process, an extensive scientific monograph. The article-based approach, considered on its own, emphasizes the importance on acculturating doctoral students to work iteratively with shared research objects embedded in an evolving network of a supervisor's research projects (Gruber, 1974) that are transmitted from one cohort of inquirers to the next. They are engaged in working with collective research objects, in defined procedures, so as to pursue the work nearer to the frontiers of knowledge instead of starting from scratch; in this way, we maintain that some degree of novelty is more likely because of the research group's involvement in goal setting. Individual efforts, very often, may partially replicate earlier investigations of which the researcher may not even be aware. The epistemic objects created through the history of a research community provide intuitive support for initiating new doctoral investigations, revealing gaps of knowledge, and indicating promising directions of inquiry.

Coauthoring is the principal method of socializing new cohorts of doctoral students to academic writing and practices of international scientific publication. Practices of coauthoring are critical because learning to take a productive part in building and creating academic knowledge is extremely difficult; it is an extended messy struggle to acquire embodied and, to a large extent, tacit or implicit capabilities rather than smoothly assimilate some well-specified competencies (Prior, 2006; Russell, 1997). Kamler (2008) has stated that students should not be left on their own to figure out how to do academic publication but require deliberate collective support and supervision. Although doctoral students are, in natural sciences, acculturated through coauthoring to write like scientists and learn to publish in high ranking journals (Florence & Yore, 2004), most students of social sciences have to learn it through personal trial-and-error efforts, often seeking "safe-spaces of publication" (Kamler, 2008), rather than rising to the highest standards.

Although all students feel personally vulnerable when being critically evaluated by external investigators, solo-published social-science students' own authority is more fragile, and they are less resilient than science students, whose data have to be gathered as part of a collective project. By guiding and supporting students' publications, the senior colleagues carry a significant part of the work of establishing authority, and thereby, make the process less threatening. In social sciences, publication of refereed journal articles often does not take place at all in absence of coauthoring (Kamler, 2008). Because of the tremendous variation in academic productivity, communities without coauthoring practices tend to become *aristocratic* in respect of 10% to 20% of investigators producing most of the publications. The article-based, collaborative approach aims, in contrast, at deliberately socializing doctoral students to the knowledge practices that high academic productivity requires.

In our interviews, research leaders, from sciences to education engaged in a collective approach, reported that their doctoral students learn to publish with seniors through pursuing article-based dissertations. Shared practices of their research communities provide significant support for scientific publication. Investigations based on already tested research methods and designs are more likely to be successful than ones created from the scratch. The supervisor and other coauthors take an active part in selecting journals and provide hands-on guidance concerning how to tailor manuscripts according to journal-specific criteria; their support for structuring and framing manuscripts is like an invisible, guiding hand enabling academic contributions. Even if a manuscript has been rewritten 20 times, sometimes by senior researchers, the doctoral student who has carried out the main responsibility for collecting and analyzing the data is usually the first author.

Senior researchers' support not only socializes the doctoral students to academic writing but also assists in ensuring that the manuscript will meet the requirements of a rigorous journal. Accordingly, a crucial aspect of academic knowledge creation is to learn to produce epistemic artifacts that pass rigorous peer review by investigators coming from more or less completely different contexts. Many interviewees emphasized that a student should never be left alone to deal with oftentimes harsh criticism; it is important to collectively decide how to respond to review feedback, after letting the student make the first suggestions. Such collective practices teach doctoral students to work productively with external reviewers, from an early point, and incorporate their critical feedback for improving quality of their manuscripts. Senior researchers' encouragement is needed to assist a student to keep the flame burning if acceptance of the first article is delayed. Overall, the community provides very tight epistemic criteria for academic work that improve the quality of knowledge produced. One educational research leader compared the contribution of supervisors with creating trails that assist a student to successfully ski across difficult terrain:

> It's really consuming to ski where nobody has skied before, there's no route and you don't know where you're going. So you can go to ski there, but it'll take a damn long time, and there's no guarantee you'll make it back alive. When you do go skiing, you'll have to do the physical work, you've got to ski for yourself, [because] that's your job. But [in the contrasting situation] you are skiing along a track that's been readymade; your skis are waxed, and you're wearing a hat. So you can think, when you've skied 50 kilometers, that you've skied it all by yourself, but you didn't build the track. So [in fact] the track is there, you've got a hat on, and the skis are sliding, you can't even begin to imagine what it would be like to ski without those things (A3).

It appears as a truly significant educational achievement of leading-edge research communities to be systematically able to train doctoral students capable of pursuing publications appearing in the highly regarded, refereed, scientific journals. At times, the best efforts of such communities lead to publication of an excellent scientific article—later, often cited—in a top-ranking journal. We consider this to be a transformation of the small-c creative expression involved in writing a locally published monograph toward pro-c (professional creativity) and sometimes even big-C (outstanding academic achievement) creativity (Kaufman & Beghetto, 2009; Kozbelt, Beghetto, & Runko, 2010; Simonton, 2010). Beyond capitalizing on established methods and practices of inquiry, successful doctoral investigations, of course, involve stretching inquiries to novel and unforeseen directions in interaction between junior and senior investigators. Even if only a few dissertation articles end up being published in the top, prestigious journals and meet the highest standards of professional creativity, deliberate enculturation of doctoral students to international publication is likely to raise epistemic standards and facilitate the scientific competence and productivity of the participants. Academic knowledge creation appears to be collectivizing in terms of an increased proportion of articles being coauthored, not only in physics and biology, but also in social sciences, such as education, psychology, and sociology.

ASPECTS OF AGENCY CRITICAL FOR KNOWLEDGE CREATION IN DOCTORAL EDUCATION

Across disciplines, doctoral students encounter daily risk and uncertainty of academic knowledge creation and associated emotional challenges. We briefly review such issues here, before elaborating on agency. In spite of having experience of interviewing many types of participants, we have never before encountered data that were so laden with emotions as those of interviewed doctoral students of medicine and physics (Hakkarainen et al., 2012b; see also Delamont et al., 2000; Stubb, Pyhältö, & Lonka, 2011). Rather than involving cool descriptions of intellectual challenges, the participants, who functioned in internationally very highly regarded research communities, shared with us extremely deep uncertainties and intellectual vulnerabilities regarding whether they are truly able to reach the required very high level of academic accomplishments, and, thereby, are worthy of collective trust and respect. The socioemotional pressures appeared to emerge from sustained struggling with frustrating and partially unanticipated failures that were initially difficult to control. In many cases, doctoral students had to work under time pressure for meeting deliberately rising standards and go through oftentimes harsh internal and external evaluation. Thus, even in a supportive community and with collaboration, there is much emotional hardship. This hardship affects the ability to carry on, to sustain one's efforts in the required manner. Sustainment is a crucial aspect of agency.

In the collective approach, we propose that particular types of agency are involved; their presence is clearly shown in our data. Doctoral students' accounts of their experiences involved frequent references to their agency, that is, experienced capacity to initiate and effectively sustain meaningful knowledge-creating activities. Relying on empirical and theoretical considerations, we distinguished three types of agentic talk representing, respectively, personal, distributed, and objective agency (Hakkarainen et al., 2012b). Less than one-third of the data referred to *personal agency*. In these text segments, the participants talked about their academic expertise and self-efficacy (Bandura, 2006).

> Yeah, like at the beginning phases I was terribly uncertain . . . about my own ideas. Like I always wanted to check with my supervisors that whether doing it like this is a good idea, and I also expected to get some kind of direct guidance (S9).

Nevertheless, functioning in a strong research community that provided a great deal of support appeared to be critical in overcoming challenges and obstacles. We found that almost half of agency-related text segments could be identified as representing *distributed agency* including references to social sharing of expertise and receiving of social support from peers and senior colleagues. After creating social connections with

> those people that were in the same room when I was writing a summary or something . . . you could ask them whatever. For example, you can ask your PhD colleagues anything, even a stupid scientific thing, and that was really nice (S4).

An essential aspect of distributed agency was also providing students a sense of collective efficacy (Bandura, 2006), that is, collective mustering of confidence that a participant is able to successfully encounter insurmountable appearing obstacles as a member of a highly regarded research community.

We identified also the third category of agentic talk, *objective agency* (shortened from "object-oriented interagency"; Engeström, 2005) that, according to our interpretation, represented an integrated and fused social system emerging within a strong research community interlinking a person's investigative efforts with those of the research community pursuing shared research objects; all being engaged in shared creation of knowledge, as we have defined it. By objects, we intend epistemic artifacts, such as theories and analytical frameworks that may be embodied, for example, in published papers. Investigators' combined efforts entail creation of a collective system in which the doctoral student's object-oriented research efforts are tightly coupled with those of supervisors and external collaborators in conjunction with metalevel awareness of such processes. Such agency goes beyond shallow sharing of cognitive efforts in deliberately focusing on advancing shared objects of inquiry (Edwards, 2005). Although such objects likely possess excellence, we are not claiming they are, of necessity, extraordinary.

An essential aspect of knowledge-creating agency is that the doctoral student comes up with his or her own conceptions of directing investigations that become a part of a shared research agenda: It was essential "first of all [that] I dared to say that I have these kinds of ideas and, and then it, and that I got some kind of feedback from them, that told me to try them" (S9). If supervisors produced most of the ideas in the beginning, "you can bring more of your ideas and you own input more and more the longer you're there" (S3).

Objective agency appears to involve going through cumulative experiences of overcoming obstacles and reaching necessary milestones (getting articles accepted) in pursuit of shared research objects. During such a transactive process (Samerroff & Mackenzie, 2003), a participant gradually grows up to meet initially insurmountable appearing, epistemic objectives and extending intellectual and creative capabilities: "many times when you're at the top of a cliff then it looks terribly hard but when you climb down, you realize that it was no problem" (S13). Climbing down entails meeting milestones that open up a novel environment of intellectual socialization and make more demanding knowledge practices accessible, adaptation to which elicits further development of knowledge-creating agency.

Although traditional studies of academic creativity focus mainly on individual characteristics of researchers, the present investigation of some leading-edge practices of doctoral education highlights the collective mediation of knowledge-creating agency. Participation in the leading-edge research communities in question allowed the doctoral students, in a concrete way, to surpass their individual capabilities by relying on the expansive resources provided by the research community. People who pursue monographs are vulnerable because they often experience being isolated outside of supporting academic networks. The interconnectedness of research activity, in contrast, gives collective doctoral students different, although possibly serious, vulnerabilities because of social dependence. For example, an interview with a student who did not appear to have a research object shared with a supervisor showed to be full of anxiety and other negative emotions. This, we understand, in our terms, is likely because a reciprocally acknowledged research object is missing.

Overall, the role of human agency is critical also in the context of collective doctoral training: Some people who appear to have been given cultural support and facilitation fail to develop higher-level competencies whereas some others succeed and excel against all odds. Some doctoral students functioning in strong collaborative research communities feel alone whereas some independent doctoral students sustain a sense of community in spite of their relative isolation (Pyhältö, Stubb, & Lonka, 2009). Prevailing cultural scripts and models do not totally, or without residue, determine the character of participants' activities or their successes. They do, however, have significant effects regarding construction of possible worlds of their anticipated future activity.

CHALLENGES OF EXPANSIVE TRANSFORMATION OF ACADEMIC KNOWLEDGE PRACTICES

Cultivation of collective knowledge practices that channel the participants' efforts of knowledge creation appears to be critically important because many aspects of academic research are difficult to learn. In spite of knowing that you must "publish or perish" in academic research, many researchers in social sciences, especially those newly arrived, find adoption of international publication practices extremely difficult. After going through the transformation, either by collective piggybacking within research communities or through sustained personal efforts, the participants experience the novel academic practices as a part of their everyday activity and sometimes find it puzzling, in retrospect, to understand what was so difficult about it. In what follows, we will briefly describe a collective process of transforming shared knowledge practices that the first author has gone through, which aroused the author's interest in collective creativity in academic research.

A research center established by the author grew from a group of two to three investigators to a relatively large community involving about 10 full-time doctoral students and postdocs. The research community learned collective practices of scientific publication across a ten-year span, see Figure 4.1. The center was completely funded by external research projects and initially constrained by applied research projects that required production of locally published extensive research reports. Without a peer review, production of thick research reports at *Stage I* did not, however, contribute to the academic record, and those publications tended, in a few years, to disappear into the cemeteries of knowledge. External performance requirements pushed the center to start pursuing full papers for international conferences at *Stage II*. These who-you-know publications did not, however, involve peer review beyond a superficial level; even one cycle of corrections was seldom required and appropriately confirmed by reviewers. Toward the end of the period examined, there emerged knowledge practices systematically focused on producing scientific journal articles. Finally, the research community decided,

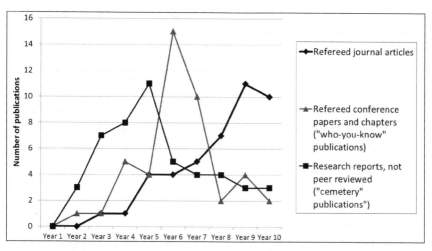

Figure 4.1 Cyclic transformation of collective publication-related knowledge practices at Centre of Research on Networked Learning and Knowledge Building (www.helsinki.fi/science/networkedlearning).

collectively, at *Stage III*, to change its knowledge practices so that every full-time doctoral student was required to pursue an article-based thesis consisting of internationally refereed and coauthored journal articles. The transformation of shared publication practices was facilitated by participation in a yearly departmental workshop in which every participant, from individual students to professors and high performing research groups, had to publicly report his or her scientific productivity.

It has been beneficial to pursue article publication because articles not only crystallize creativity of the authors—which may be simply of the bare bones type we have indicated—but also further the expertise of an expanded network of investigators, including the reviewers. Only some of the interviewed research leaders' own supervisors had mastered collective publication practices. Because of that, many of them had gone through corresponding transformation of practices of knowledge production prevailing in their research communities. These kinds of knowledge-practice transformations appear to be a paradigmatic example of cultivation of collective creativity that cannot be reduced to individual participants' knowledge and competence. Collective creativity is involved in deliberately socializing new cohorts of master and doctoral students directly to the collectively cultivated, most advanced publication practices—without having themselves to go through as difficult and troublesome developmental process as did the initial creators of the collective knowledge practices.

We have earlier described such creativity in respect of its basic novelty, its substance, and its fostering the accumulation of knowledge, as exhibited in recognized professional arenas, including journals. Undertaking such an approach, collective doctoral students, so to say, jump onto an already moving train, an action that greatly hastens the development of their academic knowledge practices. They become competent in knowledge creation, as we have termed it, even if the productions are not necessarily extraordinary or ground breaking. Appropriation of such innovative knowledge practices as an initial cornerstone of one's academic activity appears to provide a good basis for further expansive efforts of, for instance, cultivating research practices rigorous enough to meet requirements of high-impact journals. Investigations should be carried out in the future to obtain a more refined understanding of the relations between appropriating already established academic practices versus creative transformation of the tradition.

DISCUSSION

The present investigation examined practices of doctoral education prevailing in natural and social sciences by drawing on retrospective interviews of supervisors and doctoral students. The present data highlight individual experiences, giving only indirect information on personal and collective development of knowledge practices. Further, although we have emphasized contrasts, we do not see the individual and collective model of doctoral education as inimical to one another, but rather as complementary. Cultivation of group-supported practices of pursuing *dissertations* based on research objects shared with a supervisor *and* of collective pursuit of coauthored *articles* in refereed scientific journals assists in broadening the scope of doctoral education. Both types of process, as well as hybrids, are embedded in the community and context within which creativity occurs, in the sense that we have defined and investigated it. Although pursuit of journal science is very difficult to learn on one's own, research communities may cultivate creative practices that channel and structure the doctoral students' activities in a way that elicits scientific productivity as professionally recognized outside of one's own institutional setting.

Academic socialization involves parallel deliberate, conscious, and reflective top-down efforts of transforming one's habitus (Bourdieu, 1980) as well as gradual bottom-up adaptation to collectively cultivated knowledge practices being subject to constant reinvention and transformation (Knorr-Cetina, 2001). Accordingly, it is not a smooth and straightforward process, but involves questioning and problematizing prevailing activity and practices (Engeström, 1999); without creative troublemaking, it would be difficult to go beyond prevailing practices and break boundaries of established ways of doing things. Although doctoral students have to capitalize on academic tradition to be successful, innovative students deliberately seek novel theoretical and methodological lines of inquiry. This makes academic development a tension-laden process.

Academic cultures are often competitive and hierarchical in nature, and collective publication practices may reinforce the downside of institutional efforts, their resistance to change, and their obstacles, unintentionally created, to the attainment of genuine groundbreaking advances or personal fulfillment in success. For example, the approach elaborated may make doctoral students even more dependent on their supervisors than the traditional individual model. Simultaneously with enhancing academic achievements, collaborative publication cultures may represent "academic capitalism" (Slaughter & Rhoades, 2004), that is, an instrumental approach of making doctoral students a part of a *publication machine* serving interests of senior researchers and their funders, thereby, diminishing the creative potential of dissertation research. Personal and collective interests are likely to be at least in some conflict, as they are in all research communities. Although academic communities are not always functioning perfectly, growing up to distributed academic practices augments doctoral students' cognitive capacities to an extent that enables them to solve significantly more complex problems than would otherwise be possible. Such capacities are best not thought of as individual characteristics or gifts, but we argue, rather as the appropriation, within individuals, of the capabilities of the research cultures in which they function.

The basic tenet of the present article is that the creativity that matters in scientific inquiry, particularly in its present institutional form, does not come as a god-given gift to the individual; it is not in genes but embodied in academic knowledge practices that researchers undertake with one another and in objects they have in common. Our fundamental assertion is this: The practices of scientific excellence are well-founded upon the *collective creativity* involved in sharing with newcomers and fellow inquirers and the collaboratively cultivated and culturally evolved research practices that bear the accumulated knowledge and wisdom of the community. These are the crucial *processes* in the advancement of knowledge; we have argued that they appear to represent a high road to such advancement, according to the evidence of our participants. That evidence, however, is not intended to suggest comparisons of accomplishments.

Knowledge-practice transformations that change the environment of subsequent doctoral student cohorts' epistemic socialization represent *intergenerational learning* (Holmes, 2004). One generation of researchers shares its knowledge and wisdom with the following one, making academic achievements attainable. Subsequent cohorts of doctoral students can be immediately immersed with advanced research practices when entering a research community to pursue graduate or postgraduate studies without having to go through similar troublesome trial-and-error processes of creating productive academic practices that senior researchers and earlier cohorts of students had to undergo. It represents a kind of *downstream epistemic engineering* (Sterelny, 2004) that changes the scope of problems that the subsequent cohorts and generations of investigators have to solve.

Getting access to sophisticated collective academic practices cultivated across many years and decades appears to be the only known (relative) shortcut to academic excellence. Deep intellectual enculturation to practices of leading-edge research communities appears to have parallels with races on a track: "when they [students, newcomers] have the opportunity to launch themselves from such a high platform, then they can go for the Nobels and things, when they're not wasting their time and are given—like in a relay race, they get kind of a running start" (N5). In spite of tremendous personal efforts across the long periods of time required, participants getting access to higher-level knowledge practices—evolving, leading-edge methods—transmit a big advantage: Cumulative cultural advantages provided by such *collective giftedness* are likely, in the better cases, to boost one's achievements to a higher level than a strong endowment of talents and gifts—exercised individually—could produce (Gladwell, 2008).

Ordinary agents, with strong investigative drive, taking part in and socializing to such collectively cultivated, exceptional knowledge practices that greatly enhance their academic activity are likely to be able to achieve professional competence and success. The present collective-creativity approach aims to better one's understanding of those academic practices that allow innovative research communities to systematically facilitate ordinary academic excellence characteristic of highly productive investigators and their investigative collectives. From the collective perspective, it is essential, so to speak, to understand and explain how a whole forest, or a section of it, may be creatively nourished and its growth dynamically fostered, rather than merely focus on explaining why a particular tree became so magnificent.

ACKNOWLEDGMENTS

The present investigation was supported by grants 2106008 (University of Helsinki) and 127019 (Academy of Finland). We would like to thank Erno Lehtinen, Kirsti Lonka, Kirsi Pyhältö, Sami Paavola, Pasi Pohjola, Jenni Stubb, Jenna Tuomainen, and participants of our investigations for discussion regarding doctoral education.

REFERENCES

Bandura, A. (2006). Toward a psychology of human agency. *Perspectives on Psychological Science, 1,* 164–180.
Becher, T., & Trowler, P. R. (2001). *Academic tribes and territories.* Berkeley, CA: University of California Press.
Bereiter, C. (2002). *Education and mind in the knowledge age.* Hillsdale, NJ: Erlbaum.
Bourdieu, P. (1980). *The logic of practice.* Stanford, CA: Stanford University Press.
Csikszentmihalyi, M. (1999). Implications of a systems perspective for the study of creativity. In R. Sternberg (Ed.), *Handbook of creativity* (pp. 313–335). Cambridge, MA: Cambridge University Press.
Delamont, S., Atkinson, P., & Odette, P. (2000). *The doctoral experience.* London, England: Falmer.
Edwards, A. (2005). Relational agency. *International Journal of Educational Research, 43,* 168–182.
Engeström, Y. (1987). *Learning by expanding.* Helsinki, Finland: Orienta-Konsultit.
Engeström, Y. (1999). Innovative learning in work teams. In Y. Engeström, R. Miettinen, & R.-L. Punamäki (Eds.), *Perspectives on activity theory* (pp. 377–404). Cambridge, England: Cambridge University Press.
Engeström, Y. (2005). Knotworking to create collaborative intentionality capital in fluid organizational fields. In M. Beyerlein, S. T. Beyerlein, & F. A. Kennedy (Eds.), *Collaborative capital: Creating intangible value* (pp. 307–336). Amsterdam, The Netherlands: Elsevier.
Florence, M. K., & Yore, L. D. (2004). Learning to write like a scientist. *Journal of Research in Science Teaching, 41,* 637–668.
Gladwell, M. (2008). *Outliers: The story of success.* New York, NY: Little, Brown, & Company.
Green, H., & Powell, S. (2005). *Doctoral study in contemporary higher education.* London, England: Open University Press.
Gruber, H. (1974). *Darwin on man.* New York, NY: Dutton.

Hakkarainen, K. (2009). A knowledge-practice perspective on technology-mediated learning. *International Journal of Computer Supported Collaborative Learning, 4*, 213–231.

Hakkarainen, K., Hytönen, K., Makkonen, J., & Lehtinen, E. (2012a). *Promoting knowledge-creating practices of doctoral studies.* Manuscript submitted for publication.

Hakkarainen, K., Wires, S., Stubb, J., Paavola, S., Pohjola, P., Lonka, K., & Pyhältö, K. (in press). On personal and collective dimensions of agency in doctoral training: medicine and natural science programs. Studies in Continuing Education.

Holmes, F. L. (2004). *Investigative pathways.* New Haven, CT: Yale University Press.

Kamler, B. (2008). Rethinking doctoral publication practices. *Higher Education, 33*, 283–294.

Kaufman, J. C., & Beghetto, R. A. (2009). Beyond big and little: The four C model of creativity. *Review of General Psychology, 13*, 1–12.

Knorr-Cetina, K. (1999). *Epistemic cultures.* Cambridge, MA: Harvard University Press.

Knorr-Cetina, K. (2001). Objectual practices. In T. Schatzki, K. Knorr-Cetina, & E. Von Savigny (Eds.), *The practice turn in contemporary theory* (pp. 175–188). London, England: Routledge.

Kozbelt, A., Beghetto, R. A., & Runko, M. A. (2010). Theories of creativity. In J. C. Kaufman & R. J. Sternberg (Eds.), *The Cambridge handbook of creativity* (pp. 20–47). Cambridge, MA: Cambridge University Press.

Lee, A., & Boud, D. (2009). Framing doctoral education as practice. In D. Boud & A. Lee (Eds.), *Changing practices of doctoral education* (pp. 10–25). London, England: Routledge.

Miettinen, R. (2006). The sources of novelty: A cultural and systemic view of distributed creativity. *Creativity and Innovation Management, 15*, 173–181.

Nersessian, N. J. (2006). The cognitive-cultural systems of the research laboratory. *Organization Studies, 27*, 125–145.

Paavola, S., Lipponen, L., & Hakkarainen, K. (2004). Modeling innovative knowledge communities: A knowledge-creation approach to learning. *Review of Educational Research, 74*, 557–576.

Prior, P. A. (1998). *Writing/disciplinarity: A sociohistoric account of literate activity in the academy.* Mahwah, NJ: Erlbaum.

Prior, P. A. (2006). A sociocultural theory of writing. In C. A MacArthur, S. Graham, & J. Fitzgerald (Eds.), *Handbook of writing research* (pp. 54–66). New York, NJ: Guildford Press.

Pyhältö, K., Stubb, J., & Lonka, K. (2009). Developing scholarly communities as learning environments for doctoral students. *International Journal for Academic Development, 14*, 221–232.

Ritella, G., & Hakkarainen, K. (2012). Instrument genesis in technology mediated learning. *International Journal of Computer-Supported Collaborative Learning, 7*, 239–258.

Russell, D. A. (1997). Writing and genre in higher education and workplaces. *Mind, Culture, and Activity, 4*, 224–237.

Samerroff, A. J., & Mackenzie, M. (2003). Research strategies for capturing transactional models of development. *Development and Psychopathology, 15*, 613–640.

Sawyer, R. K. (2005). *Emergence: Societies as complex systems.* Cambridge, MA: Cambridge University Press.

Simon, H. (2002). Achieving excellence in institutions. In M. Ferrari (Ed.), *The pursuit of excellence through education* (pp. 181–194). Mahwah, NJ: Erlbaum.

Simonton, D. K. (2004). *Creativity in science: Chance, logic, genius, and zeitgeist.* Cambridge, England: Cambridge University Press.

Simonton, D. K. (2010). Creativity in highly eminent individuals. In J. C. Kaufman & R. J. Sternberg (Eds.), *The Cambridge handbook of creativity* (pp. 174–188). Cambridge, MA: Cambridge University Press.

Slaughter, S., & Rhoades, G. (2004). *Academic capitalism and the new economy: Market, state, and higher education.* Baltimore, MD: John Hopkins University Press.

Sterelny, K. (2004). Externalism, epistemic artifacts, and the extended mind. In R. Schantz (Ed.), *The externalist challenge* (pp. 239–254). Berlin, Germany: Walter de Gruyter.

Stubb, J., Pyhältö, K., & Lonka, K. (2011). Balancing between inspiration and exhaustion: PhD students' experienced socio-psychological well-being. *Studies in Continuing Education, 33,* 33–50.

Part II

Creative Production and Innovation as Collective Activities Crossing Epistemic Boundaries

5 Resourceful Leadership
Revealing the Creativity of Organizational Leaders

Anne Edwards and Marc Thompson

In our work with strategic leaders in children's services in England over the last few years, we have become increasingly aware of how the most successful Directors of Children's Services (DCS) engage the affect as well as the rationalities of the professionals whose work they are trying to take forward. Attention to the affective aspects of organizational change and leadership is not new (Avolio, Walumbwa, & Weber, 2009; Mumford, Connelly, & Gaddis, 2003). However, what leaders do to creatively harness the beliefs and feelings of colleagues to create a resource for successful leadership has yet to be analyzed in cultural historical terms. As we shall see, an important element in the cultural historical approach to analyzing leadership is Leont'ev's idea of the object motive (Leont'ev, 1978), which objectifies *what matters* for the actor when they work on an object of activity or problem space such as a child's trajectory.

One of the challenges for DCS is that the object motive for, for example, social workers and teachers will differ when collaborating to redirect the life trajectory of a vulnerable child. We shall, therefore, use the term *what matters* for practitioners when they act on an object of activity rather than talk in broad terms of the affective. Here we draw on the Leont'ev-inspired analyses of motives in actions in activities in practices undertaken by Hedegaard, as well as Dreyfus's recognition of the affective aspects of expertise and Knorr-Cetina's observations of the attachment and engrossment that marks the work of experts (Dreyfus, 2006; Hedegaard, 2012; Knorr-Cetina, 1997).

A key feature in our thesis is the organizational narrative that, we shall suggest, is made up of what matters for participants in organizational practices. We argue that these narratives become tools that are made and remade by participants as they together attempt to make meaning in a changing landscape of working practices. The narrative tool holds together the collective and creative envisioning of the future that shapes versions of the present. Our definition of creativity, therefore, owes a great deal to Vygotsky's.

> When, in my imagination, I draw myself a mental picture of, let us say, the future life of humanity under socialism or a picture of life in

the distant past and the struggle of prehistoric man, in both cases I am doing more than reproducing the impressions I once happened to experience. I am not merely recovering the traces of stimulation that reached my brain in the past. I never actually saw this remote past, or this future; however, I still have my own idea, image, or picture of what they were or will be like. (Vygotsky, 2004, p. 9)

Vygotsky's notion of being creative is particularly apt for a study of how individuals deal together with large-scale changes, as it goes beyond a description of individual creativity. His is a collective notion that connects the individual and the collective. He writes of "collective creativity," which he sees as combining "all those drops of individual creativity that frequently are insignificant in themselves" (Vygotsky, 2004, p. 11). It is the idea of collective creative envisioning of the future that is at the core of what we have found successful leaders to be doing as they take forward organizational change.

In this chapter, we call on two recent studies undertaken for the National College for School Leadership in England (Canwell, Hannan, Longfils, & Edwards, 2011; Daniels & Edwards, 2012). Despite the title of the sponsoring agency, the projects examined the leadership strategies and actions of leaders who were taking forward changes in new configurations of children's services, which were bringing together social work, education, educational psychology, mental health, and voluntary organizations to support the well-being of vulnerable children and young people. The chapter draws mainly on the Resourceful Leader study with some references to the follow-up, Leading for Learning. Our starting point is Engeström's suggestion that

Employees' collective capacity to create organizational transformations and innovations is becoming a crucially important asset that gives a new, dynamic content to notions of collaborative work and social capital. (Engeström, 2008, p. 199)

Like Engeström, we recognize this capacity to work creatively together to take forward organizational change does not arise spontaneously, but needs to be fostered. In this chapter, we outline how leaders of children's services fostered a collective capacity to take forward change and achieved what Engeström described as "the relationship between situated consequential decisions and future oriented visions" (Engeström, 2008, p. 214). As Engeström indicated, the dynamic is crucial. In this chapter, we discuss this dynamic, which is focused on the creation of a shared and contestable narrative and which wove together what mattered for the professionals, social workers, psychologists, etc. being led by the DCS as they worked on the problems presented by vulnerable children and their families.

THE BACKGROUND

The reconfiguring, in England, of services to enable multiagency care to be wrapped around vulnerable children and families has offered a site for examining the horizontal linkages between agencies. These services bring their specialisms to bear to disrupt the trajectories of vulnerable children and young people, so that these clients are able to benefit from and contribute to what society has to offer. Earlier studies examined the changes from the perspectives of the professionals who have had to find new ways of working (Edwards, Daniels, Gallagher, Leadbetter, & Warmington, 2009; Edwards, Lunt, & Stamou, 2010). The present studies have turned attention to how those responsible for changing the systems work creatively to do so.

The two later studies have taken place against a background of austerity policy which, since 2010, has resulted in dramatic cuts in funding for welfare services in general, which have then been presented in terms of new freedoms. The policy shift in education, for example, has been summarized by the UK government's Secretary of State for Education Michael Gove as follows: "We will ensure that all schools, whatever their status, are freed from unnecessary bureaucracy, and enjoy progressively greater autonomy, with their own funding, ethos and culture" (Department for Education, 2010, p. 50). In practice across the welfare professions, this has meant less funding for services and more responsibility for individual practitioners. In activity theory terms, the rules and division of labor have been radically disrupted.

The DCS we were studying were therefore charged with the dual task of ensuring (1) efficient service delivery within a system characterized by reduced resources and fresh demands and (2) holding together professional services for children and families at a time when practitioners had lost their identity-making certainties. Theirs was a strategic leadership role in which they had to work resourcefully, recognizing, enhancing, and using the human capital available to them in the services they were giving leadership to. Yet these were often damaged resources, because of the impact of recent policy changes. The majority of the DCS, whose work we discuss in this chapter, recognized the unsettling effects of the structural and material upheavals on practitioners' identities as expert specialists. Their solution was, as we shall see, to pay attention to releasing the personal agency of the practitioners and to aligning the professional motives, that is, the "what matters" of, for example, social workers, psychologists, teachers, and family workers with a strategic agenda, in order to achieve measurable good outcomes for children.

In tackling these priorities, the DCS were reflecting the advice of a recent review of child protection services in England (Munro, 2011). There Munro argued that: "Leaders need to be able to know their organizations well and constantly identify what needs to be realigned in order to improve performance and manage change" (Munro, 2011, p. 106). She went on to explain that organizational culture needs to recognize "the uncertainty inherent in the work" (Munro, 2011, p. 107). As we shall see, many of the DCS worked pedagogically with colleagues to weave together an organizational narrative that both reflected and sustained practitioners' identities as effective professionals and allowed them to operate constructively together to improve the lives of children and their families. In activity theory terms, this process signaled the building of what Engeström has labeled "collaborative intentionality capital" (Engeström, 2008, p. 200) as a resource for organizational development.

Bruner, working at the level of the interactions that are our focus in this chapter, has long taken a more fundamental view of the importance of narrative in being human and in being valued as a person who is personally effective and can contribute to his or her society. In particular, he has pointed to how the construction of a narrative is accomplished at the level of microinteractions. His comment on schools and culture was indicative of the ceaseless nurturing of a collective intentional narrative that we observed in the daily interactions of DCS with their colleagues.

> A system of education must help those growing up in a culture to find an identity in that culture. Without it, they stumble in their effort after meaning. It is only in the narrative mode that one can construct an identity and find a place in one's culture. Schools must cultivate it, nurture it, and cease taking it for granted. (Bruner, 1997, p. 42)

In this chapter, we, therefore, outline how successful leaders of children's services created and used narratives as tools to both realign the disrupted practices and to build collective capability to work on the problems of vulnerable children and young people. Their personal creativity and their attention to the "drops of individual creativity" (Vygotsky, 2004, p. 11) of colleagues, which in turn released their professional agency, meant that the DCS often resembled the change agents that Christensen and Lægreid (2007), echoing Bruner's attention to cultivation and nurturing, described in the following way: "The role of a successful reform agent is to operate more as a gardener than as an engineer or an architect" (p. 1063).

Elsewhere one of us has outlined three conceptual tools that help to explain interprofessional working: relational expertise, relational agency, and common knowledge (Edwards 2010, 2011, 2012). The argument there is that common knowledge, described as a respectful understanding of different professional motives, that is, what matters for the other, can become a resource that can mediate the responsive collaborations needed for work on complex problems. The work problems are described as objects of activity that can be expanded when professionals work relationally on them, bringing to bear what matters for them as professionals. This is not a straightforward Engeström activity system analysis, rather it recognizes that these interactions occur at sites of intersecting practices, where there is little sense of systemic history. The interpretations and responses to problems of practice that are made by practitioners from different practices are brought into alignment through the use of shared understandings of what matters for each collaborator.

Common knowledge of this kind, arising across the boundaries of professional practices, needs to be created and used. It can be seen in Engeström's terms as "collaborative intentionality capital" (Engeström, 2008, p. 200), through a binding together of different professional motives in, as we shall discuss, a contestable organizational narrative. The successful leaders we identified were building common knowledge between social workers, psychologists, and so on in the form of future-oriented organizational narratives that held the motives of each participating professional group and enabled them in acting agentically and jointly on demanding work problems.

THE TWO STUDIES

The first study, reported as Resourceful Leadership (Canwell et al., 2011), was given the task of identifying the knowledge, skills, and attributes of successful leaders of children's services. It used an activity theory framework (Engeström, 1999) to gather interview data in eight local authorities. The authorities were selected on the basis of their performance in the national local authority review system. Three were deemed high-performing, three were on a trajectory of improvement, and two demonstrated limited movement toward strong performance.

Each authority was visited for one day when the senior leader in children's services and several members of the leadership team were interviewed individually, using a schedule that was based on the institutional analysis afforded by activity theory, that is, they explored what each participant interpreted as the object of activity in their work; how and why they worked on them and with what; the implicit and explicit rules that shaped their work; and the division of labor. Their descriptions of their purposes and practices were fed back to them as a group for further comment at the end of the day. Summaries and initial analyses of evidence gathered during the visit were then used as the basis of in-depth telephone interviews with three members of the senior team in each local authority. These interviews were recorded in detailed notes that were typed up, and the gaps filled immediately after the conversation. Analysis was led primarily by activity theory concerns with identifying the object of activity in each children's services system, how the available tools were interpreted and used, and the extent to which the rules and division of labor sustained intentions.

The second study was a follow-up to the first. The Resourceful Leadership analysis had pointed to the pedagogic work of the more successful

DCS, yet the research brief of the earlier study had not allowed a detailed examination of the phenomenon. The follow-up study Leading for Learning (Daniels & Edwards, 2012), therefore, focused on what leaders of children's services did as they enabled the learning of their colleagues. The main phase of that study involved 10 DCS who were regarded by their peers and by local authority inspectors as "high-performing," that is, achieving good outcomes for vulnerable children and families from the services they led.

Data collection included their weekly submissions over six weeks of: (1) examples of their actions that were aimed at promoting learning in every-day activities and (2) explanations of how these actions related to their longer term strategies for the services they were leading. In cultural historical terms, we aimed at testing whether there was a link between the motives that gave shape to actions in activities with the motives that shaped the strategic practices of the organizations led by the DCS. Examples were returned using a simple reporting template and our analyses of the links between actions and strategy formed the basis of hour-long, in-depth interviews with each of them, focusing on their personal theories of leadership and learning. Analysis in this study was led by a cultural historical framing to identify motives in actions and practices (Hedegaard, 2012) and activity theory-based notions of critically aware processes of organizational change (Engeström, 1999).

RESOURCEFUL LEADERSHIP

The Vygotskian emphasis on externalization as well as internalization in learning (Vygotsky 1978) means that the cultural historical mind is outward-looking, interpreting and acting on the world. Personal sense-making is, therefore, in a dialectical relationship with public meaning-making, so that we not only are shaped by, but also shape the knowledge-laden practices we inhabit. When learning is seen in that way, learning professionals in organizations can be seen as people capable of taking creative action on problems of practice. At a time of austerity, when material resources are stripped away and workforces are drastically reduced, the expertise of the remaining workforce becomes overtly a focus for professional development and ensuring engagement with the long-term purposes of the organization. When these reductions are occurring at a time of systemic reconfiguring of the relationships between services, the need for leaders to recognize, enhance, and give purpose to the capability of colleagues at every level of the systems they lead is crucial. The sites in which we were working, therefore, amplified the need for a strong sense of organizational purpose. That purpose was built dialectically through the way personal sense-making both informed and was informed by a publicly presented narrative.

The analysis of data from the first study revealed distinct differences between authorities that were high-performing or on a trajectory of improvement when compared with those where movement was limited. In the latter, rules were used as tools to ensure adherence to tight systems of performance management, the object of activity was historically formulated and unquestioned, and there was little sense of future envisioning of either an individual or collective kind. Practitioners were resources to be ordered and deployed in relatively predetermined ways. Of course, these processes could be justified by ensuring a safe environment for vulnerable children, but they gave little room for the resourceful responsive and agentic actions of practitioners in their work with children and families. Systems with these features were not providing ideal bases for the enhanced practitioner responsibility demanded by austerity policies.

In the more successful local authorities, we discerned a far more creative response. The research brief required evidence of the knowledge, skills, and attitudes to be found among the DCS who led the systems of services, which improved outcomes for vulnerable children. However, our Vygotskian focus on the externalization of internal attributes led us to examine also *how* and *why* the knowledge, skills, and attitudes were employed as tools for developing coherent and responsive services. Here the skill of creatively resourceful leadership became apparent. We have attempted to outline the processes we observed in Figure 5.1. This is a simplified, linear model of what was an iterative process of bringing to bear leadership knowledge, skills, and attitudes in the interpretation of the practice landscape and the subsequent responsive capacity building, all of which was woven into a developing organizational narrative that captured the collaborative intentionality of the system.

We are aware that reflective reading of the organization as a system is a commonplace leadership activity; for example, management and leadership courses frequently advise "getting in the balcony" to see and reflect on the whole system (Heifetz & Laurie, 1997). However, our Vygotskian line has meant that our focus was not simply their interpretations of the practice landscape, but also what the DCS did to act on it, that is, how they used their knowledge and skills to change the landscape and why they selected particular actions. In Figure 5.1, we have outlined a dynamic process in which leaders interpreted the "figured world" (Holland, Lachicotte, Skinner, & Cain, 1998) of local children's services, identified the human capital within in them, and worked on and with practitioners to change the practice landscape (Edwards, 2012). In brief, the strategic leader recognized and enhanced the capacity of more junior colleagues to act on and shape organizational practices, in doing so the colleagues made evident what mattered for them as professionals. These motives were, in turn, woven into an organizational narrative that helped shape future directions and actions. The organizational narrative carried the purposes of the contributing practices and was used as a tool to shape the development of practitioners and practices over time.

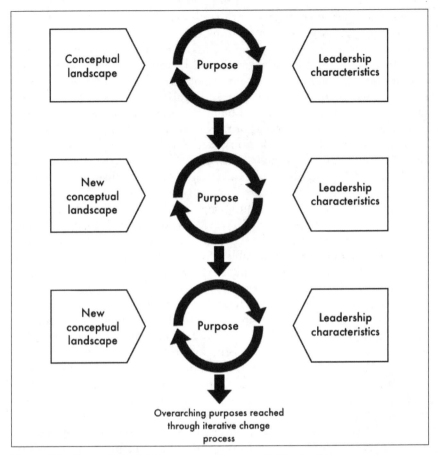

Figure 5.1   An outline of the processes of resourceful leadership.

The human capital that was worked with was the practitioner workforce. Although, as we shall suggest, user engagement in service development is currently beginning to engage the resources of clients in the coconfiguration of services. Professional development included activities such as: increasing practitioner capacity to interpret and use data as a basis for action and bringing staff from schools and social work together to expand their interpretations of the problems facing children and to find ways of collaborating to alleviate them. Practitioner development of this kind meant that the practice landscape itself was changed to become more oriented toward collaborations based on sound data and shared long-term concerns about children and families.

These changes were held together by a growing recognition that the contributing services were driven, both ethically and through systems of accountability, by a desire for the best outcomes for vulnerable children.

This focus on outcomes did not necessarily produce a neat set of intentions to which all could immediately ascribe: "There are multi-level connected systems in place. Different issues are debated and reviewed at each level" (Senior leader in authority A in telephone interview). Rather, the prioritization of outcomes and the processes that aimed at accomplishing them were negotiated and woven together into a broad set of value-laden purposes that comprised the organizational narrative.

> The DCS is heavily involved and sees her role as enhancing the quality of debate and maintaining a focus on values (another senior leader in authority A in telephone interview).

> We have good systems because we have shared values, getting shared values is hard work. We need to listen hard to each others' stories and work collectively on the priorities (senior leader in authority B in telephone interview).

Here we connect with the centrality of "common knowledge" to the process of meaning-making across professional boundaries (Edwards, 2010, 2011, 2012). Common knowledge, as we have already indicated, is described as consisting of what matters for each contributing practice, or the motives that give shape to actions in activities in each practice. Individual practitioners were making adjustments to how they worked, sometimes slightly bending rules to do the best for children. These creative changes and their motives were brought to the surface and made public in the organizational narrative. That narrative was recounted and remade regularly by DCS as it captured what mattered. What mattered for practitioners whose work was oriented toward the well-being of children was woven together creatively to direct "all those drops of individual creativity that frequently are insignificant in themselves" (Vygotsky, 2004, p. 11) toward organizational purposes.

> I try to push leadership down to the front line (Senior leader in authority C in telephone interview).

> I use hard data to bring everything up to the surface. Everyone is critical in the process. . . . I am a great believer in argument, not aggressive, but looking at how something is working, asking why, analyzing, and challenging each other (DCS in authority C in interview during initial visit).

The narrative that resulted then became a tool to be used by both the DCS and other practitioners to shape the practices and activities and actions within them to build collaborative intentionality capital and to take forward organizational intentions: "We engaged with a lot of frontline staff.

We got a tremendous amount of feedback about teams around the child and what should be the right threshold, etc. It has resulted in changes in practice" (DCS in authority C in interview during initial visit). Goals, therefore, were not simply a distant feature that enabled different practice systems to align *pace* Pickering (1995); rather they became part of a rationale for each microlevel negotiation between practitioners, between practitioners and clients, and between practitioners and the rules that shaped the practice landscape.

These findings were not incorporated in the published report in any detail as they took the research team beyond the project brief. Nonetheless, the notion of the resourceful leader as someone who could recognize and enhance the human resources already available within the children's services system and marshal them for organizational purposes, became central to the report and unsurprisingly resonated across a local authority system where material and human resources were being reduced quite drastically.

LEADING FOR LEARNING

Here we focus on the mustering of collective creativity by the 10 high-performing DCS who were the focus of the second study.[1] Every DCS had created an organizational narrative in conversations with colleagues. They recognized that for the narratives to bring cohesion to the delivery and take up of services, other voices and views needed to inform them. The narratives were, therefore, built while DCS interacted with colleagues and at times with service-users. They then used them as benchmarks, against which they evaluated their actions, and as tools for engaging others in the change process.

The narratives comprised what mattered for each contributing service and operated as stabilizing devices, helping colleagues to deal with the endemic uncertainty that Munro had alluded to (Munro, 2011). The DCS were strongly aware of the part that values and motives played in the work of their colleagues and how much the disruption of practices through financial reductions had produced a focus on what really mattered for each service in its work with children and families. The motives that gave shape to each specialist practice were made visible as they were captured in conversations and were taken into the developing interprofessional narrative: "Policy has changed—a lot of certainty has been pulled away from them. Motives are constantly under review" (DCS).

The narratives also enabled discussions of difference because they provided contestable outcomes-oriented framings that allowed people to recognize the different, but complementary, purposes of the contributing services and offered a set of intentions and values against which existing practices could be assessed, tensions and contradictions revealed, and new proposals examined.

I used the opportunity to introduce very briefly a courageous conversation by reminding PCT [Primary Care Trust, i.e., health service] colleagues of discussions we've been having about this and encouraging them in the tea break to incorporate it into feedback and then using it as hook to be able to say things about children's health that wouldn't have easily been said otherwise (DCS).

I'm a story teller; I use metaphors, trying to get people to see things they haven't seen, and I use their language to talk about what we are here for (DCS).

What was striking about these high-performing DCS was their constant attention to the purposes that were woven into the narratives. The grand vision was important, but also a continuous process of the kinds of alignment and realignment also mentioned by Munro. Their weekly responses in the templates that asked them to describe their actions in activities and relate them to their wider strategic plans illustrated directly what Engeström (2008) has described as "the relationship between situated consequential decisions and future oriented visions" (p. 214). Here is just one example taken from the weekly returns from the DCS:

Activity: I met with a newly qualified social worker to review their time in a team; what work they were undertaking and how they felt things were going.

Actions: Primarily, I listened to what the Newly Qualified Social Worker was saying—emotions and actions. I reflected and fed back my thoughts on what (I thought) was happening. I checked out my thoughts with the person for accuracy. I drew on my knowledge of the research to try to make sense of the emotions and actions that made sense to the NQSW.

Strategy: The aim is to encourage workers to be more analytic and reflective. To encourage emotional intelligence and reflexivity as part of what we do.

They were also highly self-aware about the connections they were making between their actions and broader strategies.

For sustainable change, you need to be part of the resetting and reset yourself. Resetting is not a quick fix. You need to tell a grand vision story and enable people to see their pathways. It is not as linear as you would like (DCS).

Engeström and his colleagues (Engeström, Engeström, & Kerosuo, 2003) had earlier argued that human agency is enhanced when future-oriented envisioning and actions are brought together. These DCS were clearly invigorating professional agency at a time of uncertainty and disruption by using the narrative to make visible the affordances for action represented within the vision.

CREATIVE LEADERSHIP

Conceptualizations of leadership are necessarily work in progress as changing economic models and working arrangements call for new modes of weaving together disparate contributions that specialist units might make to organizational ends. Nonetheless, the notion of heroic leaders does seem to be waning, to be replaced with one that emphasizes a broadly goal-oriented organizational culture and values and attention to human resources. As Girin puts it in a 1990 paper that was reissued in 2011:

> All literature on organizations is available to show the complexity of this universe, and it takes little to see that it is necessary to understand two aspects: the aspect of a system oriented towards some ends and the aspect of a social system or "social order" connected to the social environment. (Girin, 2011, p. 206)

In a recent review of research on leadership, Avolio and his colleagues describe leadership in a way that echoes the findings from the two studies as "depicted in various models as dyadic, shared, relational, strategic, global, and a complex social dynamic" (Avolio et al., 2009, p. 422–423). Yet their research review indicated that work was needed to clarify just what these concepts entail at the microlevel of human interaction. Indeed a group of Business School Deans has recently observed the lack of close understanding of the work that leaders do to be found in research and have, therefore, raised questions about the relevance of the evidence base of leadership programs (Canals, 2010). This is not a new problem; in 1990 Girin also pointed to both the need and the research challenges of recognizing the relevance of actions in activities where leadership may be occurring.

The dynamic of management situations is engaged and maintained by the actions of the participants. The word *action* may imply a vast series of elements such as the realization of a material task, the analysis of a problem, consulting with others, leading negotiations, reacting to an event, etc. It is difficult to more precisely define the word action, other than say that it has a beginning and an end and that it entails an *accomplishment*. The action can be more or less elementary, and observation is not enough to decide its limits. A specific perspective of analysis is needed to decide if a particular action can be isolated, or if it is only part of a larger action (Girin, 2011, p. 200).

In another review of the leadership field, Podolny, Khurana, and Besharov (2010) indicated the need for research on the more affective phenomena of the kind we described in the two studies we have presented. They called for research that explores how leaders create meaning and purpose in organizations, arguing that the concept of leadership has been *decoupled* from this focus, with most research attending primarily to individual or organizational performance. Seeing leaders as a source of institutionalized values that shape the actions of organizational members, they proposed that we need to extend our knowledge of how leaders create purpose and meaning.

We suggest that the cultural historical line adopted in this chapter addresses some of the challenges to research on leadership that have been identified in these reviews through its attention to: (1) action level data that are connected to activities and the practice of leadership and (2) how leadership can muster individual and group creativity through making and remaking an organizational narrative as a tool. In brief, the analytical approach we have taken can help unpack the relational aspects of leadership to reveal how the motives in actions, in activities, and in practices are brought into alignment with organizational strategy. It can also reveal how leaders work pedagogically in their interactions with others to achieve that alignment. Its focus, on how what matters for professionals—that is their professional motives—are woven together to create a shared yet contestable narrative, demonstrates how the individual sense-making of the purposes of professional practices becomes public meaning-making, embracing the purposes and values of the contributors to the system.

However, we suggest that cultural historical analysis can do more than simply address concerns about working at the level of action, capturing the relational aspects of leadership and the alignment of values and purposes in organizations. It can also open up a field of enquiry, as Engeström (2005) has already started to do, in which the creative aspects of leadership can be foregrounded. Writing about imagination as a central feature of creativity, Vygotsky explained that it becomes:

> the means by which a person's experience is broadened, because he can imagine what he has not seen, can conceptualize something from another person's narration and description of what he himself has never experienced. He is not limited to the narrow circle and narrow boundaries of his own experience, but can venture far beyond these boundaries, assimilating, with the help of his imagination someone else's historical or social experience. (Vygotsky, 2004, p. 17)

In the context of the interprofessional systems where we have been examining leadership, the creativity involved in the construction of a common understanding of the motives, that is, what matters for each profession is clear. Leadership here initially involves creating structures and climates in which practitioners can take the standpoints of the others and work with them (Edwards, 2010, 2011, 2012). The creativity of leadership again becomes apparent as they weave the common knowledge that is produced into a narrative that is centered on organizational purposes.

These narratives in the two studies were not benign accounts that focused on previous aims. Rather they reflected the tools discussed by Engeström and Sannino (2011) as useful for dealing with the deep-seated organizational contradictions, which might inhibit the pursuit of organizational intentions. The authors describe such devices in terms of the:

> generation of novel mediating models, concepts and patterns of activity that go beyond and transcend the available opposing forces or options, pushing the system into a new phase of development. (Engeström & Sannino, 2011, p. 371)

The DCS in the second study, for example, talked consistently about their "relentless focus on outcomes for children and families," seeing the narratives they were creating as tools for accomplishing their extremely demanding goals.

Vygotsky's broad understanding of creativity outlined in the 2004 paper brings attention to the skillful artistry that can be involved in generating the mediating models we found in use. He argued (p. 12) that the ability to combine the old (purposes) in new ways is "the basis of creativity." This combining of the old for new purposes is exactly what the successful DCS did, by listening carefully, taking seriously the motives that shaped each practice, and directing them, using the mediating device of the narrative, toward current organizational purposes.

But, there is more. As we have already indicated, the cultural historical analysis adopted here has allowed an examination of the relationships between the analytical layers of action in activity in a practice. Also our earlier comments on Vygotskian notions of externalization and the creativity involved in interpreting and acting on the world suggested that these are crucial aspects of a work culture if human resources are to be deployed to take forward organizational purposes.

The practices that made up the systems in which we were examining leadership, that is, social work, educational psychology, and so on, required practitioners to work responsively with vulnerable children and families. Practitioners were expected to interpret a situation and take action to improve a child's life chances. These actions could quite overtly reshape the practices they inhabited. Although we were carrying out the studies, the services were being reconfigured to enable interprofessional collaboration. As a consequence, frontline practitioners were finding themselves creating new ways of working that required them to act on and reshape the rules that had structured their work systems, so that they could collaborate and work jointly and responsively on the trajectories of their clients (Edwards, 2010; Edwards et al., 2009). Each time they made an adjustment, they were acting creatively to take forward what mattered for them as professionals.

In an earlier study (Edwards et al., 2009), we observed the frustration that arose when these adjustments were overlooked, and the system remained dysfunctional. The resourceful leaders who participated in the two studies discussed here could not afford to ignore evidence of the need to reshape the practice landscape, indeed they often encouraged the evidence-based reshapings that allowed for more responsive work with clients. Nonetheless, taking knowledge of this kind from the frontline to strategy can be difficult (Schulz, 2001, 2003). Examining the challenges of what we have termed *upstream learning,* one of us has shown how much more easily knowledge travels upstream from the frontline to strategy, when the affective is highlighted and the purposes understood at every level of the system (Edwards, 2010). The organizational narratives we found in the present studies did capture the *drops of individual creativity* that were reflected in the slight bending of the rules we observed in the earlier work and wove them into ways of addressing strategic intentions.

The creative and relational work undertaken by the more successful leaders in the two studies was a relentless making of the new from a badly curtailed version of the old. It was little wonder, therefore, that creative leadership focused on work within the system they were leading, with some attempts at building alliances with cognate systems such as public health. However, a great deal remains to be done to build and release the creative capital of the users of the services they were leading. There were relatively few examples of the creative coconfiguration (Victor & Boynton, 1998) of services with users in either of the studies. It seems that the creative leadership we encountered was focused on fostering a functioning system that still regarded service users as problems to be worked on. We would suggest that the next challenge for creative leadership is to recognize, engage with, and enhance the *drops of creativity* to be found among those we all too often choose to categorize as users of the services that are provided.

NOTES

1. See Daniels and Edwards (2012) for the full report.

REFERENCES

Avolio, B., Walumbwa, F., & Weber, T. (2009). Leadership: Current theories, research, and future directions. *Annual Review of Psychology, 60,* 421–449.

Bruner, J. (1997). *The culture of education.* Cambridge, MA: Harvard University Press.

Canals, J. (Ed.). (2010). *The future of leadership development: Corporate needs and the role of business schools.* New York, NY: Palgrave, Macmillan.

Canwell, A., Hannan, S., Longfils, H., & Edwards, A. (2011). *Resourceful leadership: How directors of children's services improve outcomes for children.* Nottingham, England: National College for School Leadership.

Christensen, T., & Lægreid, P. (2007). The whole of government approach to public service reform. *Public Administration Review, November/December,* 1059–1066.

Daniels, H., & Edwards, A. (2012). *Leading the learning: How the intelligent leader builds capacity.* Nottingham, England: National College for School Leadership.

Department for Education. (2010). *The importance of teaching: Schools white paper.* London, England: Author.

Dreyfus, H. (2006). Overcoming the myth of the mental. *Topic, 25,* 43–49.

Edwards, A. (2010). *Being an expert professional practitioner: The relational turn in expertise.* Dordrecht, The Netherlands: Springer.

Edwards, A. (2011). Building common knowledge at boundaries between professional practices. *International Journal of Educational Research, 50,* 33–39.

Edwards, A. (2012). The role of common knowledge in achieving collaboration across practices. *Learning, Culture and Social Interaction, 1*(1), 22–32.

Edwards, A., Daniels, H., Gallagher, T., Leadbetter, J., & Warmington, P. (2009). *Improving inter-professional collaborations: Multi-agency working for children's wellbeing.* London, England: Routledge.

Edwards, A., Lunt, I., & Stamou, E. (2010). Inter-professional work and expertise: New roles at the boundaries of schools. *British Educational Research Journal, 36*(1), 27–45.

Engeström, Y. (1999). Activity theory and individual and social transformation. In Y. Engeström, R. Miettinen, & R.-L. Punamäki (Eds.), *Perspectives on activity theory* (pp. 19–38). Cambridge, England: Cambridge University Press.

Engeström, Y. (2005). Knotworking to create collaborative intentionality capital in fluid organizational fields. In M. M. Beyerlein & F. A. Kennedy (Eds.), *Collaborative capital: Creating intangible value* (pp. 307–336). Amsterdam, The Netherlands: Elsevier.

Engeström, Y. (2008). *From teams to knots: Activity theoretical studies of collaboration and learning at work.* Cambridge, England: Cambridge University Press.

Engeström, Y., Engeström, R., & Kerosuo, H. (2003). The discursive construction of collaborative care. *Applied Linguistics, 24,* 286–315.

Engeström, Y., & Sannino, A. (2011). Discursive manifestations of contradictions in organisational change efforts. *Journal of Organizational Change Management, 24*(3), 368–387.

Girin, J. (2011). Empirical analysis of management situations: Elements of theory and method. *European Management Review, 8,* 197–212.

Hedegaard, M. (2012). The dynamic aspects in children's learning and development. In M. Hedegaard, A. Edwards, & M. Fleer (Eds.), *Motives in children's development: Cultural historical approaches* (pp. 9–27). Cambridge, England: Cambridge University Press.

Heifetz, R. A., & Laurie, D. (1997). The work of leadership. *Harvard Business Review, January–February,* 124–135.

Holland, D., Lachicotte, W., Skinner, D., & Cain, C. (1998). *Identity and agency in cultural worlds.* Cambridge, MA: Harvard University Press.

Knorr-Cetina, K. (1997). Sociality with objects: Social relations in post-social knowledge societies. *Theory Culture Society, 14*(1), 1–29.

Leont'ev, A. N. (1978). *Activity, consciousness, and personality.* Englewood Cliffs, NJ: Prentice-Hall.

Mumford, M. D., Connelly, S., & Gaddis, B. (2003). How creative leaders think: Experimental findings and cases. *Leadership Quarterly, 14,* 411–432

Munro, E. (2011). *The Munro review of child protection: Final report a child-centred system.* London: Department of Education.

Pickering, A. (1995). *The mangle of practice: Time, agency and science.* Chicago, IL: University of Chicago Press.

Podolny, J., Khurana, R., & Besharov, M. L. (2010). Revisiting the meaning of leadership. In N. Nohria & R. Khurana (Eds.), *The handbook of leadership theory and practice* (pp. 65–106). Harvard, MA: Harvard Business School.

Schulz, M. (2001). The uncertain relevance of newness: Organizational learning and knowledge flows. *The Academy of Management Journal, 44*(4), 661–681.

Schulz, M. (2003). Pathways of relevance: Exploring inflows of knowledge into subunits of multinational corporations. *Organization Science, 14*(4), 440–459.

Victor, B., & Boynton, A. (1998). *Invented here: Maximizing your organization's internal growth and profitability.* Boston, MA: Harvard Business School Press.

Vygotsky, L. S. (1978). *Mind in society: The development of higher psychological processes.* Cambridge, MA: Harvard University Press.

Vygotsky, L. S. (2004). Imagination and creativity in childhood. *Journal of Russian and East European Psychology, 42*(1), 7–97.

6 Knowledge Sharing in Professions
Working Creatively with Standards in Local Settings

Sten Ludvigsen and Monika Nerland

As concepts, learning and creativity are both strongly associated with that which is new and processes in which participants, groups, institutions, and organizations must engage in order to change their performance (Kaufman & Sternberg, 2010; Littleton, Taylor, & Eteläpelto, 2012; Sawyer, 2012a). Moreover, they are associated with short- and long-term success and survival in society, the private and public sectors. Together with innovation, these concepts are often used as buzzwords in policy and debates about societal transformation. However, to be analytically useful, we need to open these categories up and employ other relevant concepts to describe and analyze specific phenomena. Then we can have a concrete discussion about what creativity actually means in specific social and historical settings.

In this chapter, we focus on the creative actions that are involved when knowledge is shared in professions and other expert communities. In the knowledge-intensive societies of our time, social and economic well-being depends on professionals and experts who create and make use of knowledge to produce services and products (Styhre, 2011; Timmermanns & Epstein, 2010). In these activities, the construction and sharing of knowledge are some of the most important aspects that we must understand in order to explain how creative actions and solutions are realized.

Knowledge sharing is, however, not straightforward or a matter of simply distributing given knowledge. Rather, it involves creative actions and construction of knowledge to achieve solutions and make existing knowledge useful in solving new problems. Moreover, it is through the construction and sharing of knowledge that services and products can be transformed and expanded, and activities can be validated as creative over time. In this chapter, we therefore seek to understand learning as a form of knowledge construction and sharing that is emerging in social practices.

Creativity is often connected to art and innovative products (Sawyer, 2012a). Such creative work and products are recognized and validated as creative through social and historical processes after the work is performed, (e.g., Sawyer, 2012a). However, in a recent volume on creativity and creative work in contemporary work contexts (Littleton et al., 2012), it was emphasized that, in most workplace settings, we must understand how activities are constrained by routines, standards, and other forms of accumulated knowledge in order to understand how creative actions are performed (Paloniemi & Collin, 2012). Hence, sharing knowledge does not mean that there is symmetry between participants. Participants come from different positions in the sharing process, and their space for possible action is regulated by established knowledge as well as institutional histories. Moreover, rather than hindering creativity, such historical and institutional aspects may in fact enhance creative action, as they give some directions for action and, at the same time, provide resources that can be examined and transformed in different ways.

In this chapter, we explore how knowledge sharing takes place in professional work by examining how practitioners in three different professional and organizational settings develop and use standardized knowledge resources in creative ways. Creativity is understood as the actions that lead to incremental change and the improvement of future outcomes of activities, or what is called "creativity with little c" (Kaufman & Sternberg, 2010). Such processes involve creating steps toward an imagined future (Toulmin, 1999).

We use examples from case studies in three professional contexts (nursing, software development, and accountancy) that were conducted within the larger Norwegian project Learning Trajectories in Knowledge Economies. The case studies focused on knowledge practices in situations in which new tools or requirements were introduced. In such situations, what we call "stabilizing the new" and "finding solutions to present problems" are part of creative activities and cannot be taken for granted. Hence, we suggest that they should be analyzed as interactional accomplishments. In the argument that follows, we pay special attention to how practitioners go about "localizing" generalized expressions of scientific or standardized knowledge for the sake of solving local tasks.

The three cases have an illustrative function in this chapter, as our primary aim is to discuss and conceptualize how knowledge becomes shared and how this involves creative action between the participants. The research questions posed in the chapter are: How do professionals share knowledge when exposed to new standards and open-ended problems? What is the role of creative actions in such knowledge sharing?

In the following section, we discuss creativity in professional work in relation to standards and procedures. We then describe our analytic stance with regard to analyzing human activities. The three cases are then introduced and analyzed. In the discussion and conclusion section, we point out the important aspects of the three practices that can contribute to our understanding of how the work with standards involves creativity and mediates incremental change. With regard to creativity research, our work aims to contribute to a more nuanced understanding of problem identification and how creative solutions are achieved through knowledge sharing within settings that are constrained by standards. This contribution should be seen within the sociocultural perspective that emphasizes how analyzing emerging processes can give new insight to our understanding of creativity (Sawyer, 2012b) in professional work.

KNOWLEDGE SHARING AND STANDARDS IN PROFESSIONAL WORK

Work practices in professional settings are changing in several ways. New demands as well as the use of more complex tools and instruments require professionals to renew their knowledge and skills and to generate more epistemic modes of practice. Working on open-ended problems is part of professional practice in many contexts, and such problems require practitioners to develop what we term *creative solutions*. Hence, at the core of professional work today is shared expertise, knowledge sharing, and processes that lead to creative solutions in local problem solving (Adler, Kwon, & Heckscher, 2008; Styhre, 2011).

Against this background, professions can be understood to be expert cultures that are characterized by their distinct ways of sharing knowledge and finding new solutions to problems (Jensen, Lahn, & Nerland, 2012). Such cultures span site and organizational levels. Furthermore, knowledge takes a variety of forms and functions and becomes further transformed on its travels. The use of knowledge depends on local contingencies, which means that even procedures must be understood as actions that are situated within larger infrastructures of knowledge (Bowker & Star, 1999; Børte, Ludvigsen, & Mørch, 2012; Nes & Moen, 2010; Toulmin, 1999).

A global trend in professions is the increase in knowledge-constituting agencies and standardizing bodies at different levels, such as the Cochrane Collaboration and the International Accounting Standards Board. These agencies endeavor to produce universal and decontextualized expressions of knowledge that can be used in various contexts of professional and expert work. At the same time as these developments provide professionals with new tools and resources, they also generate paradoxes. On the one hand, professional work is more and more dependent on accumulated and *secured* knowledge. On the other hand, work organizations need new and creative solutions to emerging problems. Moreover, whereas universal knowledge and standards of various kinds are meant to support work performance, they cannot simply be inserted into specific situations. To follow rules is not enough: Participants need to recontextualize and expand their knowledge and find creative solutions.

This problem is described by Timmermanns and Epstein (2010) who discuss the varied forms that standards take and their implications for different areas of social and professional life. They describe standardization as a process of constructing uniformity across space and time through the generation of agreed-upon rules. However, these processes are not only carried out on sites that are external to professional work. Rather, it is an ongoing process where standards need to be deconstructed and reconstructed at different levels of practice in order to become meaningful and useful in local settings. To understand how standards work and how they may also stimulate creative action, we need to reveal how they are approached, employed, and further developed in local practices (Timmermanns & Berg, 1997).

In a study of health professions, Moreira (2005) analyzed the work of clinical guidelines groups to reveal how such guidelines are developed. He showed how the creation of guidelines was accomplished in situ by combining different repertoires of evaluation. The repertoires gave precedence to different criteria, such as robustness, usability, acceptability, and adequacy. Researchers have also directed their attention to tools and technologies that are specifically designed to facilitate the sharing of expertise by employing standardized categories, such as electronic patient records (Bruni, Gherardi, & Parolin, 2007) and oral shift reports (Winman & Rystedt, 2011). These studies show that entering information into these systems is neither straightforward nor is it sufficient for knowledge sharing. Rather, practitioners need to explore the meaning of the information and engage in creative work in order to close the gaps in infrastructure and make generalized categories useful for deciding on specific cases.

In the more technological domains, such as computer engineering, standards are often explicitly presented in everyday work and are a focal point of practitioners' attention (Nerland, 2008). This does not, however, mean that the ways in which they are dealt with and their functions are explicit. Moreover, finding ways of combining different standards in the development of technical solutions is a common challenge that requires creative modes of work (Nerland, 2008). Specific artifacts can also play a key role in such processes. For instance, Bechky (2003) showed how drawings and machines used in a manufacturing firm embedded different types of specialist knowledge that needed to be negotiated on the production floor. Engineers, technicians, and assemblers approached these artifacts and their embedded standards with different forms of understanding, and the process of negotiation involved a transformation of knowledge in problem solving as well as efforts to claim professional jurisdiction by controlling the meaning of the artifacts.

In sum, this research points to how professionals engage in knowledge sharing in a number of ways that go beyond rules and routines and call for creative encounters and actions (e.g., Chapter 8, this volume). Sharing and assessing knowledge by creating frames of relevance and interpretation lie at the core of this work.

MULTIPLE LAYERS OF HUMAN ACTIVITIES: THE SOCIOGENETIC PERSPECTIVE

We use the sociogenetic perspective to analyze three cases. This perspective makes it possible to analyze knowledge sharing as a phenomenon with multiple layers: action; activities; and the organization of social, cognitive, and cultural systems (Engeström, 1987; Engeström & Sannino, 2010; Saxe & Esmonde, 2005; Valsiner & Van Der Veer, 2000).

To understand the short- and long-term cycles of activities and artifacts and how they are embedded in specific practices and social institutions, we need a theoretical perspective that can account for phenomena at different layers of description and timescales (Engeström, 1987; Ludvigsen, 2012; Saxe & Esmonde, 2005). The three layers are socio-, micro-, and ontogenesis. Sociogenesis is understood to be how social and cultural resources are organized and become sustainable over time. To engage in nursing, estimation, or accountancy is to understand how knowledge in the profession is organized, played out, and given relevance in new activities. Even if the sociogenesis in different professions represents an accumulated body of knowledge, participants must be active and perform deliberate creative actions in order to be able to contribute to each activity. Microgenesis refers to how participants interact in social encounters and the kind of resources upon which they choose to draw in order to perform. Ontogenesis is the individual development of the participants and what they bring to activities in the workplace. It is at the intersection of these three layers that the frames of relevance and interpretation are created, and spaces are provided for how generalized knowledge becomes localized and displayed. It is at the intersection of these layers that we can understand how working with standards and procedures involves creativity and generates incremental change.

In the sociogenetic perspective, knowledge and concepts are seen as important assets in human activities. These resources come with meaning potentials (Linell, 2009), in the sense that knowledge and concepts are linked to knowledge domains and incorporate history and conventions for use. However, when used in a specific setting, a concept must be seen as a cultural resource that has specific functions and is used as part of the goals that emerge in the social situation. Semiotic mediation is at the core of the social and cognitive aspects of any activity. It also implies that cultural resources must be coordinated in specific ways in order to create shared knowledge over time. Semiotic processes are built on different forms of knowledge, artifacts, and tools that become justified when relevant to an activity. The meaning realized in situ is constrained, but not determined by the meaning potential. To understand the use of specific knowledge, we need to examine how it becomes incorporated into specific activities. Knowledge sharing needs to be understood in relation to what people aim to achieve through social interaction.

Knowledge that comes from elsewhere, whether the sources are external to the local practice or relate to previous experiences, needs to be adapted to local problem solving. This means that knowledge becomes transformed and localized through its use and serves specific functions as part of the actions performed. The acts of sharing knowledge are thus both creative and stabilizing, and they are based on frames of relevance that must be justified and accepted by the colleagues and the communities in which the professional practice is embedded. In the creation of frames of relevance, or what we can also call *problem identification,* participation moves beyond rules and creates potentially new solutions to complex problems.

THE THREE CASES: NURSING, ESTIMATION, AND ACCOUNTING

In the sections that follow, we present three cases that all focus on how professionals share knowledge and develop practice as they strive to make standards part of meaningful actions in their local problem solving. The first case examines how hospital nurses deal with a new standard introduced in their workplace through a knowledge management system. In the second case, we analyze how software professionals estimate time for unknown tasks that they must solve within a larger project timeframe. The third case examines auditors' ways of exploring and employing a new standard for risk auditing enhanced by an audit support system. In all three cases, problem identification and solutions are at stake.

The First Case: Constructing Standards in Nursing Practices

The first case that we discuss is a study conducted in a hospital in Norway (see Nes & Moen, 2010, for details and in-depth analysis) wherein professional nurses had to develop new procedures. Each procedure included step-by-step descriptions, instructions for operating devices, observations, illustrations, animations, photos, or video clips that complemented the descriptions and explanations. More than 277 new procedures had to be defined in the Norway hospital as part of the new work organization. The procedures had to be described in a new knowledge management system. They had to be disseminated across different departments within the hospital.

The hospital appointed a work group that was responsible for consolidating the hospital procedures and a group leader who was responsible for implementing the procedures across all departments. This group consisted of senior nurses from different departments in the hospital. This group reviewed all the suggestions offered by a number of work groups that were established to give input from a departmental point of view. The process of constructing the standards was completed in several steps, and the consolidation work group had responsibility for finding and building institutional consensus.

The study by Nes and Moen (2010) was based on video recordings, observations, and interviews. They focused on how different aspects of knowledge involved in the construction of the procedures were manifested in the encounters of the consolidation group. The procedures that led to heated discussions were analyzed in detail. Their analysis clearly showed that many of the procedures could not be easily adopted and implemented. Only 18% was accepted directly, whereas 72% was commented on, and

10% was rejected. Merely following the biomedical information provided on the knowledge management platform was not satisfactory. In the data displayed below, we see one example of the practitioners' efforts to resolve the problem of a clinical procedure related to infection control. One nurse explains the process as follows:

> and then *stain disinfection,* and for PPS (the software), this also applies to the procedures called "stain disinfection" and "chemical disinfection remedies." We had some very heated discussions, related to what is really said from the Norwegian Medicines Agency . . . we made contact with them . . . and we contacted the National Hospital and [naming four other Norwegian university hospitals] and, in addition, we checked the CDC—the Center for Disease Control—and Johns Hopkins [to see] what is available from the Norwegian Institute of Public Health; there are only suggested recommendations and no requirements, but they are also quite vague. We have discussed a lot back and forth in our team— specialists in infectious diseases, epidemiology, public health nurses— that what we work for is one universal, nonambiguous procedure that makes everyone do it the same way, whether the stain is spilled on a wall or on the floor, on some of the equipment or . . . whatever it is. The conclusion we reached . . . we called it [alternative procedure] stain disinfection; it is really disinfection of everything, yes . . . which adds. . . if you find the PPS procedure [referring to the group leader who put the procedures up on the computer screen]. So our conclusion is that this one [pointing to the PPS procedure on the screen] is invalidated. (Nes & Moen, 2010, p. 387–388)

As we see in this description and in the course of discussion of these particular procedures, the consolidation group examined different types of evidence. They investigated how other university hospitals, international communities, and national authorities described these procedures and defined the knowledge base for them. Because the procedure is based on the integration of knowledge from different subfields of medicine, it is also appropriate to contextualize the procedure on the basis of each department's perspective and practice of the procedure.

In order to understand these processes, the concept of local universality was used (Nes & Moen, 2010; Timmermanns & Berg, 1997). This term makes it possible to differentiate between general knowledge in the procedure (e.g., biomedical evidence) and local practice in the hospital. From a sociogenetic perspective, the creation of local universalities can be understood as accomplishments at the intersection of different layers of practice. Biomedical knowledge is organized in specific ways (Keating & Cambrosio, 2003). The different disciplines represent subfields of knowledge that have been integrated into clinical practice and standards. Evidence for the procedures is obtained from studies with accepted methodologies, methods, and analytical techniques. This knowledge base represents the connection to a collective knowledge infrastructure, which the participants can deploy and contextualize in their local work. When consensus is achieved for a procedure, it indicates that the procedure has been accepted from a medical point of view. However, in each activity performed, there are local aspects that must be taken into account. These local aspects pertain to the conventions for performing specific tasks and other patient-specific issues. Such conventions are part of local practice and serve to legitimize how a professional performs certain tasks. They are often based on norms and values for how work should be conducted.

In the example above and in the larger dataset, we see that the participants contest and challenge each other's position with regard to the relevant content and practice of the procedure. It is through such microgenetic processes that we gain insight into participants' different views of the task at hand. Such processes also shed light on what knowledge is relevant to the generalized aspects of the procedures and what aspects are important in local practice. In their communication, participants create microgenetic constructions, which build on knowledge that is validated and justified.

As part of these microgenetic constructions, we can also identify that participants bring different forms and knowledge with them (the ontogenetic layer). The participants also act as representatives of specific groups and departments in the hospital. Their individual knowledge is, in this case, also valid collective knowledge, as seen from the institutional point of view.

The idea of local universality captures how knowledge becomes used and shared at the intersection between the three layers presented here. Creative action is needed in order to achieve the common problem identification and find justified solutions. General and localized knowledge is present at all the layers—in the organization of knowledge, social interaction, and what the participants bring to the consolidation group. The work regarding the standardization of the procedure makes use of historical resources and accumulated knowledge and experience, but the procedure itself aims to regulate and stabilize the future action of the health professionals.

The Second Case: Estimation in Teams

In our society, software systems are part of our professional and personal lives. Estimation is a key factor that is important to the quality and cost of building such software systems. Estimation may be defined as a set of activities that aim to predict what is needed to program a system or parts of a system, or an attempt to plan, control, and imagine the future. It is well-known that budgets and costs are often exceeded when creating new software systems. Hence, estimation is important both for the costs and for the work that must be performed; sharing knowledge is the foundation for the work. Accomplishing an estimate is dependent on social, communication, and cognitive aspects.

This means that arriving at estimates is a social and cognitive process based on actions that can create relevant frames and interpretations for understanding the tasks to work with, or what we refer to here as knowledge sharing.

In the group that we study, they use the technique called *planning poker*, which represents accumulated knowledge and is part of the general knowledge in the field of software systems. This knowledge can be activated in the course of engaging in planning poker. The numbers on the cards are one example of such general knowledge; they serve a specific local function and are coordinated with other local resources, such as the scenario. The language used by the group is similar to everyday language. However, the group seems to use specific concepts when performing specifications. The estimating involves performing a set of actions, such as clarification, elaboration, summarization, and justification (Børte et al., 2012).

Participants working on estimates have access to a set of resources: overall project description, the scenario, the user story, and the requirement specification. These resources should be seen as part of the general knowledge that must be activated in the local discussion when doing the estimation. The data material analyzed by Børte et al. (2012) consists of video recordings from real-life estimation meetings at a Norwegian software company.

Here, we present an excerpt of one team's communication process. It begins with the group leader asking the group members to show their cards (planning poker), so that the estimate becomes known. The function of the communication could be labeled clarification and elaboration of the user story, which is supposed to lead to a set of actions.

GL: Then we have the new pension task, which is a bit confusing. If the client has some services from us, it must be *stopped*. This must be our own task. So it should come up as a task . . . and this should be stopped.

P1:   Do we have anything on this from before?

GL: No, not as case flow . . .

P2:   To stop a case, what does it mean?

P3:   It's a *specific code.*

P4:   It's *stop code in the history . . .*

P3:   Now *you talk about the GUI (graphical user interface) table?*

P4:   Yes.

P3:   And as a starting point, you would have to choose a *very precise stop for each task.* Well, the simplest here is we use the user story, and then a task, and then we show the table. (Børte et al., 2012, p. 7)

One issue that must be clarified here is the meaning of *stopped*. The stopping code is not a trivial issue in the conversation. We see that the participants, while talking about the stop, develop a set of actions that specifically addresses what stop means in this particular case. The word stop is here a meaning potential that must be realized through communication. The important communicative task here is making the relevant actions visible for all the programmers as part of the problem identification. The cultural resources involved here are all connected to the technical specification of the system, but of equal import is the issue of what functions the code will execute within the system. The code is expected to create a stop in the history of a client, which means that the employee who works on this module must initiate a set of actions. This technical knowledge works on two levels: It is the connection between the general and the specific that makes the assumptions clear.

Another example in the communication here is the use of the term *GUI table*, which is one of the few explicitly used technical terms. The use of this term serves a framing function, enabling the participants to determine how they can sequence a task. It is also important to note that the participants engage in specification as long as they perceive the need for it. The information provided by the communication does not need to be perfect but should be good enough. This is in line with the principle of communication proposed by Grice (1989), who suggests that participants communicate what is needed to further the conversation. We add that the participants do not use technical terms as long as the conversation flows smoothly and everyone in the group seems to understand. Typically, gaps and conflicts elicit the use of technical terms, which help to create relevant frames for interpretation in the communicative encounters, which are the microgenetic constructions.

It is obvious that participation is not equal (the ontogenetic layer). This is, of course, related to the status and role of the participants. It is also linked to each participant's experience and knowledge. Some participants in the group have more experience as project leaders, whereas others have mostly worked as programmers. When using the planning poker techniques, each participant is expected to show a card that indicates his or her rationale regarding what the estimate should be. Inexperienced participants can compare and contrast their own reasoning and estimates with those of the more experienced ones. Accurate estimation is the outcome of both individual and collective reasoning.

Different resources and their specifications show how estimation involves drawing on knowledge and conventions that have become organized over a long period of time. From the microgenetic interaction, we see that the specification process is a gap-closing activity that connects individual knowledge with organized and collectively formed knowledge at the intersection of socio-, micro-, and ontogenetic layers. Here the imagined future should be viewed as a creative solution to the local problem.

The Third Case: Making Use of New Standards for Risk Auditing

This case explores how auditors handle recent transformations in auditing work mediated by new knowledge management systems. In auditing work today, the problem identification and evaluation of possible risk factors is a primary concern. Current legislation and guidelines for professional practice, which emerged in the aftermath of the Enron case and other scandals, have placed risk at the core of auditing. This radically transformed auditing work by turning the profession toward more analytical ways of working (Curtis & Turley, 2007). Basically, the new standards changed the audit methodology in the sense that auditors are now asked to focus on the company or enterprise as a whole in order to identify and select possible risk factors to be investigated in depth as the audit process moves into the accounting details. Moreover, the planning phase of auditing work has become more important as the potential risk factors to be evaluated and the types of information to be collected are decided upon in this initial phase. Hence, risk auditing implies a more future-oriented and creative way of thinking and working, as the auditor is not only asked to evaluate the given state of the client but to also consider the potential values and possibilities of continuing the enterprise.

A case study by Mathisen and Nerland (2012) explored how the web-based audit support system Descartes served as a mediating tool that enhanced auditors opportunities to explore and create local expressions of the general standard for risk auditing when auditing specific clients. The study was based on observations, interviews, and stimulated talks with two auditors in different work settings; these auditors had participated in a course about Descartes and had recently put the new knowledge system to use. They were approached at two different stages of the auditing process: first, in the planning phase, when the client is explored and decisions are made about what information is needed, and then three months later, during the phase when the financial information is controlled and the client audit is accomplished.

Central to risk auditing is the act of "assigning assertions." As described in the International Standard on Auditing (2009), assertions are "representations by management, explicit or otherwise, that are embodied in the financial statements, as used by the auditor to consider the different types of potential misstatements that may occur" (p. 264). This is done by assigning concepts such as accuracy, validity, completeness, periodification, and classification to financial information. Figure 6.1 below illustrates what this may look like in the Descartes system:

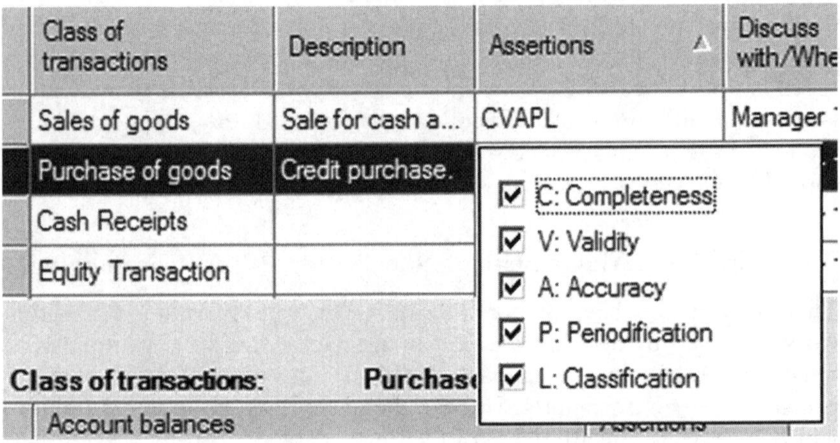

Figure 6.1　Snapshot of screen image illustrating assertions in Descartes.

Clearly, the meaning of these concepts is not transparent to everyone and rests on expertise in the profession. The auditor needs to decide upon which assertions are valid for each class of transaction, and by doing so, he or she also specifies the relevant risk factors by making decisions on what to look for when the accounting details are to be controlled at a later stage. To illustrate this process, we give an example from a stimulated talk with one of the auditors:

Researcher: Do I understand correctly that if these assertions describe what to do when you perform the audit controls later on, you should look for completeness and validity?

Auditor: Yes, in a way they do . . . like when you control costs, it's validity you should check, right?

Researcher: Yes.

Auditor: But, when you go through it, and you see, well here we have a cruise to Amsterdam, for example, hmm.

Researcher: Not quite valid?

Auditor: I suspect that perhaps it should not have been here.

(Mathisen & Nerland, 2012, p. 79)

Although this value selection may look rather straightforward at first glance, it implies an amalgamation of different information that is assessed in specific ways by employing the relevant audit standard. Descartes was seen as a work infrastructure that connects information, knowledge, standards, and work procedures across sites (Mathisen & Nerland, 2012). At the same time, this infrastructure needed to be recreated in specific ways in each audit task, through the auditors' analytical and constructive actions. The analysis showed how collective resources became visible for the auditors when they faced uncertainty and analytical modes of practice emerged. To open up the problem and make use of the generalized resources at hand, and to create frames of relevance that allowed for productive problem solving, a conceptual understanding was needed.

This points to how the ontogenesis, or the individuals' experience-based knowledge, is important for how generalized knowledge is made useful in local problem solving. Here, the study suggests that the auditors' sensitivity and knowledge is important. As shown in many studies of expertise, experience matters as it is through experience that the capacity to discriminate develops (Styhre, 2011).

This type of knowledge sharing and engagement with standards cannot, however, be understood solely from the perspective of the auditors' experiences. First, Mathisen and Nerland (2012) show how the audit of a specific client involves performing actions that can close the knowledge gaps between the information provided by the client and the assertions that are to be assigned. Here, the auditor engaged with a variety of resources, whose combination around the present problem involved creative actions. The work to identify risk factors and make sense of concepts in the specific context can be understood as an interactional accomplishment in which the auditor, the client, and the material resources provided by Descartes take part. Second, auditing rests on long traditions and established conventions that are highly formalized and shared across organizational and national boundaries. Such accumulated knowledge becomes an international and national standard that is further formalized through legislation. In the case of Descartes, the knowledge is materialized in an inscription device that also incorporates a methodology or systematized workflow. By working with and through Descartes, the knowledge and conventions of the field became visible for the auditors. Although there has been a shift toward risk auditing in this profession, this is also based on conventions that have a longer history. However, as this study shows, what must be performed is not given by the accumulated body of knowledge or standards in inscription devices such as Descartes. Inherent to the process of auditing a client, the professional also creates a future-oriented vision of how the company will perform, which is, by necessity, uncertain.

DISCUSSION AND CONCLUSION

The three cases illustrate some basic processes through which professionals share knowledge in their engagement with standards and use this to find creative solutions to open-ended problems. These problems are constrained by institutional aspects and knowledge that has been accumulated over time. Even though the three cases were taken from different professional contexts, they have some common features. At the microgenesis level, we can identify how knowledge and concepts are used as both resources and part of communication. Generalized knowledge alone does not provide sufficient levels of specification to perform the problem solving activities (Børte et al., 2012; Timmermanns & Berg, 1997). This form of knowledge represents meaning potentials from which the professional can begin to work (Mäkitalo, 2002). However, this knowledge works in tandem with the sharing processes that are important for creating solutions and imagining the future use of the standards. Both rules and creative actions are involved in the problem identification and solution process.

Another issue that seems to be common to all three cases is the form and function of the formalization involved. Formalization comes into view in generalized knowledge that is based on the artifact structure and the content of the artifacts that are activated and used: clinical guidelines in the nursing case, procedures of estimation in software development, and Descartes as a device in the auditing case. In the nursing case study, formalization was linked to the conceptualization and materialization of the procedures and the standards associated with them. In the estimation case study, the estimation techniques made the participants reason and argue for specific solutions that became *objectified* through arguments in the group. These were then promoted in the organization by the group and project leader. In the case of the accountants, their way of working was formalized in the work support system that represented a generalized meaning. Similar to a set of meaning potentials, this was then coordinated and specified to create meaning and achieve the outcome for the clients in the activities. To understand professional work in and across sites, we must account for all three layers—the socio-, micro-, ontogenetic—that are constitutive of social practices.

In all three knowledge-sharing practices discussed above, the interplay between artifacts and language is crucial. The levels of formalization and institutionalization and the use of knowledge create the meaning potential for a collective repertoire. The knowledge involved is derived from the connection of different cultural resources in the professional activities and forms of knowledge required for creative problem solving. Generalized knowledge is seen as a collective resource that is dependent on specific types of knowledge sharing in professional domains. It is through specification that the professionals' expertise becomes at least partly transparent for the participants involved. Here problem identification and problem solving are at stake. Studying professional practices involves examining the connections between the artifacts and the activated resources.

As described by Toulmin (1999), knowledge is mastered through practice, and procedures are what constitute the collective state of understanding. These are continuously approached, enacted, and developed through an interchange between "the innovations of creative individuals and their acceptance or rejection by the professional community" (Toulmin, 1999, p. 66). Hence, to understand the continuity as well as the development of professional expertise, we need to look into the details of knowledge sharing as it plays out at the intersection of different layers of practice (Sawyer 2012a, 2012b). The sociogenetic perspective offers a set of powerful analytical tools that makes it possible to analyze what is involved in creative actions and solutions with the three layers serving as the foundation for explaining and understanding human activities, action, and cognition. That is, history is also an important aspect when analyzing the social and cognitive aspects of creative actions.

In this chapter, we have defined learning as the creation and sharing of knowledge, while creativity is seen as mundane action that creates incremental change over time. In most practices, and for most people, such creativity—with the little "c" (Kaufman & Sternberg, 2010)—is what matters. It is through such actions that the past and imagined future are played out, and incremental changes take place. Of course, we also recognize the importance of major breakthroughs and large innovations; however, such large-scale innovations must also be stabilized through the creativity of everyday actions (Littleton et al., 2012). If we overlook this as mundane phenomena, we will not understand how creative actions contribute to the execution of standards in ways that differ within activities. In the wider context of this book, we recognize that our use of learning and creativity may seem to blur the distinctions between the two concepts. However, the two concepts have different origins and conceptual histories. What we have done in this chapter is to argue that learning as knowledge sharing is the foundation for creativity to take place and for creative solutions to be validated as part of the sociocultural development in specific settings.

ACKNOWLEDGMENTS

The writing of this chapter was supported by a grant from the Research Council of Norway to the project Learning Trajectories in Knowledge Economies. We would especially like to thank the participants of the Learning Trajectories in Knowledge Economies project for their inspiring discussions about the theme for this chapter and the authors of the papers from which we reused and reanalyzed data and lines of argument. In addition, we would like to thank the University of Berkeley, Center for Studies in Higher Education, and the Graduate School of Education for providing both authors with stimulating work environments during our 2012 sabbatical winter and spring terms.

REFERENCES

Adler, P., Kwon, S.-W., & Heckscher, C. (2008). Professional work: The emergence of collaborative community. *Organization Science, 19*(2), 359–376.
Bechky, B. (2003). Sharing meaning across occupational contexts: The transformation of understanding on a production floor. *Organization Science, 14*(3), 312.
Bowker, G. C., & Star, S. L. (1999). *Sorting things out*. Cambridge, MA: MIT Press.
Bruni, A., Gherardi, S., & Parolin, L. (2007). Knowing in a system of fragmented knowledge. *Mind, Culture, and Activity, 14*(1–2), 83–102.
Børte, K., Ludvigsen, S., & Mørch, A. (2012). The role of social interaction in software effort estimation: Unpacking the "magic step" between reasoning and decision-making. *Information and Software Technology, 54*(9), 985–996.
Curtis, E., & Turley, S. (2007). The business risk audit: A longitudinal case study of an audit engagement. *Accounting, Organizations and Society, 32*, 439–461.
Engeström, Y. (1987). *Learning by expanding: An activity-theoretical approach to developmental research*. Helsinki, Finland: Orienta-Konsultit.
Engeström, Y., & Sannino, A. (2010). Studies of expansive learning: Foundations, findings and future challenges. *Educational Research Review, 5*(1), 1–24.
Grice, H. P. (1989). *Studies in the way of words*. Cambridge, MA: Harvard University Press.
International Standard on Auditing. (2009). *Identifying and assessing the risks of material misstatement through understanding the entity and its environment*. Retrieved from http://web.ifac.org/download/a017–2010-iaasb-handbook-isa-315.pdf

Jensen, K., Lahn, L. C., & Nerland, M. (2012). Professional learning in new knowledge landscapes: A cultural perspective. In K. Jensen, L. C. Lahn, & M. Nerland (Eds.), *Professional learning in the knowledge society*. Rotterdam, The Netherlands: Sense Publishers.

Kaufman, J. C., & Sternberg, R. J. (2010). *The Cambridge handbook of creativity*. Cambridge, England: Cambridge University Press.

Keating, P., & Cambrosio, A. (2003). *Biomedical platforms: Realigning the normal and the pathological in late-twentieth-century medicine*. Cambridge, MA: MIT Press.

Linell, P. (2009). *Rethinking language, mind, and the world dialogically*. Charlotte, NC: Information Age Publishing.

Littleton, K., Taylor, S., & Eteläpelto, A. (2012). Creativity and creative work in contemporary working contexts. *Vocations and Learning, 5*, 1–4.

Ludvigsen, S. (2012). What counts as knowledge: Learning to use categories in computer environments. *Learning, Media and Technology, 37*(1), 40–52.

Mathisen, A., & Nerland, M. (2012). The pedagogy of complex work support systems: Infrastructuring practices and the production of critical awareness in risk auditing. *Pedagogy, Culture and Society, 20*(1), 71–91.

Mäkitalo, Å. (2002). *Categorizing work: Knowing, arguing, and social dilemmas in vocational guidance*. Gothenburg, Sweden: Acta Universitatis Gothoburgensis.

Moreira, T. (2005). Diversity in clinical guidelines: The role of repertoires of evaluation. *Social Science and Medicine, 60*(9), 1975–1985.

Nerland, M. (2008). Knowledge cultures and the shaping of work-based learning: The case of computer engineering. *Vocations and Learning: Studies in Vocational and Professional Education, 1*, 49–69.

Nes, S., & Moen, A. (2010). Constructing standards: A study of nurses negotiating with multiple modes of knowledge. *Journal of Workplace Learning, 22*(6), 376–393.

Paloniemi, S., & Collin, K. (2012). Discursive power and creativity in inter-professional work. *Vocations and Learning, 5*, 23–40.

Sawyer, K. (2012a). *Explaining creativity: The science of human innovation*. Oxford, England: Oxford University Press.

Sawyer, K. (2012b). Extending sociocultural theory to group creativity. *Vocations and Learning, 5*, 59–75.

Saxe, G., & Esmonde, I. (2005). Studying cognition in flux: A historical treatment of "fu" in the shifting structure of oksapmin mathematics. *Mind, Culture, and Activity, 12*(3–4), 171–225.

Styhre, A. (2011). Knowledge Sharing in Professions. Farnham, England: Gower Publishing Limited.

Timmermanns, S., & Berg, M. (1997). Standardization in action: Achieving local universality through medical protocols. *Social Studies of Science, 27*, 273–305.

Timmermanns, S., & Epstein, S. (2010). A world of standards but not a standard world: Towards a sociology of standards and standardization. *Annual Review of Sociology, 36*, 69–89.

Toulmin, S. (1999). Knowledge as shared procedures. In Y. Engeström, R. Miettinen, & R. Punamaki (Eds.), *Perspectives on activity theory*. Cambridge, MA: Cambridge University Press.

Valsiner, J., & Van Der Veer, R. (2000). *The social mind: Construction of the idea*. Cambridge, England: Cambridge University Press.

Winman, T., & Rystedt, H. (2011). Electronic patient records in action: Transforming information into professionally relevant knowledge. *Health Informatics Journal, 17*(1), 51–62.

7 Researching Technologies for Enhancing Collective Creativity in Interagency Working

Harry Daniels and Peter Johnson

This chapter is concerned with understanding how multiagency organizations work together, why on occasions they fail to work together, and what might be done to improve that. We consider the ways that they share and create information and knowledge. How awareness and understanding is achieved. How and what they report. How instructions and *commands* are issued and received. How decisions and their consequences are made and considered. These are all questions that need to be understood if we are to improve how people from different organizations can work together in a collective and creative manner.

We investigate two types of multiagency working: one in which the service user is relatively easily identifiable (i.e., children's services) and another in which the notion of service user is more general (i.e., disaster response emergency services). In considering these two types of multiagency working, we contrast a number of different properties including service type, organization structure and function, end user populations, patterns of communication, contexts in which the services are provided, and types of risk.

We make theoretical advances in understanding these multiagency service (MAS) systems and provide insights into improving the agility, reflexivity, and learning capacity of MAS. These theoretical insights achieve improvement through their implications for the sociocultural leadership and operational aspects of how MAS work and the development of interactive technologies that can support those improved ways of working. These technologies include: (1) modeling tools to support reflective design and functioning of services, (2) protocols and tools for sharing and representing knowledge, reports and intent and command, across and between service providers and service users to increase awareness, and (3) decision support tools that increase engagement and reflexive thinking in decision making and decrease risk in situations where outcomes are not always or entirely predictable.

The chapter investigates a number of instances of MAS operations in different situations that extend our understanding of complex and creative behavior and collective capability. These investigations and the theoretical understandings of complex and creative behavior and collective capability lead us to insights on those sociocultural practices that can lead to collective creativity and how to support it through particular digital technologies.

The challenge we face in extending our understanding of complex and creative behavior and collective capability is witnessed in the writing of this chapter. One of us is an educationalist, the other is a computer scientist. We are attempting to develop a novel synthesis of our ideas that, to some extent, are complementary and, to some extent, are divergent. In the interpersonal exchanges in which we have engaged, there has been a process of mutual transformation. As Van der Veer and Valsiner (1991) note from a Vygotskian perspective, reasoning against other viewpoints can lead to a breakpoint for novel "synthesis" (p. 393). They also argue that as we make the ideas of others our own, we do not merely copy them rather they are "analyzed and reassembled in novel ways—the individual is a co-constructor of culture rather than a mere follower of the enculturation efforts of others" (p. 395). This is nontrivial because the mediational means of our disciplinary backgrounds provide alternative forms of representation. On the basis of the complementarity that exists between us, we have sought to transform and synthesize our legacy understandings to generate a novel perspective on a common interest. In this sense, we have engaged in the processes that are the object of the chapter.

Increasingly end-user services are provided by collections of agencies each producing services that then both poorly fit together and collectively do not meet the various users' needs. An important point of impact is to provide service design, planning, and delivery through collaboration and collective technologies that enable multiple agencies to work together to provide seamless and fit-for-purpose end-user and customer services, providing collective capability to respond to complex challenges. This capability and the responses it produces need to be, by definition, innovative and creative. Collective creativity raises a number of challenges.

One challenge is how to provide the best possible integrated service to meet the multiple individual and dynamically changing user needs, reducing duplication of provision and increasing service delivery effectiveness. Another challenge is engaging the multiple stakeholders, including service planners, service deliverers, and service end users, in service design and delivery to increase the quality and effectiveness to all stakeholders. Frequently, these challenges are not met: The citizen or customer or end-user experience suffers as the services fail to fit together, duplicate, or miss important aspects of needs. Multiagency service failings are increasingly found in education, welfare, transport, energy, utilities, health and well-being, defense, and emergency response services. Failure results in dissatisfaction, poor service quality, lack of trust, and inadequate take-up of services and can cost lives, resources, and reputations. There are underlying generic problems in such multiagency services that result in their inability to meet these challenges and give rise to these failures. Our research exposes and addresses these underlying generic problems. We discuss the background to this work in detail later in the chapter.

To address these challenges, we need both new forms of leadership and working, and technologies that enable them to work as collaborating collectives. These technologies include collaborative modeling tools of service organization that can be used to describe and analyze the different existing modalities and predict possibilities of future configurations of complex services. Such tools enhance collective system design by providing explicit shareable representations of the emergent design to the multiple stakeholders. A central feature of these representations is the portrayal of criteria and options for communication and participation in decision making in the processes of service planning and service provision.

Central to the design requirements of these technological supports is that they should make it possible to explicate and overcome the tensions, contradictions, and lack of awareness across service providers, between providers and users, and with the demands of the contexts in which the services are required to operate. From a theoretical position, it is here that cultural-historical activity theory is developed and deployed in intervention studies with selected services. From our analyses, we develop a framework for collective creativity processes and identify their technological implications. These technological requirements have implications for knowledge creation and sharing technologies.

We begin by reflecting upon two studies in which MAS have both problems and failures that need to be understood. From understanding the problems that face these cases, we can begin to understand the requirements that have to be met. Those requirements then put constraints and challenges on sociocultural practices in and across those organizations, work processes, and technologies that enable new ways of working to be achieved.

TWO CASE STUDIES OF MULTIAGENT SYSTEMS AND THEIR CURRENT WORKING

Case Study One: Emergency and Disaster Relief

In the case of emergencies on the scale of disasters such as Hurricane Katrina and, more recently, the Fukushima nuclear power plant crisis, both military and civilian groups work closely together with each other and the local community to respond to the emergency and bring about a safe and stable situation. There are significant challenges and issues with the current way that these agencies work. In both the case of Katrina and Fukushima, there are rich examples of failures in the agencies involved to (1) work together, (2) recognize when ways of working were creating problems, (3) develop new ways of working, and (4) act responsively and in ways appropriate to the needs.

Fukushima. First let's consider Fukushima when Daiichi Nuclear Power Station (NPS) was struck with an earthquake and tsunami. This resulted in a nuclear emergency that was made worse by communication gaps between the government, nuclear industry, and the general public. First, a very brief overview of events:

> March 11, 14:46: 9–0 earthquake; nuclear power station automatically shuts down.
> March 11, 14:48: Power substation out of service.
> March 11, 15:27: Tsunami 1.
> March 11, 15:35: Tsunami 2.
> March 11, 15:32: Station blackout (whiteboard memo).

> Emergency diesel generators rendered inoperable due to flooding in basement.

> March 12, 15:00: Power connected.
> March 12, 15:36: Hydrogen explosion(s); Unit 1 loosing containment.
> March 14, 11:01: Hydrogen explosion; Unit 3 loosing containment.
> March 15, 6:00–6:10: Hydrogen explosion; Unit 4 loosing containment.

Following the earthquake, Yoshida, the site head, pumped seawater into the NPS reactor to prevent the core from overheating. Around 12:00, Yoshida decided to make preparations to start a seawater pump and ordered an in-house firefighting team to start to research the configuration for a line configuration or seawater injection (Fukushima Nuclear Accident Independent Investigation Commission, 2011). At this point, apparently, no one at Tokyo Electric Power Company (TEPCO) was opposed to injecting seawater. When the NPS ran out of fresh water at 14:53, March 12 (Asia and Japan Watch, 2011), it needed to start pumping seawater into Unit 1 (Fukushima Nuclear Accident Independent Investigation Commission, 2011) to cool the reactor. Such an important decision normally requires the president of TEPCO to sign off on it (Asia and Japan Watch, 2011).

The start of the seawater pump was approved by TEPCO president Masataka Shimizu. At around 14:54, Yoshida ordered the seawater to be pumped into the unit (Fukushima Nuclear Accident Independent Investigation Commission, 2011). At around 15:18, Yoshida reported to government bodies that they would start injecting seawater once fresh water supplies were gone (Fukushima Nuclear Accident Independent Investigation Commission, 2011). Kan asked about the criticality of the damaged fuel in the

Unit 1 reactor that may result from pumping seawater. The chairman of the Nuclear Safety Commission, Madarame, replied that after the seawater injection such a possibility "could not be denied" (Funabashi & Kitazawa, 2012). Therefore, the decision to continue pumping seawater became difficult. As a result, the government notified the TEPCO head office that further water injection should be avoided until the government had decided on a course of action (Funabashi & Kitazawa, 2012). TEPCO president Shimizu communicated this to Yoshida on site via teleconference (Asia and Japan Watch, 2011) at the nuclear power plant. The decision was made to stop pumping seawater. Yoshida insisted on restarting injections as soon as possible (Funabashi & Kitazawa, 2012).

> During a teleconference, Yoshida called the employee in charge of the seawater injections to his side and whispered in his ear so the microphone for the teleconference with the head office would not pick up his voice that though he would now order a halt to the seawater injections, the employee should disregard the order and continue. Thereupon, Yoshida loudly declared to all teleconference participants that water injections would be interrupted. (Funabashi & Kitazawa, 2012)

This was possibly to avoid any further confrontation with the government. At this point, the on-site workers were going directly against the instructions from the government. Kan instructed the seawater to resume pumping at 8:20 p.m. (Asia and Japan Watch, 2011). However, the pumping of seawater had never stopped. Now let's consider another dimension of the events of Fukushima with respect to developing and adopting alternative technologies.

Crowd-sourced radiation detection. The Japanese government's radiation detection system (SPEEDI) predicts local radiation levels (Chino, Ishikawa, & Yamazawa, 1993). Information concerning radiation levels, provided by SPEEDI, was withheld from the general public (Digges, 2011). The reports produced by the system were sent to Japan's nuclear safety agency. However, the reports were not acted upon. As a consequence, a school predicted to receive dangerous levels of radiation was turned into an evacuation shelter. Due to a lack of trust in official reports, the general public in Japan felt there was a growing need to take matters into their own hands.

Crowd-sourced geiger counter readings from all over Japan were and are still being aggregated on the Pachube platform online (Courtland, 2011), now called Cosm (Developers, 2012). The Cosm platform works by allowing users to collaborate in many ways, including (1) build and connect their own devices, (2) control, monitor, and analyze data, (3) search for other devices, (4) browse and search data to find out what is happening, and (5) build communities and conversations around data. Websites such as Safecast (Safecast, 2012) allow users to submit their own readings and view their readings alongside others. The aim of Safecast is to empower people with information about their environment (Safecast, 2012). Individuals have generated maps based on the data. For instance, Kozhuharov generated a map displaying mobile data using Google fusion tables (Kozhuharov, 2011). Also, Bergeret (2013) created an interpolation map that uses existing geiger counter readings and attempts to fill in the space between individual readings.

In these reports from Fukushima, we can see the challenges and failings that the government and industrial agencies experienced. The lack of shared awareness across the plant operatives, the company officials, and the government officials resulted in conflicting commands and commands not being obeyed, together with reporting failures. Similarly, the reliance upon central data collection and information distribution resulted in inaccurate and distrusting information about radiation levels. This resulted in the appropriation of an emergent technology by individuals becoming the trusted and relied-upon source.

Katrina. Hurricane Katrina was one of the costliest natural disasters to strike the United States in recent years. The total property damage is estimated at $81 billion and at least 1,836 people lost their lives. The rescue missions that took place following the events were subdivided into search, rescue, evacuation, and supply and delivery. Temporary organizations were created. The command structure is both dynamic and readjusted to the events as they unfold and also must not interfere with already established command structures. This is based on the description of the events as given by Moffat (2011):

> One day after landfall, on [the] 30th [of] August 2005, the Joint Task Force (JTF) Katrina was established. States forwarded their requests for assistance to federal civilian officials, and these requests then moved through a series of military channels. Inherent in this process was the need for time to assess the capabilities required by each request and to design an appropriate military response. There was, at this early stage of events, an incorrect situational awareness and understanding at the DoD level. Civilian and military decision makers throughout the government apparently judged that the projected flow of National Guard units would be sufficient. Only on the 30th of August did the Deputy Secretary of Defense give the commander in charge a "blank check" for any DoD resources, and on [the] 31st [of] August, a high level military officer still "did not believe that federal ground forces were needed." (p. 86)

Federal military forces lacked situational awareness of which National Guard units were in the area and how they were operating. The command of the National Guard units and the federal level could not exchange information due to incompatible communication systems.

No unified command system was put in place during the search and rescue, evacuation, and supply delivery missions. The effect was that of having multiple rescue teams operating in the same area while other areas were left uncovered. This is an example of *conflicted command* and occurred over the first week after landfall, from [the] 29th [of] August to approximately [the] 4th [of] September. At the initial stage then, *conflicted command* was in place. Only after some days were National Guard and active-duty units deliberately deployed into different geographic areas where they carried out various relief and rescue missions using separate command structures, increasing the command approach to *de-conflicted command*. (p. 87)

Moffat (2011) reports the only example of what he calls "edge command" (i.e., agile responsive behavior) as follows:

This was the response of an individual pharmacist to the crisis in medical supplies in New Orleans. He raided the flooded pharmacies and repositioned these supplies in local downtown hotels. His rich understanding of the situation led to a local response consistent with the overall intent—saving lives. (p. 89)

These are just some of the reported challenges and failings that the civilian and military agencies were faced with during Hurricane Katrina. The rules, structures, and procedures of the different agencies prevented the distribution of information, the formation of collective knowledge, and the dearth of agile responsive behavior.

From both of these disaster emergency response case studies, we can begin to identify requirements to overcome the shortcomings of the sociocultural and working practices of these agencies. We argue that these sociocultural and working practice requirements carry with them requirements for improved communication, reporting, commanding, and data gathering, knowledge sharing, and decision making technologies.

Case Study Two: Local Authorities and the Troubled Families Program

Local authorities face many challenges as they seek to identify and work with troubled families. These families almost always have other often long-standing problems that can lead to their children repeating the cycle of disadvantage. They are defined as households who are involved in crime and antisocial behavior, have children out of school, have an adult on unemployment benefits, and raise costs of social service budgets (Communities and Local Government, 2012). At a minimum, this work involves agencies concerning crime, education, and employment. However, central government is also encouraging local authorities to use their discretion to work with local partners, such as health, police, and others, to determine what is the range of issues that they must prioritize and to identify the families. This includes families with a child who is on a Child Protection Plan, families of a looked-after child, families subject to frequent police callouts or arrests, and families with health problems such as emotional and mental health problems, drug and alcohol misuse, and long-term health conditions caused by domestic abuse or teenage pregnancy.

Policy requires local authorities to take a systematic and strategic approach to these challenging families, who concern different services. The first step involves complex and challenging MAS work, as the local authorities compile a list of families who will be a part of their subsequent intervention program. It also involves professionals collecting information and sharing it within and between services, in order to identify families with complex needs. This involves the collection of sensitive personal data by caseworkers with a statutory demand for secure collection, transfer, and retention of the data. Current data storage and representations of needs vary across services and have, in the past, proved to be very difficult to share (Edwards, Daniels, Gallagher, Leadbetter, & Warmington, 2009).

In earlier work on practices of professional learning in and for MAS, it was noted that practitioners described taking risks involving rule bending as responses to contradictions between emergent practices and systems of rules, protocols, and lines of responsibility. They demonstrated the need to question the legitimacy of the existing rules in relation to their professional actions on increasingly complex objects of activity and the necessity of making visible the ways in which they worked around the barriers to action. For example, systems of referral that meant that organizations passed on "bits of the child," as one practitioner put it, from one to the other, were opened up for scrutiny and criticism of how slow the respective organizations were in enabling parallel, interprofessional collaboration that was the most responsive to the needs of children. Rule bending was sometimes observed, reflecting practitioners' frustrations about the responsiveness of systems to new demands of child-centered collaborations. These were likely to be a matter of bypassing organizational hierarchies in order to make direct contact with the practitioner in another service that could help quickly.

IMPLICATIONS OF THE CASE STUDIES

So, what can we conclude from these very different and very exceptional case studies? Although they are very extreme events and very different in their nature, they are the very things that test the capability of our trusted services to act properly when called upon to do so. Those services are intended and strategically planned to be able to cope with and respond to these extreme and serious situations. The procedures, policies, and ways of working are there to ensure that they deliver the services that we must rely upon. As a consequence, we are very concerned when we find that there are some very common properties of each, which transcend the differences and which we have observed in further situations. Each of these case studies is an example of what has been termed *complex* and *wicked* problems, where the nature of the problem itself is never fully understood or is sometimes understood only after the event.

This was the case of Baby Peter, in which the mistreatment leading to the death of Peter by his caregivers occurred despite repeated visits by various social, welfare, health, and other services in the United Kingdom. The nature of each of these case studies and the nature of complex, wicked problems is that a known answer from a known expert is not appropriate or available because the nature of the problem itself is not understood. Only through the unfolding of attempts to take action is the nature of the problem further disclosed. This brings with it a number of consequences listed below.

1. The failure to notice, report, and share what turns out to have been important data. This often occurs through preconceived notions of what is relevant in the individual or the culture and processes of the organizations.
2. The lack of agility and the reluctance or fear of trying something new that is outside the known bounds of practice. This occurs through structural pressures on the individual and organization, and the lack of a mechanism to sanction, assure, or approve such actions.
3. The failure of the whole to learn rapidly during the event. This occurs through rigid and stove-piped lines of communication, false or non-reporting in order to comply, to avoid rebuke and/or to save time and get on with it.
4. An overreliance upon the formal, established specialist resources and processes and an inability to make effective use of the unofficial, novel, and available. This occurs through the misplaced ownership of the problem being in the hands of a few.
5. The resultant breakthroughs that contribute to solution and future ways of working come from outside the current known expertise, processes, and responsibilities.
6. The mechanisms to share, question, reflect, and propose alternatives are not available to all but a few, and often in highly abstracted and prescribed forms. This occurs from the lack of trust, a fear of information overload, the lack of lightweight mechanisms, and the inability to construct *provenance* from novel sources.
7. The nature of leadership and command is often rigid, inflexible, and prescriptive. This occurs from a belief that command and leaders must always appear to know the right answer and be the ultimate experts. This results in the suppression of new ideas and improved problem solving, and prevents a culture of empowered discovery.

8. The processes and tools are often inappropriate and inflexible, and the ability to appropriate new or changed tools and processes is poor. This occurs from the lack of available, easily reconfigured, and adaptable tools and processes and the inability to allow appropriation of external tools and processes for fear of damaging the system.

COLLABORATIVE CREATIVITY: A VYGOTSKIAN PERSPECTIVE

Taking the findings from these different case studies, we now consider how different theoretical positions might provide insight to help us understand the complexities of working together in agile collectives that enable creative action. First, we consider the Vygotskian perspective followed by the *collective intelligence* perspective.

The work of a group of early twentieth-century Russian social scientists, including Vygotsky, Luria, and Leont'ev is influencing a great deal of contemporary thinking on the social formation of mind including those aspects of human functioning that are said to witness creativity (Vygotsky, 1978). In this discussion of collaborative creativity, we engage with questions concerning what counts as collaboration and creativity. On the basis of this discussion, we outline a position for the formative effect of new technologies in collaborative creative practices.

Vygotsky (1978) developed accounts of human action and activity in which cultural artifacts, such as speech, mediated human engagement with the world. These artifacts or tools are human products that are taken up, developed, and transformed in the course of human activity. The emphasis is on the social production of artifacts that can be used as tools of both personal and social development and change. In the case of the writing of this chapter, these tools reflect the conceptual, metaphorical, and rhetorical foundations of our respective disciplines.

Social and cultural tools are historical products, and creativity involves their deployment in the cultural context of the here-and-now. This perspective can be brought to bear on the topic of creativity. Vygotsky (2004) started with a conception of creativity as "a historical, cumulative process" (p. 30). This sense of creativity capitalizing on the past is exemplified in the following, more recent statement "the most eminent are those creators who best utilize the social and cultural tools and best fit with the social and cultural expectations of their time" (Moran & John-Steiner, 2003, p. 80).

The concept of zone of proximal development (ZPD) was developed by Vygotsky as a means of discussing the way in which social and participatory learning takes place (John-Steiner & Mahn, 1996). The argument for the primacy of the social is made clear in Vygtotsky's (1978) "general genetic law of genetic development:"

> Every function in the child's cultural development appears twice: first, on the social level, and later, on the individual level; first between people (interpsychological), and then inside the child (intrapsychological). This applies equally to voluntary attention, to logical memory, and to the formation of concepts. All the higher functions originate as actual relations between human individuals. (Vygotsky, 1978, p. 57)

Vygotsky was concerned to develop an account in which humans were seen as "making themselves from the outside." Through acting on things in the world, they engage with the meanings that those things assumed within social activity. Humans both shape those meanings and are shaped by them. This understanding is exemplified in recent research on creativity when it is understood as: "studying the intrapersonal dynamics of creative processes *in the context* of the inter-personal relations that make it possible" (Glăveanu, 2010, p. 63).

However, Vygotsky insisted that there is no necessary recourse to physical presence in accounts of support within the ZPD. With the following quotation, he announced the possibility of virtual collaboration without the physical presence of the adult or teacher.

> When the school child solves a problem at home on the basis of a model that he has been shown in class, he continues to act in collaboration, though at the moment the teacher is not standing near him. From a psychological perspective, the solution of the second problem is similar to this solution of a problem at home. It is a solution accomplished with the teacher's help. This help—this aspect of collaboration—is invisibly present. It is contained in what looks from the outside like the child's independent solution of the problem. (Vygotsky, 1987, p. 216)

If we accept the notion of support without presence as discussed by Vygotsky (1978, p. 216), we are then faced with the fundamental question of the extent to which the mind can be considered as an individual attribute. Clearly, Vygotsky's reference to virtual support raises some important issues. First, it raises the question as to whether any aspect of human functioning is ever truly asocial. With respect to the notion of collaboration, it causes us to reflect not so much on whether something is collaborative or not, but rather on the kinds of collaboration that have a beneficial effect. Second, in the case of our own work, it prompts us to reflect on the power of new technologies in the facilitation of novel forms of actual and *virtual collaboration*. This is particularly important when we consider that if support within the ZPD may come from the voice of an absent tutor, then surely there is a place for several voices within a particular ZPD. If this is the case, then each voice or influence may not necessarily be in agreement. As Cheyne and Tarulli (1999) noted, in a discussion of the work of Bakhtin and Vygotsky,

> A dialogical mind does not itself constitute a common apperceptive mass, but rather a community of different and often conflicting voices that may not be resolved into one comprehensive self . . . it is in the struggle with difference and misunderstanding that dialogue and thought are productive and that productivity is not necessarily measured in consensus. (p.89)

One of the most important differences to be found between Vygotsky and Bakhtin is then with respect to the difference of the other. For Bakhtin, it is through and in difference and misunderstanding in dialogue that the contradictions that generate development are to be found. Vygotsky often seems to be concerned with a ZPD as a space where the learner is brought into the *knowing* of the other. The emphasis on multiple voices engaged in the construction of a form of meaning, which is not necessarily located within the individual, characterizes many current interpretations of Bakhtin's influence on a Vygotskian account. It becomes an important component of a theoretical framework that might be used to interrogate the use of actual and *virtual voices* mediated by new technologies.

If the Bakhtinian approach is to some extent a reasonable model of possible activity, within the ZPD, we are faced with the prospect of the learner actively making decisions about actions or pathways to progress. At a particular time, a person makes decisions with the benefit (or otherwise) of the influence of others both present and absent. This position opens the way for a nondeterminist account in which the person finds a way forward through what may be contradictory influences. This does not deny the possibility of the single voice of influence. There may be times when a person follows a single path through a ZPD as a diligent apprentice to an all-powerful master. However, this is not a necessary concomitant of the ZPD model: (1) the person's own prior understanding may come into conflict with the support given and (2) the person may receive influence from several conflicting sources.

This speculation on the nature of support within the ZPD raises questions about broader social influences. Multiple and possibly conflicting discourses with different social cultural historical origins may be in play within the ZPD. This view of the ZPD as the nexus of social, cultural, and historical influences takes us far beyond the image of the lone learner with the directive and determining tutor. It provides a much expanded view of the *social* and the possibility of a dialectical conception of interaction within the ZPD.

With respect to creativity, Newman, Griffin, and Cole (1989) argued that the ZPD arises in negotiation between the more advanced partner and the learner, rather than through the donation of a scaffold as some kind of prefabricated climbing frame. Cole and Griffin (1983) mount a strong criticism of the scaffolding metaphor based on the extent to which the child's creativity is underplayed. The argument that different settings and activities give rise to *spaces*, within the ZPD for creative exploration rather than pedagogic domination, is at the heart of their position: "Adult wisdom does not provide a teleology for child development. Social organization and leading activities provide a gap within which the child can develop novel creative analyses" (Griffin & Cole, 1983, p. 62).

In a seminal work, Vygotsky (2004) recognized the importance of the development of creativity through schooling and also rejected the notion of creativity as the product of sudden inspiration. He argued that the active promotion of creativity was a central function of schooling:

> We should emphasize the particular importance of cultivating creativity in school-age children. The entire future of humanity will be attained through the creative imagination; orientation to the future, behavior based on the future and derived from this future, is the most important function of the imagination. To the extent that the main educational objective of teaching is guidance of school children's behavior so as to prepare them for the future, development and exercise of the imagination should be one of the main forces enlisted for the attainment of this goal. (Vygotsky, 2004, pp. 87–88)

His analysis of the development of creativity is marked by an emphasis on interfunctional relations that resonates throughout his work. He argued that children are not necessarily more creative than adults, rather that they have less control and critical judgment over the products of their imagination. He suggests that as rational thought develops so does critical judgment, and that the tendency is for adolescents to become increasingly dissatisfied with the products of their imagination if they do not acquire appropriate "cultural and technical factors" or tools with which to engage in creative activity.

Adults dismiss their creative output if they are not given the tools to do this sort of work. In the context of this chapter, this position forces us to reflect on the ways in which new technologies can provide new tools for creativity not least by virtue of their capacity to bring multiple perspectives explicitly into view. Vygotsky argues that creativity is a social process that requires appropriate tools, artifacts, and cultures in which to thrive. The activity theory literature emphasizes the importance of focusing on the *object* of the activity system in collaborative, distributed work settings. In other words, its principal concern is with identifying what professionals are working on and their perceptions of the ends that are to be achieved. The object serves as a centering and integrating device in complex, multivoiced settings; it becomes a way of conceptually framing diffuse professional groups, individual agents, and complex practices and services. However, specific tools for collaborative, interagency practice are lacking at an operational level.

Current developments in activity theory are concerned with producing conceptual tools to enable understanding of dialogue, multiple perspectives, and networks of interacting activity systems. Central to activity theory's analysis of learning in practice is the notion of *expansive learning* among both professionals and service users. Expansive learning can be defined as the capacity to reinterpret and expand the definition of the object of activity. By rethinking their goals and activities and their relationships with other service providers and clients, professionals may begin to respond in enriched ways, thus producing new patterns of activity, which expand understanding and change practice.

Thus, object centered analyses of interagency working are "post-bureaucratic," in that they move beyond simply offering systemic prescriptions for managing collaboration and also avoid focusing exclusively on actors and their discursive interactions at the expense of focusing on object formation. This approach is pertinent to the radically distributed forms of *joined up* working intended to counter social exclusion, wherein clients may encounter multiple agencies and individual practitioners over extended periods. In much of the reviewed literature, current shifts toward radically distributed work and expertise are underacknowledged. The increasing tendency for professionals to work in loose, constantly shifting configurations is often depicted as a barrier to effective interagency working, rather than a shift to a new, expansive form of work. It is still often implied that the conflicts generated by interagency working must be denied, and that the ideal work form is conventional team working, wherein professional expertise coalesces into tight, consensual communities of practice.

The emphasis placed upon consensual models of working may place constraints on expansive learning in practice and, in particular, may tend to underacknowledge the importance of the internal tensions generated by activity systems as mechanisms for transforming practice. As a consequence, Engeström, Brown, Christopher, and Gregory (1997) stress the importance of developing tools "for disagreement": Ways of working that allow practitioners to capitalize upon interprofessional tensions and tensions between providers and clients. Existing practices, designed for single service provision, may not suffice. The authors emphasize the special importance of "future-orientated tools": Practices and instruments that do not merely address immediate working needs but which suggest means by which to expand learning and practice, so as to encourage continual innovation.

Engeström's (2000) work emphasizes the importance of the notion of the object in the study of collaboration that he argues may be studied and analyzed as *object formation*. This approach lays great stress on the significance of models and representations as tools of object construction. Acknowledging that an object is constantly being renewed and changed, Miettinen (1998) argues that future-oriented artifacts, so-called where-to tools, were important in the transformation of the object.

This understanding is extended by Engeström (2000) who proposes that we should analyze a whole system of instruments, or instrumentality (i.e., a constantly evolving set-up of multiple cognitive artifacts, semiotic means, and primary tools used in daily life; old tools being continually modified; and new ones created). Thus there is a clear role for technologies for modeling, reflecting, and representing through its capacity to enhance and expand the virtual community of learners, whose often disparate and contradictory views and repertoires of cultural tools form the seedbed of creative practice.

COLLECTIVE INTELLIGENCE AND COLLECTIVE CAPABILITY

Collectives can outperform the average individual and often the expert. Figure 7.1 illustrates the relative utility of the individual and the collective (Johnson, 2008). If the problem is simple, individuals solve the problem well. But as complexity increases, the expert typically has skills or information that increase their utility. However, at some threshold of complexity—or what is often termed wicked problem—even the experts (or groups or organizations, depending on the scale of the problem) are challenged and their utility declines. The notional curve for the collective captures why we think collective intelligence (CI) is important.

Hence Johnson (2008) warns that engaging experts to solve moderately complex problems can be adequate; however, when the complexity increases, an expert is likely to be out of their depth without realizing it,

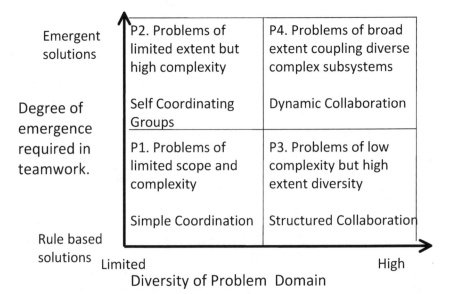

Figure 7.1 The problem space for collective intelligence and dynamic collaboration.

hence a diverse collective is needed in these situations because not just the problem, but the scope of the problem, is going to be itself complex and not fall within the remit of existing expertise. However, and here is the rub, "we think the way to get a diverse collective working well together is through cooperation" (p. 270). Johnson takes inspiration from studies of self-organizing systems that develop through a three-stage process of first formative competitive processes, followed second by synergizing individual differences, and finally, third, convergence on optimal solutions.

In cases where synergy is not reached, the group remains competitive and becomes self-destructive. Another possible outcome is that the synergistic stage is omitted, and the group converges on a consensus (as in group-think) with a view that has not been challenged, redefined, and evolved. Hence these stages are predictable and need to be enabled by allowing divergence of opinion, not forcing consensus and not accepting the optimized and low diversity, especially in the synergistic and convergence stages.

There are of course implications for the leadership required to achieve a collective capability. For many leaders, collective capability is a threatening concept: How can a leader be a leader if they defer their intelligence to the collective? This requires leaders to not be those who sustain leadership by rules, to recognize the need for distributed leadership through enabling divergence and synergistic processes.

In Figure 7.1, the landscape is shown in terms of the diversity of the problem domain and the degree of emergence required in the team working. This landscape is divided into four quadrants. Quadrants P1 and P2 represent respectively the areas where classical types of leadership: localized power or structure and emergent leadership as in a hero. The quadrants P3 and P4 capture the areas where there is a need for two extremes of CI: the structural-based CI such as democracies or information-enabled CI to the emergent forms of CI discussed above.

This landscape can also usefully summarize CI. Diversity is the essential requirement for CI performance. Therefore, as leadership resources move to the right of the landscape, diversity of the collective must be developed and expressed, and leaders must become facilitators of the collective wisdom. As the complexity of problems increases, the collective will perform better and be more resilient to change. Therefore, to better address the modern challenges of faster change and greater interdependence, the CI leadership resources required for areas (P3–P4) must be better understood, developed, and utilized. Finally, the greatest challenge, but also the greatest opportunity, is to enable the leadership processes of emergent CI (P4) where global solutions are found by individuals solving their own local problems, but where the emergent solution is possibly beyond individual understanding. "To enable emergent CI, individuals must not only express their diversity, but also share a common worldview" (Johnson, 2008, p. 274).

So how can we begin to achieve this type of creative, distributed problem solving that maximizes diversity, progresses to synergy, and develops convergence? What tools can we provide individuals and leaders with that can allow them to both create and utilize collective capability? Johnson (2008) observes that

> The Internet has three significant, arguably unique, capabilities beyond prior human-technology systems: (1) *breadth*—the ability to connect quickly, globally heterogeneous systems, (2) *depth*—the ability to capture and retain details of the access and use of information and (3) *accuracy*—the ability with minimal loss to relate and transmit information. All of the modern implementations of CI on the Internet exploit these unique capabilities. For example, the Amazon's product referral system requires rapid access to detailed purchasing histories of individuals (and not bestseller aggregations) with no loss of information. The same is true for Google's recommender system. These unique capabilities overcome the prior thresholds of size and extent previously observed in human-technology systems. And it captures knowledge that was previously lost: When you retrieve a reference from a book on your shelf, only you benefit from it—on the Internet, all can benefit from it. It is fortuitous that the same Internet that created the global challenges of faster change and greater interdependence also provides humans with the resources to meet these challenges. (pp. 265–256)

Hence we argue here that collective capability recognizes that this requires the development of three fundamental and integral foundations, conceptual foundations, sociocultural infrastructures, and enabling technological infrastructures. In the following, we consider the development of the technologies for collective capabilities in response to the advancing conceptual and sociocultural dimensions.

COLLECTIVE CAPABILITY: EVOLVING TECHNOLOGIES

Here we consider the evolution and use of technologies to enable the power of collectives to solve wicked or complex problems. Progress in the development of how to utilize and evolve technologies to support the growth of collective capabilities is growing but is still largely in its infancy. The likes of Amazon, Google, Facebook, and the various micro-blog technologies have recognized the needs and possible advantages in creating the foundations for technologies to enable collective capabilities. Essentially, they have each recognized the need to enable an emergent capability that depends on being able to pool and connect many people's diverse data, information, interpretations, comments, and debates around issues. They have recognized that this is relevant not only to individuals but to many organizational contexts, where it is important to work with contested data, information, knowledge, and decisions, due to the different intellectual traditions and competing individual and organizational objectives, while overcoming the related problems of information overload, incompleteness, ambiguity, uncertainty, reliability, and provenance.

As we have seen from the above discussion, appreciating the value and power of divergent perspectives, inconsistencies, ambiguities, and disagreements is fundamental to the development of collective capability to address complex and wicked problems. Recognizing that in well understood problem spaces, there is indeed an optimal or correct response; in wicked and complex problems, there is always going to be contention and disagreement over the right answer, over the problem itself, and what constitutes success. This leads to multiple debates, competing evidence, and different rationales. Engelbert (1963) recognized the need for tools such as dynamic knowledge repositories to enable a more global intellect to be developed. The need to develop tools for *sense-making* or giving form to interpretations through externalizable representations that allows the unfolding and evolving of understanding, possibilities, and implications to be created.

Similarly, Weick (2006) has shown the dangers of entrained thinking in which experts fail to notice or recognize a novel and important phenomenon because of their prior expectations and existing categorizations. Hence Weick sees the need for sense-making support systems that draw attention to the novel, to exceptions, and ensure that they remain open to a multiplicity of perspectives for as long as possible. More recently, De Liddo, Sándor, and Buckingham Shum (2012) focus upon contrast, surprise, novelty, critical thinking, and knowledge building. Building upon earlier and other work on argument mapping (Van Gelder, 2002), Structured Evidential Analysis (Lowrance et al., 2008) and Analysis of Competing Hypotheses (Heuer, 1999), De Liddo and colleagues (2012) have developed an integrated platform that includes two tools. One of these tools is COHERE, which is a social semantic web tool for people to annotate web material and create knowledge maps. A second tool is Xerox Incremental Parser that is in essence a computer program for automatic text analysis. These tools enable computer-supported human analysis and computer analysis of arguments, disagreements, contentions, and contrasting ideas across wide-ranging bodies of documents.

Elsewhere work on utilizing the power of individuals to come together in collectives is gaining ground. Recent work by Vieweg (2012) explores the use of Twitter during mass emergencies with an eye toward informing the creation of tools to automatically identify information that contributes to situational awareness. This is part of a much larger endeavor at the University of Colorado to understand the possibilities and to develop tools to enable greater use of information to and from the public in times of mass emergency. Similarly in Japan, the Fukushima emergency and threat from the nuclear plant led to the creation of Safecast (2012), which was a people-generated map of radiation and allowed individuals from all over the world to contribute data on radiation levels that resulted in the creation and utilization of maps of radiation severity levels by individuals.

Hence, we see a diverse range of technological developments aimed at and enabling collective capability to be realized. That work is now gaining ground rapidly, but it is still early days as we increase our understanding of how to enable collective capability to contribute to complex and wicked problems, to develop the conceptual foundations of collective capability and the sociocultural understanding of the organizational, leadership, and community infrastructures, and to facilitate collective capability and the technological tools and environments to support it.

SUPPORTING CREATIVE COLLECTIVE CAPABILITY THROUGH TECHNOLOGY

From our discussions so far, it should be clear to see that we are interested in supporting people in complex situations where the nature of the problems they are faced with are "wicked problems" (Churchman, 1967). We are advocating that in complex, wicked problems, there is a need for people to both realize that they are in such a situation and to recognize that any and each one of them may discover the way forward. This requires them to know that existing procedures and processes may not be appropriate, that they need to increase their awareness of the situation and the other actors, and to be aware of what we call potential framing effects, which cause the problem to be misunderstood. To notice and understand what may previously have been unnoticed or thought irrelevant, to be open to new possibilities, to be free to test new possibilities, and, overall and most important, to be able to take and share their different ideas, impressions, data, results, and reflections with each other, recognizing the need for contrasting analysis and synthesis before convergence. To do all that requires a culture to be established in which relational agency (Edwards & Daniels, 2010) is fostered throughout the collective, new tools are needed that allow individuals to notice the unnoticeable; to share their ideas, their data, and their results; to reflect and critique, to analyze, and, from all of this, to create a new synthesis of understanding. These situations demand technologies that allow creative interaction between people.

Creative work can be understood inclusively as a tension between divergent and convergent thinking (Baer, 2003) in a cyclical process of ideation, representation, and evaluation (Coughlan & Johnson, 2006). Whereas in creative work constraining motivations, tools, and conceptual structures are necessary to direct and support creative activities, what is more important is that the ongoing questioning and development of these structures is central to the process of creative problem solving. Schön's (1987) analysis of creative problem solving in professional practice describes a process of reflection in and on action, involving the external representation and evaluation of ideas.

KNOTWORKING AND BOUNDARY CROSSING

The demands of MAS exceed current conceptualization of work-related learning, in that standard concepts of learning in practice still often rely upon conventional notions of partnerships, teams, networks, and communities of practice. In MAS settings, the emergent form of work is characterized by *knotworking,* which is intensely collaborative activity but relies upon constantly changing combinations of people coalescing on multiple, different, and changing tasks. Utilizing developmental work research methods, Engeström and colleagues (1997) have explored the facilitation of knotworking at a more formal level, by introducing rules and tools explicitly designed to structure knotworking interactions. In short, this work raises the question of how professionals can be supported by training, leadership, and technology to knotwork.

The notion of *boundary crossing* offers a means of conceptualizing the ways in which collaboration between workers from different professional backgrounds might generate new professional practices. Standard notions of professional expertise imply a vertical model, in which practitioners develop in competence over time, as they acquire new levels of professional knowledge, graduating *upward* in their own specialism. By contrast, boundary crossing suggests that expertise is also developed when practitioners collaborate *horizontally* across sectors. Where practitioners from diverse professional cultures are engaged in shared activities, their professional learning is expanded as they negotiate working practices that cross traditional professional boundaries.

In short, the working practices required to support disaster emergency relief, or at-risk young people and families, are not the discrete province of any one profession but require planned configurations of complementary expertise drawn from across professional services. Engeström's (2001a, 2001b) notions of boundary crossing suggest that developing collective capability in MAS should focus upon the potential spaces for renegotiation of professional practice that are opened up when workers from traditionally separate sectors begin collaborating. A related debate is whether MAS will encourage professionals from diverse sectors to become adept at operating within the discursive practices of colleagues from other backgrounds or whether more fundamental reconfigurations of professional practice might lead to the emergence of hybrid professional types. Of course, this creates tension for organizations required to have deep, single expertise while providing a broad range of expert services.

In activity theory, *boundary objects* are the focal points for understanding boundary crossing practices. Boundary objects may take the form of physical objects, pieces of information, conversations, goals, or rules. These become boundary objects when they are worked upon simultaneously by diverse sets of actors. For example, a child's care plan may be negotiated by teachers, social workers, health workers, and educational psychologists. In such a situation, the care plan assumes particular importance in the learning of these diverse professionals because it sits at the intersection between different professional practices or cultures. It can be used differently by the corresponding communities, providing a means to think and talk about an idea in multivoiced fashion, without the necessity of any one community completely adopting the perspective of the other. A boundary object provides a mechanism for meanings to be shared and creates collective collaboration across professional boundaries. Hence, we see that interagency working is rarely found; instead, we see instances of stove-piped hierarchical working.

To overcome this, we must enable rich interconnected MAS through developing cultures, leadership, and technologies that enable multiagency collective capability.

UNDERSTANDING THE CHALLENGES AND ENABLING COLLECTIVE CAPABILITY IN MULTIAGENCY SERVICES

Our aim is to enable multiple agencies (people and groups) to work as a collaborative creative whole, achieving their objectives in an effective, efficient, and agile manner and increasing their ability to use local initiatives and create greater shared knowledge and learning. Although policy aspires to develop this, often the different motivations, operational processes, and technologies of agencies working together inhibit achievement of these aspirations. This in turn causes practitioners to fail or to construct workarounds that are costly, inefficient, and localized.

Working with practitioners in their contexts and everyday practices we must understand their ways of working, the processes and technologies, their constraints and limitations, and the reasons why those practices, work-arounds, and technologies have been developed, how they fail, and why they work. Also, we must codesign with practitioners practices and technologies to help them meet their needs, policies, and aspirations for working together. Finally, we must develop uptake through working in different multiagency problem areas. Such processes and technologies must be aimed at creating connections between disconnected people, information, and knowledge to enable a disconnected multiagency system to achieve collective capability.

To achieve this, research must investigate the sociotechnological, environmental, and contextual factors in which processes and technologies will have to work to support collective capability in MAS. We argue that developing the collective capability of MAS will improve (1) the levels of local and global awareness and utility of information and knowledge, (2) the quality and trustworthiness of decision making and consideration of alternatives, (3) the ability to increase the level of shared understanding through the development of lightweight but richer information-capture mechanisms; and (4) the ability to globally exploit and learn from local knowledge.

We have argued that MAS is best thought of in terms of professional learning (Daniels & Edwards, 2011; Edwards & Daniels, 2010; Edwards et al., 2009). The 2011 Munro Review (Munro, 2011) of children protection services pointed to the need for a focus on learning organizations.

The review argued that services should be seen as learning and adaptive systems, and leadership should be committed to promoting learning but remain accountable.

In meeting these challenges, we draw upon research that addresses issues of sharing and representation of information and knowledge to improve awareness (e.g., Hourizi & Johnson, 2004). Hourizi, Middup, Nemetz, Nosier, and Johnson (2008) developed information and knowledge sharing requirements that improved small group collaboration. Johnson, Hourizi, Carrigan, and Forbes (2010a, 2010b) developed an analytical modeling framework that enables large-scale collaborations to be modeled in terms of their points of potential conflict and through this to design deconflicted systems. Hence from these models, we can predict and overcome points of information and knowledge conflict.

Elsewhere, the work on digital notice boards (Taylor & Cheverst, 2012) to promote community awareness has found that it still remains a challenge to enable people to create and share their own information and knowledge. Our work on professional learning in and for MAS has demonstrated the importance of mediating artifacts in the construction of common knowledge, as professionals seek to work across agency boundaries (Daniels & Edwards, 2011; Edwards & Daniels, 2010; Edwards et al., 2009). Drawing upon this, we see a need for technologies that allow individuals to create, share, and manipulate information as they build common knowledge through using these mediating artifacts. Our research has developed the conceptual understanding of collective capability and how to enable it through new processes and technologies.

MEETING THOSE CHALLENGES

We hypothesize that new processes and technologies can enable collective capability by providing improved creation gathering, representation, and sharing of information that enhance the following:

1. Local and global awareness of individuals, teams, and agencies in the collective.
2. The power and utility of information knowledge sharing.
3. The ease of collection, richness, and rapid assessment of locally gathered information for global learning.
4. The decision-making process concerned with the production and sharing of information by individuals and groups, and the collective analysis and assessment of that information.

We believe that this will lead to improvements in MAS collective capability in terms of improved capability and greater effectiveness. More specific, we postulate that greater shared awareness and utility of information, collective analysis, and assessment for decision making will increase the capability and agility of MAS. It is important to note that these effects will also be complex (i.e., greater shared awareness will affect collective analysis and assessment for decision making and more collective decision making will in turn lead to greater shared awareness).

Collective capability will produce collaborative, agile, responsive, and efficient collaborative working. To achieve this, research must investigate the sociotechnological, environmental, and contextual factors that support collective capability in MAS. Such research must employ a range of theoretical and methodological perspectives. We argue that much understanding and insight is to be gained from bringing together activity theory, collective intelligence, and human computer interaction theory, and the methods to understand the interaction between the processes, technologies, the end users, their work, and collective capability.

ACKNOWLEDGMENTS

We are grateful to Dr. Rachel Burrows for help with the Yokishima case study and to Dr. Ana Calderon and Dr. Jo Hinde for the Katrina case study.

REFERENCES

Asia and Japan Watch. (2011). *Nuke plant manager ignores bosses, pumps in seawater after order to halt.* Retrieved from http://ajw.asahi.com/article/0311disaster/fukushima/ AJ201105270252

Baer, J. (2003). Evaluative thinking, creativity, and task specificity. In M. A. Runco (Ed.), *Critical creative processes* (pp. 129–151). Cresskill, NJ: Hampton Press.

Bergeret, L. (2013). *Safecast interpolation map.* Retrieved from http://gamma.tar.bz/maps/static/

Cheyne, J. A., & Tarulli, D. (1999). Dialogue, difference, and the "third voice," in the zone of proximal development. *Theory and Psychology, 9,* 5–28.

Chino, M., Ishikawa, H., & Yamazawa, H. (1993). Speedi and wspeedi: Japanese emergency response systems to predict radiological impacts in local and workplace areas due to a nuclear accident. *Radiation Protection Dosimetry, 50*(2–4), 145–152.

Churchman, C. W. (1967). Guest editorial: Wicked problems. *Management Science, 14*(4), 141–142.

Cole, M., & Griffin, P. (1983). A socio-historical approach to re-mediation. *Quarterly Newsletter of the Laboratory of Comparative Human Cognition, 5*(4), 69–74.

Communities and Local Government. (2012). *The Troubled Families programme financial framework for the Troubled Families programme's payment-by-results scheme for local authorities.* Retrieved from http://www.communities.gov.uk/documents/communities/ pdf/2117840.pdf

Coughlan, T., & Johnson, P. (2006). Interaction in creative tasks: Ideation, representation and evaluation in composition. In R. Grinter, T. Rodden, P. Aoki,

E. Cutrell, R. Jefferies, & G. Olson (Eds.), *Proceedings of the SIGCHI conference on human factors in computing systems* (pp. 531–540). Berkeley, CA: ACM Press.

Courtland, R. (2011). *Radiation monitoring in Japan goes diy*. Retrieved from http://spectrum.ieee.org/tech-talk/energy/environment/radiation-monitoring-in-japan-goes-diy

Daniels, H., & Edwards, A. (2011). Resourceful leadership in learning organisations. *RD543-2: National College for School Leadership and Children's Services*.

De Liddo, A., Sándor, Á., & Buckingham Shum, S. (2012). Contested collective intelligence: Rationale, technologies, and a human-machine annotation study. *Computer Supported Cooperative Work, 21*(4–5), 417–448.

Developers, C. (2012). *Connect to your world*. Retrieved from https://cosm.com/

Digges, C. B. (2011). *Japan ignored its own radiation forecasts in days following disaster, imperiling thousands*. Retrieved from http://www.bellona.org/articles/articles_2011/rad_forcasts_ignored

Edwards, A., & Daniels, H. (2010). *Developing interagency working for children and families*. London: Consortium of the Local Government Association, IdEA, and Local Authorities Research Council Initiative.

Edwards, A., Daniels, H., Gallagher, T., Leadbetter, J., & Warmington, P. (2009). *Improving inter-professional collaborations: Multi-agency working for children's well being*. Oxford, England: Routledge.

Engelbert, D. C. (1963). A conceptual framework for the augmentation of man's intellect. In P. W. Howerton & D. C. Weeks (Eds.), *Vistas in information handling* (pp. 1–29). Washington, DC: Spartan Books.

Engeström, Y. (2000). From individual action to collective activity and back: Developmental work research as an interventionist methodology. In P. Luff, J. Hindmarsh, & C. Heath (Eds.), *Workplace studies*. Cambridge, England: Cambridge University Press.

Engeström, Y. (2001a). Expansive learning at work: Toward an activity theoretical reconceptualization. *Journal of Education and Work, 14*(1), 133–156.

Engeström, Y. (2001b). *The horizontal dimension of expansive learning: Weaving a texture of cognitive trails in the terrain of health care in Helsinki, Finland*. Paper presented at the international symposium, New Challenges to Research on Learning, University of Helsinki, Finland.

Engeström, Y., Brown, K., Christopher, C. L., & Gregory, J. (1997). Coordination, cooperation and communication in the courts: Expansive transitions in legal work. In M. Cole, Y. Engeström, & O. Vasquez (Eds.), *Mind, culture and activity: Seminal papers from the laboratory of comparative human condition* (pp. 369–388). Cambridge, England: Cambridge University Press.

Fukushima Nuclear Accident Independent Investigation Commission. (2011). *Investigation committee on the accident at the Fukushima nuclear power stations*. Retrieved from http://www.nirs.org/fukushima/naiic_report.pdf

Funabashi, Y., & Kitazawa, K. (2012). Fukushima in review: A complex disaster, a disastrous response. *Bulletin of the Atomic Scientists, 68*(2), 9–21.

Glăveanu, V. P. (2010). Creativity as cultural participation. *Journal for the Theory of Social Behaviour, 41*(1), 48–67.

Heuer, R. J. (1999). *Psychology of intelligence analysis*. Retrieved from https://www.cia.gov/library/center-for-the-study-of-intelligence/csi-publications/books-and-monographs/psychology-of-intelligence-analysis/PsychofIntelNew.pdf

Hourizi, R., & Johnson, P. (2004). Designing to support awareness: A predictive, composite model. In E. Dykstra-Erickson & M. Tscheligi (Eds.), *Proceedings of ACM CHI conference on human factors in computing systems* (pp. 159–166). Berkeley, CA: ACM Press.

Hourizi, R., Middup, C., Nemetz, F., Nosier, A., & Johnson, P. (2008). Towards autonomous systems that collaborate. In B. Bardo (Ed.), *Proceedings of EMRC/ SEAS DTC conference* (pp. 208–218). Edinburgh, Scotland: EMRC.

Johnson, N. (2008). Science of CI: Resources for change. In T. Malone, T. Atlee, & P. Lévy (Eds.), *Collective intelligence creating a prosperous world at peace* (pp. 265–274). Oakton, VA: Earth Intelligence Network.

Johnson, P., Hourizi, R., Carrigan, N., & Forbes, N. (2010a). *Collaboration and conflict: A framework for large-scale collaborations.* Paper presented at the international symposium on collaborative technologies and systems (CTS 2010), Chicago, IL.

Johnson, P., Hourizi, R., Carrigan, N., & Forbes, N. (2010b). A framework to manage the complex organisation of collaborating: Its application to autonomous systems. In J. Bryans & J. Fitzgerald (Eds.), *Proceedings of the second workshop on formal aspects of virtual organisations* (pp. 51–63). Eindhoven, The Netherlands: Open Publishing Association.

John-Steiner, V., & Mahn, H. (1996). Sociocultural approaches to learning and development: A Vygotskian framework. *Educational Psychologist, 31*(3–4), 191–206.

Kozhuharov, K. (2011). *Map of current radiation data.* Retrieved from http:// gamma.tar.bz/maps/main/

Lowrance, J., Harrison, I., Rodriguez, A., Yeh, E., Boyce, T., Murdock, J., Thomere, J., & Murray, K. (2008). Template-Based Structured Argumentation. In A. Okada, S. Buckingham Shum, & T. Sherborne (Eds.), *Knowledge Cartography: Software Tools and Mapping Techniques* (pp. 307–333). London: Springer.

Lowrance, J., Harrison, I., & Rodriguez, A. (2001). Capturing analytic thought. In *Proceeding of the first international conference on knowledge capture* (pp. 84-91). Berkeley, CA: ACM Press.

Miettinen, R. (1998). Object construction and networks in research work: The case of research on cellulose-degrading enzymes. *Social Studies of Science, 28*(3), 423–463.

Moffat, J. (2011). *Adapting modelling and simulation for network enabled operations.* Retrieved from http://www.dodccrp.org/files/Moffat_Adapting. pdf

Moran, S., & John-Steiner, V. (2003). Creativity in the making: Vygotsky's contemporary contribution to the dialectic of development and creativity. In R. K. Sawyer, V. John-Steiner, S. Moran, R. J. Sternberg, D. H. Feldman, H. Gardner, . . . M. Csikszentmihalyi (Eds.), *Creativity and development* (pp. 61–90). Oxford, England: Oxford University Press.

Munro, E. (2011). *The Munro review of child protection: Final report "A child-centred system."* London, England: Department for Education.

Newman, D., Griffin, P., & Cole, M. (1989). *The construction zone: Working for cognitive change in school.* Cambridge, England: Cambridge University Press.

Safecast. (2012). *Safecast.* Retrieved from http://blog.safecast.org/about/

Schön, D. A. (1987). *Educating the reflective practitioner.* San Francisco, CA: Jossey-Bass Publishers.

Taylor, N., & Cheverst, K. (2012). Supporting community awareness with interactive displays. *IEEE Computer, 45*(5), 26–32.

Van der Veer, R., & Valsiner, J. (1991). *Understanding Vygotsky: A quest for synthesis.* Oxford, England: Blackwell.

Van Gelder, T. J. (2002). Enhancing deliberation through computer-supported argument visualization. In P. Kirschner, S. Buckingham Shum, & C. Carr (Eds.), *Visualizing argumentation: Software tools for collaborative and educational sense-making* (pp. 97–115). London, England: Springer.

Vieweg, S. (2012). *Situational awareness in mass emergency: A behavioral and linguistic analysis of microblogged communications* (Doctoral dissertation). University of Colorado at Boulder.

Vygotsky, L. S. (1978). *Mind in society: The development of higher psychological processes.* Cambridge, MA: Harvard University Press.

Vygotsky, L. S. (2004). Imagination and creativity in childhood. *Journal of Russian and East European Psychology, 42*(1), 7–97.

Weick, K. (2006). Dear editor: A reply to Basbøll and Graham. *Ephemera, 6*(2), 193.

8 Creative Encounters, Collaborative Agency, and the Extraordinary Act of the Meeting of a Need and an Object

Reijo Miettinen

The psychology of creativity has long regarded the creative individual as a source of novelty. The systems view of creativity (Feldman, Csikszentmihalyi, & Gardner, 1994)—often also called the sociocultural approach—suggests that the locus of creativity is in the interactions between an individual, a cultural domain, and a field. Even this approach, however, tends to remain individual-centered. The domain provides resources and raw material for creativity, the individual creates, and the field evaluates the products. The Vygotskian tradition has analyzed the development of creativity as a central dimension of individual development that is realized in successive zones of proximal development. Vygotsky (e.g., 1998) analyzed the emergence of imagination in play, its merger with concept formation and its transformation into adult creativity realized through internalization-externalization cycles in science, art, and work (Moran & John-Steiner, 2003). John Steiner (2000) took a step toward the understanding of the collaborative nature of creative agency in studying the significance of collaboration between artists and scientists for creative work. Sawyer's work (2003) on the creative power of collaboration focuses on creative group work within organizations and opens up the discussion of the wider collaborative creativity that is realized in interorganizational networks and Internet communities.

Innovation studies have analyzed the development, commercialization, and implementation of new technologies and products.[1] One of its main findings of innovation studies in the 1980s was that the locus of innovation is no longer a single organization but rather an interorganizational collaboration or an innovation network (Freeman, 1991; Rothwell, 1992). Increased global competition, increased specialization, and division of labor as well as the increased complexity of products forces business firms to collaborate. By combining dispersed complementary knowledge, interorganizational collaborative networks make possible novel combinations of knowledge and expertise needed in innovations (Smith-Doerr & Powell, 2005). Evolutionary economists have characterized this phenomenon as a generative relationship or an interactive emergence (Lane & Maxfield, 1996; Noteboom, 2000). I want to contribute to the understanding of this phenomenon by studying the emergence of creative collaborative agency. While studying research-based technical innovations inspired by activity theory, my research group recurrently came across a mechanism of such an emergence: An encounter between two partners from different organizations that gave birth both to a new product idea and to a collaborative product development project (e.g., Miettinen, 2009; Miettinen, Lehenkari, Hasu, & Hyvönen, 1999; Miettinen, Lehenkari, & Tuunainen, 2008). I suggest that such a creative encounter provides a proper event for the study of the nature and conditions of interactive emergence and collaborative creativity.

I proceed in this chapter as follows. First, I discuss the *intrinsic motivation* thesis proposed by the social psychological approach of organizational creativity. I suggest that as such it does not suffice to explain the emergence of collaborative agency and creative interaction. I analyze their interactive emergence through creative encounters using the idea of Leont'ev (1978), according to which the meeting of a need with an object gives rise to motivation and agency. To distinguish this approach from individualist approaches, I define the concept of need as emerging out of contradictions in human activities. I regard the joint object as a hypothesis for the solution of such a contradiction. In addition, I suggest that the idea of complementarity of the knowledge and resources of partners is important in explaining the emergence of collaborative agency. I present a model of a creative encounter and use data from two product development processes to substantiate and illuminate it.

ORGANIZATIONAL CREATIVITY AND THE MOTIVATIONAL FOUNDATION OF CREATIVITY

Social network literature analyzes the effects of network structures, network positions, and the nature of ties between the network nodes on innovativeness. This literature, however, does not study the quality of interactions between the actors nor how interactions emerge and evolve. A recent paper by Sosa (2011) asks, "Where do creative interactions come from?" Characteristically to social network literature, it analyzes interaction in terms of information processing where the roles of the actors in an interactive dyad are those of a provider and a recipient of knowledge. This does not help to make sense of the emergence of an instance of collaborative agency, that is, a mutual development of a joined vision of a new product or service and a joint commitment to a project to realize the vision in practice.

A prominent approach in the literature of organizational creativity is an interactional model, which analyzes how the features of a group or an organization influence individual creativity (Amabile, 1983; Ford, 1996; Woodman, Sawyer, & Griffin, 1993). The three components of the creative performance of an individual in Amabile's (1983) componential model of creativity are domain-relevant skills, creativity-relevant skills, and task motivation. Among the organizational factors that facilitate individual creativity (Perry-Smith & Shalley, 2003) are the absence of a constraining reward system, a supportive leadership style, norms that promote risk taking, autonomy, and external competition. These factors are thought to feed back to the creative behavior of individuals, and the overall creativity of organization is a result of these interactions. As Amabile herself has suggested (Kurtzberg & Amabile, 2001), the interactive model has not paid attention to team-level creative synergy, in which ideas are generated by groups. The theory of intrinsic motivation is the cornerstone of her theory. The intrinsic motive hypothesis (Amabile, 1996) states, "the intrinsically motivated state is conductive to creativity, whereas the extrinsically motivated state is detrimental" (p. 107). Amabile substantiates this hypothesis with experiments in which the effects of external evaluation and rewards on the creative performance of student groups in heuristic tasks are studied.

Several authors have criticized the intrinsic motivation thesis (e.g., Besser-Jones, 2012; Ochse, 1990; Yaroshevsky, 1974). The results of classroom experiments are inconclusive (Eisenberg & Shannock, 2003) and can hardly be generalized to the persistent, long-lasting motivation that is characteristic of creative work in real life (Ochse, 1990). Historical studies and the sociology of science have shown again and again that external, social, and outcome-related motives are all an essential part of scientific and artistic work (e.g., Allport, 1961; Yaroshevsky, 1974). Among these is the seeking of professional and scientific recognition, becoming esteemed in society, finding approval for the work from others, helping other people, as well as ambition, fame, reputation, and economic reward. According to Merton (1973), the joy gained through scientific discovery and recognition from others is made of the same psychological coin. In creative work, both personal and external, social motives are inextricably mixed. Although intrinsic motivation (or a flow experience) may fittingly characterize the state of subjects involved in creative work, it hardly provides an explanation of the emergence, direction, and normative orientation of creative agency (Besser-Jones, 2012).

In my account of interactive emergence and collaborative agency in product development, I will resort to the concepts of contradiction and the object-orientedness of activity as well as the idea of the complementarity of the historically formed expertise and resources of the partners of an encounter. It is well known that Leont'ev (1978) regarded the meeting of a need with an object as "an extraordinary act" that leads to the emergence of a motive. This is "an act of objectifying need, 'filling' it with content derived from [the] surrounding world. This is what brings need to a truly psychological level" (Leont'ev, 1978, p. 54).[2] In order to apply the idea of the meeting of a need with an object to an analysis of a creative encounter, I think that two conceptual clarifications are needed.

First, the concept of need requires to be redefined as emerging out of contradictions of several activities. Leont'ev refers to this possibility when he says that specifically human activity, including motives, "is indigenously social, that is, developing only under cooperation and sharing by people" (Leont'ev, 1978, p. 59).

Second, because contradictions evolve historically, they become recognized and defined only gradually. At first they typically are expressed—to use the term of Bratus and Lishin (1983)—as a *need state,* "an indeterminate, temporary objectless desire" (p. 43). In collective practices, a need state can be regarded as an intuitive, only partly conscious, grasp of an emerging contradiction in an activity. Its full articulation often requires new conceptual resources, as will be shown later. A need state becomes a motive when it meets an object (that is, a projected solution to the contradiction) that opens a horizon for inventive actions. A gradual recognition of a contradiction cannot be analyzed as rational decision making. Rather, it is expressed as what has been called anticipatory directionality (Fogel, 1993) and precedes the full articulation of an object of activity.

THE EMERGENCE OF COLLABORATIVE AGENCY THROUGH CREATIVE ENCOUNTERS

A creative encounter is an event or a process in which two or more persons representing different activities meet face-to-face and recognize the complementarity of their expertise and resources for the creation of a new artifact that can solve a contradiction in a human activity. A creative encounter leads to the emergence of collaborative agency, which assumes the form of a joint project. Although the term creative encounter has occasionally been used (e.g., Lorenzen, 2007), only few attempts have been made to define it. Bruun (2000) uses the concept of "epistemic encounter" in studying multidisciplinary collaboration, which is designed as "attempts to circulate knowledge components between epistemic frameworks/approaches" (p. 34). Long (2002) found an encounter to be a critical event in a space of a dialogue "that ties together a number of spatially distant, institutionally complex and culturally distinct activities" (p. 84). Beech, MacIntosh, and MacLean (2010) introduce the term "generative dialogic encounters," in which "researchers and practitioners work together in order to develop solutions to problems in the world of practice" (p. 1342). They base this definition on theories of dialogue that focus on epistemological and communicative dimensions of interaction, such as mutuality, shared understanding, and the transmission of knowledge and models of action from one actor to another. They do not extend their explanation to the commitment of the partners to shared transformative projects.

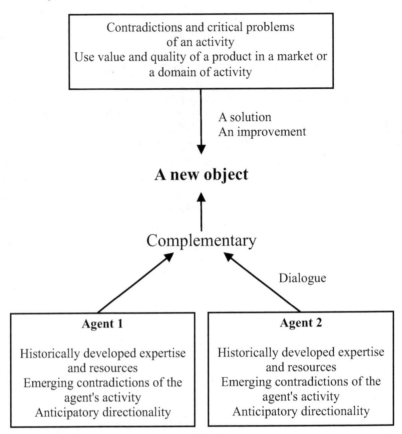

Figure 8.1   The structure of a creative encounter.

In Figure 8.1, the three constitutive elements of an encounter and the emergence of collaborative agency are outlined: (1) The gradual development and recognition of contradictions in an activity are expressed as dissatisfaction concerning some elements of the activity and as a gradual formation of anticipatory directionality, that is, a preliminary orientation looking for a solution. (2) An encounter with a partner leads to the formation of a shared object idea as a solution to the contradiction and to the emergence of collaborative agency that assumes the form of a joined project. (3) The complementarity of the expertise, resources, and interests of the partners make the formulation of a joint object and the establishment of a joint project possible. Each phase in the process, from a contradiction to the construction of an artifact—the recognition of a contradiction of an activity, the formulation of a constructive problem, the development of an inventive idea, and product development—embodies learning in different forms. Vygotsky's (1978) idea of learning as remediation may be used to characterize the process of developing new technologies and products.

In the following, the three elements of an encounter will be elaborated by using theoretical resources from creativity research, the history of technology, and the economics of innovation. Their meaning is clarified by taking examples from two product development processes. A Finnish firm Wallac developed the Delfia immunodiagnostic method in collaboration with the Department of Molecular Endocrinology of Middlesex Hospital, University College London in the 1980s (Miettinen, 2000; Miettinen et al., 1999). An unplanned encounter between the CEO of the Finnish biotechnology firm Finnzymes and the leader of a research group from the Technological Institute of Iceland led to the development of the Dynazyme enzyme product in the beginnings of the 1990s (Lehenkari, 2006; Miettinen et al., 1999; Miettinen et al., 2008). Both cases are examples of interactive emergence that grew up from the complementary knowledge and expertise of the partners.[3]

CONTRADICTIONS AND FUNCTIONAL FAILURES AS SOURCES OF INVENTIVE IDEAS

The tradition of materialistic dialectics regards the historically emerging contradictions of human activities as a source of development (Ilyenkov, 1977). In organizational research, the dialectic approach regards contradictions (Benson, 1977), or more recently institutional contradictions (Hargrave & Van de Ven, 2010; Seo & Creed, 2002) as the source of change. In activity theory, Engeström (1987) has developed a theory of expansive learning in which contradictions constitute the driving force of development and learning in human activities. The contradiction between use value and exchange value permeates economic activity in capitalism (Engeström, 1987). Contradictions between elements of activity, primarily between the means (instrumentalities) and the object of activity, constantly emerge.

Other practice-oriented philosophies also use terms compatible with contradiction to explain change. Phenomenology and pragmatism regard *breakdowns* or *disharmonies* of practices (Koschmann, Kuutti, & Hickman, 1998; Spinosa, Flores, & Dreyfus, 1997) as a starting point for world-making and reflective transformation of practices. These terms can be interpreted as expressions of contradictions in human practice. Historians of technological systems (Constant, 1984; Hughes, 1988) view contradictions as the main source of technological change. They have developed their own terms for contradiction out of empirical research without resorting to the philosophical tradition of dialectics. They, however, provide convincing accounts of the workings of contradictions in the development of technology-mediated activities. Hughes (1988) has used the term *reverse salient* to refer to the weakest point in an expanding technological system: "An analysis of a growing system often reveals the inefficient and uneconomical components, or reverse salients" (p. 80). An example of a reverse salient requiring development can be taken from the early history of telephone communication (Hoddeson, 1981). In the first decades of the twentieth century, the Bell Telephone Company was unable to provide calls from coast to coast in the United States because the signal weakened as it ran along the cables. This phenomenon was a hindrance to the development of telephone services and business. The hindrance was removed in 1915 when physicist Harold Arnold developed a triode that successfully functioned as an amplifier in the cable system.

Edward Constant uses the term *functional failure* to refer to a system's inability to function in new and more demanding circumstances, which serves as a major impetus for technical change (Constant, 1984). Both a reverse salient and a functional failure can be regarded as a contradiction between a technical means and the object of activity of a product and service provider caused by the changes in user activities of the product in question. In the activity of a firm, it is expressed as a crisis of profit making that jeopardizes the business activity and forces it to search for new possibilities.

Economic historian and theorist of innovation, David Rosenberg (1976), suggests that *imbalances* between the components of a technological system are a major reason for further innovations. Typically, the utilization of a new technology requires the development of complementary technologies and new organizational arrangements. Rosenberg extends the imbalance to cover the relationships between technology and economic and political processes. Strikes, wars, and embargos have been an important source of innovation. Rosenberg (1976) cites Marx's *Poverty in Philosophy*:

> In England, strikes have regularly given rise to the invention and application of new machines. Machines were, it may be said, the weapon employed by the capitalist to quell the revolt of specialized labour. The *self-acting mule*, the greatest invention of modern industry, put out of action the spinners who were in revolt. (p. 118)

Perez's theory (2002) of technological revolutions suggests that there is a *gap* between technological and organizational-institutional change. New technologies are typically introduced to organizational structures developed during the previous technological paradigm. For instance, in the 1980s and 1990s, ICT was brought into hierarchical organizations of mass production, which greatly impeded the full deployment of the new technology. Perez's theory and the evolutionary economics of innovation were inspired by Kuhn's (1962) theory of scientific revolutions adopting the concept of paradigm from it. In Kuhn's theory, the reason for a change of paradigm is the accumulation of *anomalies,* which also can be regarded as a specific type of a developmental contradiction.

To explain the emergence of collaborative agency, in addition to a contradiction in a user or object activity, the contradictions and challenges in the activities of design partners need to be analyzed to explain why they commit themselves to a joint project. The reasons may be related to the need to expand expertise; find a new product, raw material, or market; or resolve a specific problem evolving in their activity (Miettinen, 1998). In the formation of collaborative agency, the contradictions and dilemmas of several activities are intertwined.

DELFIA: CONTRADICTIONS IN IMMUNODIAGNOSTICS AND PRODUCER-USER INTERACTION GIVE RISE TO A NEW IMMUNODIAGNOSTIC METHOD

Since the 1950s, radioimmunoassay (RIA) has been the main method used in immunodiagnostics, in which human antibodies are used to recognize molecules and begetters of diseases in blood samples. In RIA, radioactive labels are used to mark the antibodies to allow the measurement of the quantity of biological agents. In the 1970s, a small Finnish enterprise, Wallac, a manufacturer of devices that measure radioactivity, developed an alternative immunodiagnostic method in which radioactive labels were replaced by fluorescence compounds. The new product, under the trademark of Delfia, was introduced to the market in 1984. The new product changed Wallac from a producer of measuring instruments into a producer of immunodiagnostic kits.

In the 1960s, Wallac produced measurement instruments for multiple purposes. The turnover of their traditional main product, Geiger counters used in the measurement of radioactive fallout from nuclear tests, strongly declined. This was an emerging contradiction in Wallac's business activity that forced it to look for alternative products and markets. One of Wallac's products, a gamma calculator, was used in immunodiagnostics. Dr. Erkki Soini, a physicist and the research manager of Wallac, started to become acquainted with immunodiagnostics (a step toward anticipatory directionality). In 1971 Soini visited a client and user of their measurement device, Professor Roger Ekins from the Middlesex Hospital Medical School, located in London. Ekins was one of the key developers of RIA technology. This encounter led to a long-standing collaboration between Wallac and Ekins' department and to a friendship between Professor Ekins and Dr. Soini (a creative encounter). After the general purpose measuring instruments for radioactivity were soon found to be cumbersome in immunodiagnostic testing, Wallac designed a gamma calculator specifically for RIA. This was a further step in anticipatory directionality and learning about immunodiagnostics.

During this collaboration, Wallac gradually learned that RIA had several limitations, which constrained the use and development of immunodiagnostics. The sustainability of the radioactive labels was poor, often limited to six to eight weeks. They were awkward to handle and involved health risks requiring special safety equipment, and after use became hazardous waste. Dr. Soini recollects how he saw the situation:

> It was already clear that the use of radioactive labels in chemistry and biomedical research was difficult, because the researchers couldn't use them freely. They always had to go to a laboratory that was inspected and certified. There were systems of control, and so forth. It was clear that had it been possible to use these methods without radioactivity, their use would have expanded, and so would the market, of course.

This statement includes a description of a reverse salient in the immunodiagnostic testing practice and its transformation into a technical problem to be solved: "Had it been possible to use these methods without radioactivity, their use would have expanded, and so would the market, of course." The dilemmas of RIA use were, of course, well-known to practitioners, but as long as RIA was the most sensitive method—and the only possible one for several applications—and no alternative method was being developed, the disadvantages were taken as a necessary evil and as belonging to the state of art of that practice. Its recognition as a contradiction required a vision of an alternative. Soini and Wallac were able to provide such an alternative. By 1974 he became convinced that the solution should be based on fluorescence, a specific emission of light.

The recognition of the reverse salient emerged out of the discussions between Wallac and Professor Ekins and included a strong element of learning from a totally new field of expertise.

Professor Ekins: I was invited to visit Turku. . . . They (Wallac) wished me to provide knowledge of the requirements radioimmunoassay poses to the calculator, and they also wished more general knowledge of the development of radioimmunoassay.

Dr. Soini: Professor Ekins tried hard to teach us what radioimmunoassay is and what it requires. We didn't understand very much about radioimmunology at that time . . . . An average hospital chemist wouldn't have realized the future, which Ekins was able to see. This advice was worth millions. Had you put some marketing man to conduct a market study, the verdict would have been: There is no need or demand.

These citations show that the recognition of the reverse salient and formulation of an inventive problem (finding an alternative label) was also a learning process in which the physicists gained an understanding of immunodiagnostics. The idea of replacing the radioisotope with a fluorescent label was a working hypothesis with which the contradiction of immunodiagnostic testing could be resolved and a new market created. The testing and realization of this hypothesis, however, required four more years of experimentation, learning, and collaboration with diverse partners (Miettinen, 2000). Eventually, Delfia became the main product of Wallac. For the partner, it was a step forward in the development of immunodiagnostics.

FROM A NEED STATE TO THE FORMATION
OF A SHARED OBJECT IDEA

The process from a need state to the formation of the object has been analyzed in creativity studies in terms of a "problem of the problem" and in the history of technology in terms of the interconnectedness of a contradiction, an inventive problem and the formulation of an inventive idea. One of the pioneers of creativity studies, Getzels (1982), suggested that the problem of the problem is the key issue in creativity studies. Instead of problem solving, the process in which indeterminate dilemmas are turned into a creative or constructive problem is essential.[4] Getzels (1982) states that "transforming the dilemma into a fruitful problem— putting the right question, as the saying goes—may be no less an intellectual achievement than attaining the effective solution once the productive problem is posed" (p. 38). Researcher of innovation, Noteboom (2000) articulates a similar idea: "The main point of the discovery procedures finding out where problems lie, which preserve priority, what might be promising and viable elements of solution, where they are to be searched for" (p. 256).

Seidel (1976) suggests that the study of the social and economic history of problems is needed to solve the problem of the problem. Emerging economic and social inadequacies of human practices are turned into "inventive" problems. Seidel himself studied the invention and early development of the steam machine. He showed that the development of a workable steam machine was a response to the worsening water problem in the coal mines in England. A new power machine for water pumping was badly needed, and the first steam machine designed by Thomas Newcomen in 1712 was used as a pumping device.

In his theory of inventive activity, Hughes (1978) regards "critical problems" as bridges between imbalances of current technology use and inventive activity. The formulation of the problem already implies a hypothesized direction of a possible solution (Hughes, 1978). In terms of activity theory, the development of a contradiction in a field of human practices constitutes a foundation for the formulation of "productive" problems and projects. Because both the development of contradictions and their recognition are gradual processes, the definition of the problem is preceded by anticipatory directionality, a nonspecific dissatisfaction with and concern about what is happening and a preliminary orientation of where to look for solutions. An encounter with a partner with complementarity knowledge and resources may constitute a decisive springboard for the formulation of the solution, that is, an idea of an artifact that provides a solution to a contradiction in a practice. The object to be constructed—or the open hypothesis for a possible new product and solution—constitutes a joint motive of collaboration.

One partner alone may not be able to generate a solution, even if he or she is familiar with the inadequacy or the emerging contradiction in the activity. On the other hand, this familiarity provides a preparedness to create a joint object when the complementary knowledge and resources of the partner enables the articulation of a new possibility. In innovation studies, Van de Ven, Polley, Garud, and Venkataraman (1999, p. 26) characterized the formation of anticipatory directionality in terms of an extended "gestation period" during which the need for change is gradually recognized as a result of multiple coincidental events.

The *generative* potential of an encounter is realized through discussions in which the complementarities of knowledge and the resources of the partners are recognized, mutual interests are articulated, and trust in the partner is constructed. To become a real motive, an object idea must turn into a project in which the partners combine their knowledge, resources, and efforts.

ANTICIPATORY DIRECTIONALITY, CREATIVE ENCOUNTERS, AND COLLABORATIVE AGENCY IN THE DEVELOPMENT OF THE DYNAZYME DNA POLYMERASE ENZYME

Finnzymes, a small Finnish biotechnology firm established in 1986, produces and sells reagents, enzymes, and instruments for genetic engineering and research. It started its activity by selling enzymes produced from a North American partner in northern Europe. The company itself only produced one type of enzyme, a restriction enzyme used to cut DNA strands in specific sites. The firm's early period was a time of learning how to follow and seek developments and opportunities in the field, as described by the CEO of the firm:

> We learned the patterns of the import and export businesses, but simultaneously, we learned the trends in the field. We found out what is nonpermanent and withers away. We also learned to recognize product opportunities on the basis of market demand. Consequently, we learned to orientate ourselves in the field.

Very soon the management of Finnzymes realized that business based on the production of restriction enzymes and the distribution of enzymes produced by other companies would not allow the firm to survive (a contradiction in the business activity). Finnzymes started to look for alternative markets and products by following developments in molecular biology. One important development in the field was PCR technology, invented in the mid-1980s. It serves as a copy machine for DNA, producing millions of copies of a specific DNA sequence in a test tube. PCR technology was developing into a new generic technology in molecular biology at the late 1980s. The CEO of Finnzymes recollects the situation: "We familiarized ourselves with the PCR in the early phase in the late 1980s, and we immediately started to search for conventions for selling PCR instruments because we saw its importance."

The newly developed instruments and enzymes used in the PCR technique became an important part of Finnzymes' import business. This contributed to the formation of a deeper understanding of the technology. Learning about the field and the new technology comprised the anticipatory directionality that preceded and paved the way for the development of enzymes used in PCR technology. The DNA replication in a PCR is catalyzed by a thermo stable (high-temperature resistant) DNA polymerase enzyme. The quality (purity, stability) of this enzyme was a reverse salient in the development of the reliability of the new method (a contradiction in the development of the utilization of PCR). Finnzymes had expertise in developing and producing high-quality enzymes. However, because it did not have access to sources of thermo stable enzymes, this directionality did not materialize in the product design.

In 1989 the CEO participated in a meeting of a Nordic biotechnology research program and encountered (for the first time) the leader of an Icelandic research group working at the Technological Institute of Iceland, IceTec. The Icelandic group had expertise in hot spring bacteria. The CEO immediately saw this group as a potential producer of the thermo stable DNA polymerases required in PCR technology. The leader of the Icelandic group became excited about the opportunity to study thermo stable enzymes, and they decided to start a joint screening and enzyme development project.

In 1990 a member of the Icelandic group visited Finnzymes to learn the screening methods for DNA polymerases and restriction enzymes and for determining their activity. After the visit, a joint project was initiated. The Icelandic partner isolated, cultivated, and preanalyzed bacteria strains living in hot springs. The results were sent to Finnzymes, which did the final analysis of the thermal resistance and accuracy of the activity. In this research, several new restriction enzymes were found, and a new DNA polymerase enzyme was derived from the *Thermus Brockianus* bacterium. The partners wrote eight joint articles for scientific journals and conference publications. The enzyme with the marketing name Dynazyme became Finnzymes' leading product. The attribute that made Dynazyme competitive in the market was its thermal stability. Dynazyme tolerated longer heating phases than its rivals (many of them extracted from bacteria from Yellowstone hot springs) when used in PCRs, which diminished reaction failures. This, in turn, was vital for the users. Both partners learned much from the process. Furthermore, the joint project was based on the different but complementary expertise of the partners: expertise in hot spring bacteria (microbiology) and the purification and production of enzyme products (process engineering).

The already recognized contradiction in the business activity, knowledge of technological developments, and a potential new direction for enzyme production did not lead to product development because of the absence of the relevant expertise and resources. The encounter with the microbiologists of IceTech reversed this situation: a collaborative agent and a realistic project for developing polymerase enzymes emerged.

THE COMPLEMENTARITY OF KNOWLEDGE AND THE RESOURCES OF PARTNERS AS A SOURCE FOR OBJECT FORMATION AND THE EMERGENCE OF COLLABORATIVE AGENCY

The third element of a creative encounter and a key condition for the emergence of collaborative agency is the recognition of the potential inherent in the complementarity of knowledge and resources of the partners. In innovation studies, Teece (1986) has suggested that because of the increasing specialization and complexity of products, complementarity of knowledge and resources is an increasingly important source of product development. It is needed for the recognition of contradictions and opportunities, in the formulation of the idea of a new object and in the actual product development. Correspondingly, John-Steiner (2000) analyzes disciplinary and temperamental complementarity as an essential mechanism in collaborative scientific creativity.

A classic example of the power of complementarity is the emergence of one of the most important technologies of the last century, gene transfer technology. This technology emerged out of an encounter between Stanley Cohen (Stanford University) and Herbert Boyer (University of California, San Francisco) in a conference in Hawaii in 1972. While listening to Boyer's presentation on restriction enzymes that cut DNA strands in specific sites, the idea of gene technology occurred to Cohen. He was a specialist in plasmids, molecules that are able to carry sequences of DNA inside the cell (Cohen, 1982). He talked with Boyer, and they established a project that subsequently led to the development of the new technology. They had complementary areas of expertise and therefore, a strong mutual interest in joining forces. Although Boyer recognized how to create a new DNA molecule, he did not know how such a molecule would behave without introducing it into a living cell. Cohen and his assistants developed a method of introducing plasmids into a bacterial cell, but they did not have the means of splicing new genetic information into the plasmids.

The same situation was seen in both of the product development processes described in this paper. The experience and expertise of two partners were needed for the articulation of the contradiction of an immunodiagnostic testing activity. The knowledge of an alternative by an outsider, physicist and instrument maker Dr. Soini, was needed to fully recognize the contradiction and turn it into a critical problem and an inventive idea. In the case of Dynazyme, Finnzymes already had an orientation to the development of polymerase enzymes. The expertise of the Icelandic research group and its access to hot spring bacteria turned this orientation into a joint object and a collaborative project.

CONCLUSIONS

Different versions of an individual-centered approach have dominated the psychology of creativity. In drive theories, biological and innate drives energize and direct human conduct and are transformed into motives. This tradition survives in applied psychoanalytic theories of creativity and humanistic psychology. Amabile's concept of intrinsic motivation is also an heir of the individualistic tradition. She (Collins & Amabile, 1999) regards intrinsic motivation as the state of an individual and as a "personal character and trait" (p. 301). The environment can hinder or facilitate the realization of such a motive. In this paper, I have looked for an alternative solution from the concepts of a contradiction and an object of activity.

The critics of drive theory in the 1950s formulated a theory of exploratory activity, which involves attention to an object in the environment and action upon this object (White, 1959). Lewin (1935) suggested that objects in the environment have valences. Leont'ev (1978) took a step forward in introducing the double nature of an object of activity, both as something historically given and as imagined and projected by a human agent. To develop this idea further, human needs require to be analyzed in terms of emerging contradictions in human activities in which the individual participates and to which he or she is connected to. The development of a full-fledged joint object of activity and agency in product development can be defined in terms of a process: a contradiction of an activity, its recognition as a constructive problem, the formulation of a working hypothesis or object or product idea, and the establishment of a project to realize it. As suggested by a historian of technology, these moments of emergence are deeply intertwined in creative activity, carrying the continuity between the past, present, and future. The agent needed to carry out this process is increasingly a collaborative agent.

In making sense of the early phase of the *meeting of a need and an object,* a type of cognition characterized as anticipatory directionality is needed. Anticipatory directionality is a bridge between the deepening contradiction and the full articulation of a new object. It covers the growing dissatisfaction in a dimension of an activity as well as a non-specific and open-ended search for alternatives. An important challenge is to study the nature of learning during the search activity and anticipatory directionality. This type of learning surely differs from that in which a well-defined problem is a starting point. The pragmatist concept of abduction may provide tools for its further analysis (e.g., Paavola, 2004). On the other hand, the Davydovian idea of the genetic method in the formation of theoretical concepts may well be applied to search activity in work (e.g., Miettinen & Virkkunen, 2005). It would include interpreting cues of diverse complex developments in technology, politics, markets, and user activities that together constitute the terrain both for the development of contradictions and for new opportunities.

The increasing significance of an interactive emergence is a result of increased specialization, division of labor as well as the increasing complexity of the problems that need to be resolved in society. Their solutions emerge in the dialogue and collaboration between people representing different fields of knowledge and having complementary skills and resources to contribute to joint projects. An important means of fostering creativity is the development of spaces within which a certain kind of interaction across epistemic boundaries can take place. In addition to traditional spaces such as conferences, professional meetings, associations, and trade fairs—new types of spaces, such as regional meetings, may foster encounters between heterogeneous agents, user-producer seminars, and living labs. It would also be interesting to study to what extent Internet communities and platforms of various kinds enhance creative encounters and the emergence of collaborative agency.

NOTES

1. Creativity and innovation are often used interchangeably. In economics of innovation, the term innovation refers to an economically utilized new product, service, or production method. It differs from the concept of creativity in psychology in three senses. First, the novelty of an artifact is evaluated in economic terms, by its success in the market. Second, it implies the study of the relationship between producers and users. Third, whereas creativity is often studied as the production of ideas (creative thinking), innovation covers the process of product development, the development of a material artifact that requires several cycles of experimentation and learning. Innovation also implies the process of diffusion, which in business firms takes place through marketing.
2. About the relationships between the concepts of need, object of activity, and motive, see Miettinen (2005).
3. Because of the limitations of space, the short accounts of cases serve as examples providing empirical foundation for the model of a creative encounter. For extended analyses of the cases with the descriptions of the interview and documentary data used in the studies, see Lehenkari (2006), Miettinen (2000), and Miettinen et al. (1999, 2008).

4. Getzels and Csikszentmihalyi (1976, p. 81) think that instead of the problem-solving process, creativity research should focus on how important problems are being found and formulated: "The problem solver must become a problem finder . . . . To turn a problem solver into a problem finder, one must feel that there is a challenge needing resolution in the environment, one must formulate this feeling as a problem, and then attempt to devise appropriate methods for solving it . . . . Not only the solution but the problem itself must be discovered."

REFERENCES

Allport, G. W. (1961). *Pattern and growth of personality*. New York, NY: Holt, Rinehart and Winston.

Amabile, T. (1983). A social psychology of creativity: A componential conceptualization. *Journal of Personality and Social Psychology, 45*, 357–376.

Amabile, T. (1996). *Creativity in context*. Boulder, CO: Westview Press.

Beech, N., MacIntosh, R., & MacLean, D. (2010). Dialogues between academics and practitioners: The role of generative dialogic encounters. *Organization Studies, 31*(9–10), 1341–1367.

Benson, J. K. (1977). Organization: A dialectical view. *Administration Science Quarterly, 22*, 1–21.

Besser-Jones, L. (2012). The motivational state of the virtuous agent. *Philosophical Psychology, 25*(1), 93–108.

Bratus, B. S., & Lishin, O. V. (1983). Laws of the development of activity and the problems of psychological and pedagogical shaping of personality. *Soviet Psychology, XXV*(2), 91–103.

Bruun, H. (2000). *Epistemic encounters: Intra- and interdisciplinary analyses of human action, planning practices and technological change*. Gothenburg, Sweden: Göterborg University.

Cohen, S. N. (1982). The Stanford cloning patent. In W.J. Whelan and S. Black (Eds.), *From genetic experimentation to biotechnology—the critical transition* (pp. 213–216.). Chichester: John Wiley & Sons.

Collins, M. A., & Amabile, T. (1999). Motivation and creativity. In R. J. Sternberg (Ed.), *Handbook of creativity* (pp. 297–312). Cambridge, England: Cambridge University Press.

Constant, E. W. (1984). Communities and hierarchies: Structure in the practice of science and technology. In R. Laudan (Ed.), *The nature of technological knowledge: Are models of scientific change relevant?* (pp. 27–46). Dordrecht, The Netherlands: Reidel, Sociology of Sciences Monographs.

Eisenberg, R., & Shannock, L. (2003). Rewards, intrinsic motivation, and creativity: A case study of conceptual and methodological isolation. *Creativity Research Journal, 15*(2–3), 121–130.

Engeström, Y. (1987). *Learning by expanding: An activity theoretical approach to developmental research*. Helsinki, Finland: Orienta Konsultit.

Feldman, D. H., Csikszentmihalyi, M., & Gardner, H. (1994). *Changing the world: A framework for the study of creativity*. Westport, CT: Praeger.

Fogel, A. (1993). *Developing through relationships: Origins of communication, self, and culture*. Chicago, IL: The University of Chicago Press.

Ford, C. M. (1996). A theory of individual creative action in multiple social domains. *Academy of Management Review, 21*(4), 112–1142.

Freeman, C. (1991). Network of innovators: A synthesis of research issues. *Research Policy, 20*, 5, 499–514.

Getzels, J. W. (1982). The problem of the problem. In H. Hogarth (Ed.), *New direction in the methodology of social and behavioral science: Question framing and response consistency* (pp. 37–49). San Francisco, CA: Jossey-Bass.

Getzels, J. W., & Csikszentmihalyi, M. (1976). *A creative vision: A longitudinal study of problem finding in art.* New York, NY: Wiley.

Hargrave, T. J., & Van de Ven, A. H. (2010). Institutional work as creative embrace of contradiction. In T. B. Lawrence, R. Suddaby, & B. Leca (Eds.), *Institutional work: Actors and agency in institutional studies of organizations* (pp. 120–140). Cambridge, England: Cambridge University Press.

Hoddeson, L. (1981). The emergence of basic research in the Bell telephone system, 1875–1915. *Technology and Culture, 22,* 512–544.

Hughes, T. P. (1978). Inventors: The problems they chose, the ideas they have, and the inventions they make. In A. Kelly & M. Kransberg (Eds.), *Technological innovation: A critical view of current knowledge* (pp. 166–182). San Francisco, CA: San Francisco Press.

Hughes, T. P. (1988). *Networks of power: Electrification of western world 1880–1930.* Baltimore, MD: The John Hopkins University Press.

Ilyenkov, E. V. (1977). *Dialectical logic: Essays on its history and theory.* Moscow, Russia: Progress Publishers.

John-Steiner, V. (2000). *Creative collaboration.* New York, NY: Oxford University Press.

Koschmann, T., Kuutti, K., & Hickman, L. (1998). The concept of breakdown in Heidegger, Leont'ev, and Dewey and its implications for education. *Mind, Culture, and Activity, 5*(1), 25–41.

Kuhn, T. S. (1962). *The structure of scientific revolutions.* Chicago, IL: Chicago University Press.

Kurtzberg, R. R., & Amabile, T. (2001). From Guilford to creative synergy: Opening the black box of team-level creativity. *Creativity Research Journal, 13*(3–4), 285–294.

Lane, D., & Maxfield, R. R. (1996). Strategy under complexity: Fostering generative relationships. *Long Range Planning, 29*(2), 215–231.

Lehenkari, J. (2006). *The networks of learning in technological innovation: The emergence of collaboration across fields of expertise* (Doctoral dissertation). University of Helsinki, Helsinki, Finland.

Leont'ev, A. N. (1978). *Activity, consciousness, and personality.* Englewood Cliffs, NJ: Prentice Hall.

Lewin, K. (1935). *A dynamic theory of personality.* New York, NY: McGraw Hill.

Long, N. (2002). *Development sociology: Actor perspectives.* London, England: Routledge.

Lorenzen, M. (2007). *Creative encounters in the film industry: Contents, cost, chance, and collection.* Frederiksberg, Denmark: Samfundslitteratur.

Merton, R. (1973). *The sociology of science: Theoretical and empirical investigations.* Chicago, IL: The University of Chicago Press.

Miettinen, R. (1998). Object construction and networks in research work: The case of research on cellulose degrading enzymes. *Social Studies of Science, 38,* 423–463.

Miettinen, R. (2000). *The problem of creativity in technology studies: Invention as artifact construction and culturally distributed work.* Helsinki, Finland: Center for Activity Theory and Developmental Work Research.

Miettinen, R. (2005). Object of activity and individual motivation. *Mind, Culture and Activity, 12*(1), 53–68.

Miettinen, R. (2009). *Dialogue and creativity: Activity theory in the study of science, technology and innovations.* Berlin, Germany: Lehmanns Media.

Miettinen, R., Lehenkari, J., Hasu, M., & Hyvönen, J. (1999). *Osaaminen ja uuden luominen innovaatioverkoissa: Tutkimus kuudesta Suomalaisesta innovaatioista [Knowledge and the creation of new in innovation networks: Study of six Finnish innovations].* Helsinki, Finland: Taloustieto.

Miettinen, R., Lehenkari, J., & Tuunainen, J. (2008). Learning and networks in product development: How things work for human use. *Management Learning, 39*(2), 203–219.

Miettinen, R., & Virkkunen, J. (2005). Epistemic objects, artifacts and organizational change. *Organization, 12*(3), 437–456.

Moran, S., & John-Steiner, V. (2003). Creativity in the making: Vygotsky's contemporary contribution to the dialectic of development and creativity. In K. Sawyer, V. John-Steiner, S. Moran, R. J. Sternberg, D. H. Feldman, J. Nakamura, & M. Csikszentmihalyi (Eds.), *Creativity and development* (pp. 61–90). New York, NY: Oxford University Press.

Noteboom, B. (2000). *Learning and innovation in organizations and economies.* Oxford, England: Oxford University Press.

Ochse, R. A. (1990). *Before the gates of excellence: The determinants of creative genius.* Cambridge, England: Cambridge University Press.

Paavola, S. (2004). Abduction as a logic and methodology of discovery: The importance of strategies. *Foundations of Science, 9,* 267–283.

Perez, C. (2002). *Technological revolutions and financial capital: The dynamics and bubbles and golden ages.* Cheltenham, England: Edward Elgar.

Perry-Smith, J. E., & Shalley, C. E. (2003). The social side of creativity: A static and dynamic social network perspective. *Academy of Management Review, 28*(1), 89–106.

Rosenberg, N. (1976). *Perspectives on technology.* Cambridge, England: Cambridge University Press.

Rothwell, R. (1992). Successful industrial innovation: Critical factors for the 1990s. *R & D Management, 22,* 3, 221–239.

Sawyer, R. K. (2003). *Group creativity: Music theatre, collaboration.* Mahwah, NJ: Erlbaum.

Seidel, R. (1976). *Denken. Psychologiche Analyse der Entstehung und Lösung von Problemen [Thinking: Psychological analysis of the emergence and solving of problems].* Frankfurt, Germany: Campus Verlag.

Seo, M.-G., & Creed, W. E. D. (2002). Institutional contradictions, praxis, and institutional change: A dialectical perspective. *The Academy of Management Review, 27*(2), 222–247.

Smith-Doerr, L., & Powell, W. W. (2005). Networks and economic life. In N. J. Smelser & R. Swedberg (Eds.), *Handbook of economic sociology* (pp. 379–402). Princeton, NJ: Princeton University Press.

Sosa, M. E. (2011). Where do creative interactions come from? The role of tie content and social networks. *Organization Science, 22*(1), 1–21.

Spinosa, C., Flores, F., & Dreyfus, H. L. (1997). *Disclosing new worlds: Entrepreneurship, democratic action, ands the cultivation of solidarity.* Cambridge, MA: MIT Press.

Teece, D. J. (1986). Profiting from technological innovation: Implications for integration, collaboration, licensing and public policy. *Research Policy, 15,* 285–305.

Van de Ven, A., Polley, D. E., Garud, R., & Venkataraman, S. (1999). *The innovation journey.* New York, NY: Oxford University Press.

Vygotsky, L. S. (1978). *Mind in society: The development of higher mental functions.* Cambridge, MA: Harvard University Press.

Vygotsky, L. S. (1998). Imagination and creativity in the adolescent. In R. W. Rieber (Ed.), *The collective works of Vygotsky: Child psychology* (Vol. 5, pp. 151–166). New York, NY: Plenum Press.

White, R. W. (1959). Motivation considered: The concept of competence. *Psychological Review, 66*(5), 297–333.

Woodman, R. W., Sawyer, J. E., & Griffin, R. W. (1993). Toward a theory of organizational creativity. *The Academy of Management Review, 18*(2), 293–321.

Yaroshevsky, M. (1974). The external and inner motivation in scientific creativity. *Social Sciences, 1*, 58–72.

Part III

Interventions Mobilizing Creative Efforts in Collective Problem Solving and Development of Activities

9 Creative Tools for Collective Creativity

The Serious Play Method Using Lego Bricks

Klaus-Peter Schulz and Silke Geithner

When considering learning and development processes in the workplace, organizations often make use of their creative potential through integrating various stakeholder groups into collective activity (Reed, Storrud-Barnes, & Jessup, 2012; Sanoff, 2000). In these contexts, new ideas are likely to emerge out of mutual reflecting and practicing (West, 2002; West & Farr, 1990). Hence, heterogeneous groups can be seen as a source for collective creativity (Amabile, 1996; West, 2002). Despite the creative potential of such activity, participants are confronted with their different perspectives and understandings, concerning the object of the activity, clients, teamwork, and management issues. It is, however, the very diversity of the participants combined with their ability to share meaning and understanding that provides creative potential (Cropley, 2006; West, 2002). Therefore, we see in collective learning and development an initial challenge of bridging different participants' perspectives in order to provide mutual understanding and idea generation (Chesbrough, 2003; Von Hippel, 2006).

Bearing in mind an activity-theoretical approach to learning and development (e.g., Chaiklin, Hedegaard, & Jensen, 1999; Engeström, 1987, 2001, 2005; Engeström & Sannino, 2010; Sannino, Daniels, & Gutièrrez, 2009), such diversity is likely to bring about contradictions with regard to the existing practice as a prerequisite for learning as development (Bateson, 1972; Engeström, 1987, 2001). However, the contradictions need to be identified, explicated, and made understandable among the participants of a development and learning process. Following the concept of expansive learning (Engeström & Sannino, 2010), contradictions can be solved through developing new activity that accompanies the change of existing background assumptions and understandings of the participants. This collective conceptualization can be seen as the central creative activity at early stages of the development and learning process.

Questions, however, arise as to how such creative potential can be fostered and the necessary preconditions can be set that make foster collective creative behavior more likely. Namely, how can a collectively shared understanding be created, contradictions be identified and explicated, and solutions be developed using the creative potential of the group? Considering current research in the field of organizational change, we particularly see a considerable gap in discussing collective creativity and learning from a methodological perspective. Mechanisms of creativity have been widely researched within various disciplines (e.g., Csikszentmihalyi, 1990) and with respect to collectivity (e.g., Von Held, 2012). The process of improvisation within groups and organizations has been considered by innovation researchers and organizational theorists with the focus to describe creative group processes (Fisher & Amabile, 2009; Vera & Crossan, 2005; West, 2002). Furthermore, the use of manual tool kits in creative processes has been intensively studied in industrial design (Cross, 2011; Sanders & Stappers, 2008). However, we argue that methods need to be drawn up and applied that focus on the process of expressing and sharing meaning within groups as well as inspiring participants to conceive and reify ideas.

Traditional settings of group collaboration are based on verbal communication, partially supplemented by written charts, power point slides, tables, or figures. Hence, participants create and express meanings through verbal explanations, gestures, or sketches. Understanding is created through such ongoing communication and exchange as a process of "growing together" (Baitsch, 1993; Sleeswijk Visser, Van der Lugt, & Stappers, 2007). However, in the case of heterogeneous groups, it remains unclear to what extent a common ground for understanding can be reached among participants. Contradictions may remain unconscious and their explication difficult to establish. In terms of learning and development, it is doubtful that such settings foster an inspiring atmosphere that is characterized by an intuitive and creative inquiry with the object of consideration (Csikszentmihalyi, 1990). Methods that perceive creative inquiry as playful interaction with the object make use of metaphors that are easily created and understood. Sketching, cardboard modeling, or sculpting are frequently used methods (e.g., Cross, 1999, 2011). They are, however, largely individualistic and often assume a certain level of crafting capabilities of the creators. Gaps can, therefore, emerge between users dependent on these capabilities. An alternative method frequently applied in architecture and product development processes consists of nominating a process designer who simultaneously visualizes and documents the ongoing discussion (Brown, 2009). Such a method, however, places the reflection and interpretation of the creative process in the hands of one or two persons and calls upon their individual perceptions.

In response to these shortfalls, we introduce a conceptual approach that aims to actively integrate all stakeholders of the learning and development processes, allowing them to gain awareness and express and exchange their ideas within a group. The approach includes the cocreation of physical models through *tool kit based modeling*, which means in our case simple tool kits such as children's building blocks that are used to create and discuss prototypes (Sanders & Stappers, 2008). The creation process itself can be described as *serious play* (Roos, Victor, & Statler, 2004; Statler,

Heracleous, & Jacobs, 2011). This concept addresses the paradox between intentionality and playfulness with the aim to foster the creative expression of ideas. Abstract models are created intuitively by the user as he or she carries out a general task. We particularly consider the use of LEGO building blocks, which can easily be assembled and disassembled without any prerequisites needed from the user. Furthermore, the serious play method using LEGO bricks addresses manual building and verbal expression.

The built items are mere metaphors for meaning. The meanings are transported through the story that is told by the creator of the model (see also Orr, 1996, 2006). The meaning can easily be grasped by the other team members, and feedback questions can be asked. In addition to the individually created metaphors, the models can be put together to create a collectively shared model. To subsume, the tool kit based modeling on serious play is itself a creative approach that "enables people to express themselves creatively and to develop as creative thinkers" (Resnick et al., 2005, p. 3). Whereas general tasks or challenges are given, directions are not. The models emerge out of the manual creation in combination with the verbal expression of meaning. The subsequent shared models express both collective connection and diversity between participants.

In this paper, we start with a theoretical discussion of learning as development, an activity we consider as inevitably collective and creative. In the next section, we explain serious play and tool kit-based modeling as ways to facilitate collective creativity within learning and development processes. We then refer to the LEGO Serious Play method and discuss its prerequisites, process performance, and outcomes through a case study. The case is about a workshop on developing a future concept of a research laboratory. We discuss and assess the application of LEGO Serious Play and present our analysis of the relative merits of this method with respect to learning as a creative collective development.

LEARNING AS EXPANSIVE DEVELOPMENT

Learning as expansive development (Engeström, 1987, 2001, 2005; Engeström & Sannino, 2010; Lompscher, 1999, 2004) refers to collective activity that requires creativity from the learners. Expansive development implies a fundamental change in thinking and acting, stemming from the effort of dealing with contradictions in the existing activity and understanding of the learners. Collective exchange in groups with diverse views and backgrounds can especially bring about such contradictions as long as the members of the groups are able to share their possibly of different understandings. Therefore, expansive development goes far beyond adaptive problem solving or methodological learning (Bateson, 1972). Particularly the solving of contradictions through a change of mind-sets and the conceptual development of new practice requires creative collaboration among group members.

Referring to Vygotsky (1978), who described learning on an individual level, Engeström (2001) characterized the developmental process of an activity, in other words expansive learning, as a "collective journey through the zone of proximal development" (p. 137). This zone is the distance between the actual developmental level as determined by independent problem solving and the level of potential development as determined through problem solving under guidance, or in collaboration with more capable peers (Engeström, 1987; Engeström & Sannino, 2010; Vygotsky, 1978). Based on this premise, Vygotsky (1978, 1997) conceptualized the notion of *double stimulation,* which has strongly influenced interventionist methodology in activity theory (Sannino, 2011) and leads to expansion in the sense of the zone of proximal development. Instead of merely assigning a task to the learner to be solved, he provided both a demanding task, also called *first stimulus,* and a neutral or ambiguous external artifact as a *second stimulus.* Thus, the subject could fill the task with meaning and turn it into a new mediating sign that would enhance his or her actions, and potentially lead to reframing of the task (Engeström & Sannino, 2010). Therefore, challenging tasks on the one hand, and artifacts on the other, play important roles within the developmental process. In a collective learning process, a challenging task (first stimulus) could be the explication of particularities of the existing work situation. Building blocks or other tool kits could, therefore, be used as a second stimulus for model creation.

Vytgotsky's methodological principle of double stimulation leads to a concept for designing developmental projects that can be used as a blueprint for the above-mentioned tool kit-based modeling process. In line with Engeström (2011), we summarize this as follows:

Starting point: The subjects face a problematic and contradictory challenge; the contents are not known ahead of time.

Process: The content and course of the project or intervention are subject to negotiation.

Outcome: The aim is to generate something new (e.g., new concept) that may be used in other settings as frames for the design of locally appropriate new solutions.

Facilitator's role: The researcher or facilitator aims at provoking and sustaining an expansive transformation process led and owned by the practitioners.

The above-described principles of learning and development of double stimulation provide a conceptual basis for collective tool kit-based modeling.

Tool Kit-Based Modeling

Originating mainly in graphical and industrial design, idea creation by representational modeling has been a common practice for some time (Best,

2006; Cross, 1999, 2011). Sketching, cardboard modeling, and sculpting are frequently applied methods. Within a discipline whose members are experienced in applying a certain method (e.g., designers producing sketches), using idea creation can be easy and very efficient. Within a heterogeneous group originating from different professions, and with participants of different skills, applying such methods can, however, prove to be time-consuming and produce an unsatisfying imbalance in the quality of solutions (Lee, 2008). This problem has become more obvious since representational modeling was transferred from design to more abstract fields of application such as business strategy or organizational change (Brown, 2009). Case users and nondesign experienced practitioners are asked to contribute to the learning and development process. Methods used for modeling should be easy to handle and suited to providing high informative value. Accordingly building bricks, cardboard, geometrical shapes, symbolic characters, or icons are appropriate tool kits, because they are simple to use and meaning is generated easily (Sanders & Stappers, 2008).

Based on a conceptual formulation, the tool kits are used to build physical models that are subsequently verbally explained by the creator, by way of storytelling. Through such storytelling, model builders make sense of their individual assumptions as well as of the social dynamics in the learning processes. The stories are important parts in the production, reproduction, transformation, and deconstruction of beliefs, understandings, and assumptions (Boje, 1991). The model building and its explanation can be individual or collective, and adapted to the task, whether of abstract or concrete nature. The physical building of models is therefore only a "metaphor for meaning" (Heracleous & Jacobs, 2011). The meanings are transported through the story that is told by the creator of the metaphor (Roos et al., 2004, see also Orr, 1996, 2006). Such meaning can easily be grasped by the other participants; as a consequence, feedback should naturally arise. Hence, meanings are created and expressed through a manifest representation, the physical model created with a tool kit, and the volatile one that is the story about the model. The entire meaning of the model requires both steps: a process of building and verbal explanation (Lektorsky, 2009; Polanyi, 1969).

The tool kit-based modeling is considered to be a successful methodology at early stages of development processes in particular (Sanders & Stappers, 2008). It necessarily relies on full participation from all concerned. The outcome of the creative process is based on the reification of ideas through the model, its verbal explication, and subsequently its reflexive development.

Serious Play as a Creative Modeling Process

The use of tool kits does not necessarily imply creativity; tool kits may, for example, merely help to explain an issue. However, when the tool kit is used for intuitive modeling, the processes set in motion may be described as creative and akin to *playful interaction*. The creator is immersed in applying the given tools to build a model. Because this playful action has an objective and is goal-oriented, it is referred to as *serious play* (Roos et al., 2004; Statler, Roos, & Victor, 2009). To bring about creative solutions, serious play by way of tool kits invites the users to "think with the hands" (Roos & Victor, 1999). The basic assumption of serious play, according to Polanyi's (1969) idea of tacit integration, is that possible answers are already present in the minds of the creators without them being conscious of such interplay. Hence, the answers come through an intense and intuitive interaction between tool kit and creator, motivated through the task itself (Csikszentmihalyi, 1990). Such intuitive practice is characterized through unawareness and improvisation in acting. In contrast to a conscious composition of the model, serious play is an improvisation (Fisher & Amabile, 2009) where the creator develops the model intuitively inspired by the hands-on interaction with the tool kit and bears in mind the given task.

According to Vygotsky (1976) *play* is a dynamic and complex activity that represents an interactive social form of embodied imagination, in turn generating complex symbolic constructions and the production of collectively shared knowledge (John-Steiner, Connery, & Marjanovic-Shane, 2010). Play can be seen as a creative action of adapting and developing new skills (Brown, 2010). Considering play at the work place and in organizational development processes, the term *serious* is emphasized because it serves a purpose and necessarily follows rules and agreements among the participants. However, the term serious also indicates somewhat a paradox, because the playfulness is accompanied by a general motive: the intention provided (Heracleous & Jacobs, 2011; Statler et al., 2011). The concept of serious play can be of individual and collective nature. It can give way to a process of playing and self-reflection with certain limits, often with a restricted playtime. It can also be a collective process, as playful interaction inspired by parallel building and subsequent exchange with others. Serious play as idea creation requires a physical tool kit because the interaction or communication with the object of creation needs to be set up. Without the reification of ideas in a physical model, the outcomes of the playful improvisation could not be maintained and would be lost for reflection and further development.

The serious play method also bears in mind the important role of *imagination* for learning. Following Vygotsky (2004), imagination is located at the core of learning and development and originates within social interactions (John-Steiner et al., 2010). Imagination becomes the means by which a person's experience is broadened, because he or she can imagine what he or she has not seen and can conceptualize something from another person's narration and description of what he or she him- or herself never directly experienced (Vygotsky, 2004). Creative imagination is especially fostered by serious play because participants are invited to think beyond their existing assumptions to combine, recombine, or develop items or concepts.

LEGO Serious Play: Tool Kit-Based Modeling to Promote Collective Creativity

Vygotsky (2004) emphasized the role of *social interaction* for learning and development as well for creativity. He criticized that, traditionally, creativity has been studied as an individual process, as a result of predisposition, talent, and apprenticeship of individuals (Vygotsky, 1971). However, Vygotsky highlighted the dialectical relationship between the individual and his or her world (John-Steiner et al., 2010). Creativity has indeed a collective dimension. This can be grasped through tool kit-based serious play that enables collective exchange in a playful manner through different stages.

The so-called LEGO Serious Play uses LEGO bricks as artifacts for modeling. LEGO Serious Play was developed in the mid-1990s as a specific in-company executive education program in the LEGO company (Roos et al., 2004). It integrates the elements of tool kit-based modeling and the principle of serious play; metaphors and models are manually built with LEGO bricks and verbally explained afterward. It can, therefore, be considered as a creative improvisation of the builder (Fisher & Amabile, 2009). The serious play method using LEGO bricks benefits furthermore from the building part of playing. Knowledge is gained through building something. Learning is fostered when participants actively construct brick models (Papert & Harel, 1991). The relationship between hand and brain coordination (Jensen, 2005) can be seen as a central principle. Through the "think through the hands" principle (LEGO Serious Play facilitator manual), spontaneous creative acting is enabled and models open up perspectives that go beyond those attained by merely mental processing. The characteristics of LEGO building blocks enable an easy modeling process without specific craft capabilities required. Furthermore, the playful interaction is fostered through the possibility of quick connection, release, and reconnection of the material.

Applying LEGO Serious Play in a development and learning workshop may include the following basic elements of individual and collective model building:

1. Basic modeling to become familiar with the method and topic: Models are created by each participant and the meaning of the metaphors is explained to the others. The individual model creation includes the following steps:
    (a) Posing the question: The participants are challenged by a question that should have no obvious or easy solution. This challenge can be seen as the first stimulus in the sense of Vygotsky (1978).

(b) Designing a model: The participants make sense of what they know and what they can imagine by constructing a model using LEGO bricks and materials. The bricks are the second stimulus in the sense of Vygotsky (1978).

(c) Explicating and sharing: The participants conceive a story covering the meaning in the model. The stories are shared between the participants. At this stage, contradictions within the model and between participants may appear.

(d) Reflecting: As a way of internalizing and grounding the story, reflection upon what was heard or seen in the model is encouraged.

2. Concrete model building based on a workshop task: Each participant builds a complex model representing an artifact, a process, or an abstract concept that is subsequently explained to the others following the above steps.

3. Model connecting: The individual models are connected to a shared one in which the participants consolidate or negotiate their individual mock-ups into one collective model. The shared model must represent the diverse perspectives of all participants. Contradictions are to be solved collectively. In this last stage, the participants explain the collective model.

Playful modeling using LEGO blocks as a tool kit allows for creativity and collectivity from different points of view:

(a) The playful improvisation of the creator is involved in developing the model and in bringing about meaning while explaining the model.

(b) The metaphor told by the creator inspires the storytelling and subsequent modeling steps of the other creators.

(c) LEGO blocks allow groups to connect individually by building models to create a collective one, allowing for adjustment and modifications along the way. Such manual and verbal interaction combined with the challenge of optimizing collectivity and diversity inspire participants to develop further ideas.

Applying LEGO Serious Play, therefore, follows a choreography which, in most cases, includes the above main elements adapted to the group requirements and task. The process needs to be supported by a facilitator who guides the participant through the process and follows a workshop specific *roadmap* outlining the development of the task, time management, and reflection, all of which are predesigned. Therefore, the framework of creative activity is designed for serious play, whereas the activity itself is subject to improvisation, through playful interaction (see also Fisher & Amabile, 2009).

The serious play method using LEGO can prove to be a powerful methodology facilitating the expansive development of individuals, groups, and organizations. The above-described principles of double stimulation can be seen as a blueprint for serious play. In a LEGO Serious Play setting, a challenging task (first stimulus) could be the explication of particularities of the existing work situation or the development of a future vision of something. Building blocks are used as a second stimulus for model creation. These models are metaphors for meaning that help to clarify different understandings within a community, as well as enable a common understanding between the members. Moreover, the participants engage in modeling with their hands, construing metaphors and stories, thus developing their creative potential.

The application of LEGO Serious Play in learning and development processes is described in the following. We discuss in depth one LEGO Serious Play workshop; however, our conclusions are based on a number of applications carried out in university, industry, and public administration settings.

CASE STUDY: CONCEPTION OF A FUTURE ORGANIZATION FOR A RESEARCH INSTITUTE

In the following, we refer to an example from a work context in which LEGO Serious Play was applied in a one-day workshop as part of a larger research program of a research institute. The research institute is in the field of product development and design and is affiliated to a traditional university in Germany with a total of about 4,000 employees. Researchers carry out basic as well as applied research and product development for public and private partners. At the time of the research project in question, around 50 people worked directly in the institute. The workload of these researchers differed greatly. Often freelancers were employed to assist the researchers. On the one hand, the project characteristics strongly depended on the actual needs of the customers or requirements of the applied research projects. And on the other hand, there were specific general trends and basic developments in the fields in which the institute had vested interests, and consequently pursued research activities. Hence, a future vision had to be developed to more efficiently assist the research institute in coping with emerging challenges.

Requirements for the vision development process included the integration of team members from different disciplines and also partially external cooperation partners. Furthermore, creative ideas were to be encouraged and integrated in a shared vision that ultimately was to represent general directions rather than concrete concepts. Mutual inspiration through discussing views from different angles was one of the main requirements of the institute. The goal was to develop and explicate a vision by the end of the one-day workshop.

Design and Analysis of the LEGO Serious Play Workshop

LEGO Serious Play was chosen as the method. There was no systematic activity prior to the workshop, but the research group leaders had been discussing future strategies for some time. According to the above principles of playful modeling and explaining the models to others, the workshop was designed around the tasks to be carried out and divided in two sections. At the beginning, the existing research world was represented, following which a future world was designed. Both were connected with principles on how to move from the now to the future. Initially, the goal was pursued to reify understandings and views, whilst in the second part a new model was developed. Participants were not informed of the subsequent tasks in advance. The two workshop sections were organized as follows:

(1) Reifying the existing world

Individually:

(a) Creating and explaining basic metaphors about ideal research work.
(b) Creating and explaining a model of the existing research institute.

Collectively:

(c) Connecting the individual models to form a shared one of the existing research institute.
(d) Supplementing the shared institute model with main agents influencing work in the institute.

(2) Developing a future model of the research institute

Individually:

(e) Creating a model of the future research institute.

Collectively:

(f) Connecting the individual future models to a shared vision of the research institute.
(g) Transferring and modifying the influencing agents from the existing to the future model.
(h) Developing guiding principles on how the transformation process could be carried out.

The workshop was facilitated by two researchers experienced in applying LEGO Serious Play. The participant's group of 10 people included engineers, industrial designers, business administrators, an architect, and a psychologist.

Observations, photo and video analysis, were used as research methods and carried out by an additional researcher. Results were documented using an observation manual. The process of modeling, learning, and development was investigated. The following findings refer directly to the workshop. No further study about the diffusion of workshop results in operational practice has been carried out to date. With regard to collective creativity and learning, the following processes were analyzed:

1. Generation of a collective understanding among participants.
2. Development, explication, and reflection of the individual models.
3. Connecting the individual results especially with regards to dealing with different views and contradictions, and how views develop.
4. Collaboration and mutual influence of participants with regard to the development of models.

Outcomes

After an introduction on methodology, participants quickly developed metaphors about their picture of an ideal workplace. The focus was on how to handle the tool kit and fulfill the task rather than deeply discuss the outcomes. Results represented a variety of different views about work. The metaphor was modified, and in the subsequent step, each participant individually developed a model depicting how he or she perceived the existing research institute. This task was more complex and the models far more elaborate. At this point, a playful interaction with the tool kit took place. Participants acted upon intuition in contrast to their previous rule-based behavior in the initial stage. Moreover, the stories told at this stage had a more emerging character than those told initially. The individual models were discussed intensively; however, the discussions were of an explanatory and less inquiring nature. Figure 9.1 displays individual models.

Figure 9.1 Individual model representing the current situation of the research institute.

Subsequently, it was required that the individual models merge to form a collectively shared model. Participants began to simply group the models around each other. After an intervention of the facilitator, they started to connect them closely. The whole process of building a shared model involved discussion and negotiation. The task to integrate all views led to an intense discussion over which models were comparable and whether they all had to be recognized. Through modifying size, position, and shape of the individual models, the group tried to solve contradictions. The group considered it as a challenge to integrate, on the one hand, all the different viewpoints and, on the other, to end up with an agreed collective solution. The overall design represented an integrated model rather distant from the individual ones. For the outside observer, the individual models could hardly be identifiable within the shared model. However, all the group members felt represented by the final model. The model acquired its real value through the telling of the story by participants. Through the explanation, some remaining contradictions could be solved by verbally putting the model characteristics into perspective. The storytelling was a collective process where several participants completed the statements of the one person taking the lead. The model was supplemented by agents outside of the organizational boundaries who exerted an influence on the institute. The agents were briefed on the exercise and connected with the model. In Figure 9.2, the existing model is represented including the connected agents.

Participants commented that they had never seen their institute in such a comprehensive and multifaceted light before. They also stated that the model reifies the actual situation integrating various perspectives.

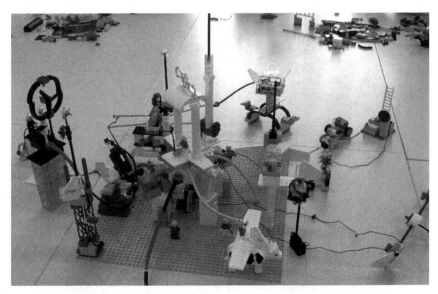

Figure 9.2   Shared model representing the current status of the research institute.

In the following action, the process of individual modeling was repeated with the task of designing a future model of the research institute. The modeling process was characterized through a more goal-oriented focus; the models themselves are elaborate in design and the stories more complex. The reflection of the group at this stage was far more intense than at the earlier stage with regards to questioning the contents of the models.

The physical model quality, in terms of design, differed between the participants as well as the quality of the explanations. In sum, however, the explanatory value of the models did not differ significantly. Especially for the design of future visions, participants allowed themselves to be inspired by the models of others as well as via explanations. When participants were asked personally about their models right after finishing them, they explained them in a much more simple way than they were to do at the later stage.

The fusion of the *future vision* models to build a shared one went more smoothly but followed the same pattern as when developing the current situation. Diversity, however, was evident in the dimension and the horizon of the vision. Because some participants tended to modify the current situation, others developed entirely new tasks or organizational principles. Hence, the shared model included different stages of development. The future vision was completed with modified agents and finally with principles on how to follow the path from reality to future. Figure 9.3 shows the future vision of the model including the agents.

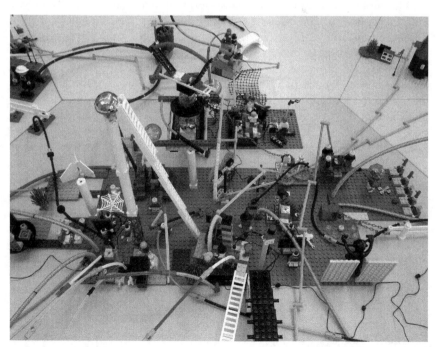

Figure 9.3 Shared model representing the future status of the research institute.

DISCUSSION

Combining serious play with the tool kit was considered as one of the key aspects in the creative process. Intuitive playfulness could, however, not be recognized right from the beginning of the workshop. The first steps in using the tool kit to fulfill the given task were of rule-based and conscious nature (Dreyfus & Dreyfus, 2005). Playful behavior of the participants emerged out of the process as the participants gained experience on how to use the tool kit (Dreyfus & Dreyfus, 2005). The participants were motivated through the challenging nature of the task itself. The abstraction and variety in forms and colors of the LEGO blocks further led to a stimulating interaction between the tool kit and the builder (Csikszentmihalyi, 1990; Vygotsky, 1978) with the models gaining in quality over time. The modeling process, however, was not restricted to the manual building but also included the explanation of the model that evolved by way of intuitive and spontaneous developmental action (see also Orr, 1996). The LEGO Serious Play principle also included a methodological switch. Whereas individual model creation was characterized by an intuitive and playful mode (Roos et al., 2004), the assembling of a shared model followed a conscious process of negotiating and working out contradictions (Engeström, 2011).

Based on Vygotsky's (1978) principle of double stimulation and Engeström's (2011) conceptualization of developmental project design, the LEGO Serious Play workshop spontaneously challenges participants with problematic tasks and contradictive issues. Outcomes represent novel ideas and concepts that can be used to frame further action. Essential in this process is the facilitator's role as supporter, process guide, and provoker within the workshop. LEGO Serious Play itself can be seen as a creative tool. Using it in a workshop requires a clear choreography of subsequent steps carefully planned in advance according to the object of the workshop. Therefore the tool LEGO Serious Play itself is of compositional nature. The participants are, however, unaware of the subsequent workshop steps and tasks; they are motivated to act spontaneously and intuitively. Hence, participants' activity is characterized through improvisation. An LEGO Serious Play workshop, therefore, integrates two aspects of creative behavior: the facilitator's contribution of *composition* and the participant's contribution of *improvisation* (Amabile, 1996; Fisher & Amabile, 2009).

As the case study example shows, the first steps include designing a model of the current situation that leads to sharing understandings and resolving contradictions due to different perspectives (Baitsch, 1993; John-Steiner et al., 2010; Schulz, 2008). The *shared model*, however, is not a merge toward one perspective; it represents commonality and diversity at the same time. At this point in particular, the LEGO tool kit shows its added valued through the ability to flexibly connect and release all kinds of blocks as desired. Furthermore, the models of the current situation (individual and shared) not only support the emergence of a shared understanding but also represent the world of the participants in a way they have not previously seen and therefore act as a stimulus for creative development. For the current situation, the models develop largely through a creative process and therefore represent creative ideas.

The LEGO Serious Play workshop as a whole is an example of collective creativity and development. The very design and explanation of the individual models inspires the other participants. Ideas are considered; explanations are objects of reflection and discussion. Most particularly, the step from the individual model to a shared one is a collective process characterized by a bundle of emerging contradictions that need to be solved. The goal can only be reached through spontaneous and creative adaption, modification, and integration of the single models, a characteristic for team creativity (Vera & Crossan, 2005). Specific value in the LEGO Serious Play process lies in the fact that each participant is recognized in almost the same way. Artistic skills may improve the sophistication of the brick model, but they do not influence the explanatory quality of the model-story combination. As a consequence, building brick-based serious play is a method in overcoming hierarchical and skill differences. Therefore, each person's potential creativity is taken into account.

Considering learning, the example shows that the participants explicate their current views through the model, making it understandable for others. Through such process and through the connection of the individual models with the task to build a shared view or vision, contradictions emerge and are discussed intensively. Concerning the explication of contradictions, three phenomena should be distinguished: First, contradictions are consciously represented through the model; second, the creator becomes aware of contradictions when explaining the model; and third, contradictions are exposed within the group through the comparing of models and stories. Because both manual construction and verbal expression are used, different skills are brought into play. Hence, the stimulation takes place individually both through the dialogue with the serious play tool kit and the succeeding explication. Collectively, the shared storytelling and the model reflection stimulates further building action. This is, however, only successful if participants fully engage with the method and the tool kit, and also if they consider the model to be a real representation of their understandings.

In the described process, it can be observed that participants developed the capacity for broadening their viewpoints. Through discussing a shared model, exchanging points of view, they engaged in the active process of negotiation. The design of a shared model, in our example the future vision of the research institute, can be seen as a process of developing new activity (Engeström, 2001, 2005), albeit on a very abstract level. With the use of LEGO Serious Play as tool kit-based modeling, expansive learning is likely to take place. However, observations also indicate that the emergence of expansive learning is subject to the composition of the workshop and the support within the process that needs to be of a challenging nature.

CONCLUSION

In this article, we discussed how tool kit-based serious play as a method of collective creativity can facilitate learning and potentially expansive development (Engeström, 1987, 2001; Engeström & Sannino, 2010). We referred to the principles of tool kit-based modeling (Cross, 1999, 2011; Sanders & Stappers, 2008) and serious play (Heracleous & Jacobs, 2011; Roos et al., 2004; Statler et al., 2011) as a method of intuitive and task motivated idea development (Csikszentmihalyi, 1990).

The combination of manual playful design with verbal explanation enables creative outputs. The LEGO tool kit we chose provides the opportunity for abstract design that is easy to combine, release, and recombine without any preknowledge required from the applicant. The LEGO tool kit is of course limited due to the very characteristics of the material, which is hard, colorful, and geometric. Therefore, the principle of serious play may be applied with any other tool kits; the facilitators should, however, take into account the prerequisites of the group and intention of the process. One central benefit, in using fixable building blocks like LEGO, lies in the ability to further combine them to shared models. This opens up rich perspectives for discussion on collective aspects and for negotiating points of views and addressing emerging contradictions.

Physical modeling in a modus of serious play, evident also in other cases of ours, addresses collective creativity and the activity of learning. Although some tasks were individual, the subsequent exchange and the mutual inspiration lead to creative behavior and learning. In these processes, contradictions emerge and are solved through discussion and modeling. Collective creativity culminates in the development of a shared model, which integrates inspiration, discussion, connection, and modification. Such collectively creative processes are likely to change mind-sets and to lead to learning as a developmental activity (Engeström, 2001; Engeström & Sannino, 2010).

Collective creativity in our case is a result of the tool kit, storytelling, facilitation process, and spontaneous interaction between participants. Inspiration and creativity, therefore, not only are restricted to the guided modeling process, but are a general attitude that emerges from a serious play workshop and include various kinds of discussion and creation, also discussion and creation that go beyond the intended model building.

The tool kit-based modeling in serious play can be particularly successful at early stages of development processes (Sanders & Stappers, 2008), where thinking is metaphorical and ideas need to be created. The abstraction of the tool kit allows focusing on an intuitive interaction between model and creator. The more concrete the tasks are, the more participants focus on the model design and less on the creation of metaphors; an aspect that preempts the easy and prerequisite free use of the tool kit. Especially at later stages of development processes, the limitations of the LEGO tool kit become evident. Indeed, if design details, material properties, structures, or impressions of spaces are objects of consideration, other methodologies and skills are required.

REFERENCES

Amabile, T. M. (1996). *Creativity in context*. Boulder, CO: Westview Press.
Baitsch, C. (1993). *Was bewegt organisationen? Selbstorganisation aus psychologischer perspektive* [What drives organizations? Self-organization from a psychological perspective]. Frankfurt, Germany: Campus-Verlag.
Bateson, G. (1972). *Steps to an ecology of mind*. New York, NY: Ballantine Books.
Best, K. (2006). *Design management: Managing design strategy, process and implementation*. Lausanne, Switzerland: AVA Academia.
Boje, D. M. (1991). Organizations as storytelling networks: A study of story performance in an office-supply firm. *Administrative Science Quarterly, 36*, 106–126.
Brown, T. (2009). *Change by design. How design thinking transforms organizations and in-spires innovation*. New York, NY: HarperCollins.
Brown, S. (2010). *Play: How it shapes the brain, opens the imagination, and invigorates the soul*. New York, NY: Penguin.
Chaiklin, S., Hedegaard, M., & Jensen, U. (Eds.). (1999). *Activity theory and social practice: Cultural-historical approaches*. Aarhus, Denmark: Aarhus University Press.
Chesbrough, H. (2003). *Open innovation: The new imperative for creating and profiting from technology*. Boston, MA: Harvard Business School Press.
Cropley, A. J. (2006). In praise of convergent thinking. *Creativity Research Journal, 18*, 391–404.
Cross, N. (1999). Natural intelligence in design. *Design Studies, 20*(1), 25–39.
Cross, N. (2011). *Design thinking: Understanding how designers think and work*. Oxford, England: Berg Publishers.
Csikszentmihalyi, M. (1990). *Flow: The psychology of optimal experience*. New York, NY: Harper & Row.
Dreyfus, H., & Dreyfus, S. (2005). Expertise in real world contexts. *Organization Studies, 26*(5), 779–792.
Engeström, Y. (1987). *Learning by expanding*. Helsinki, Finland: Orienta-Konsultit.
Engeström, Y. (2001). Expansive learning at work: Towards an activity theoretical reconceptualization. *Journal of Education and Work, 14*(1), 133–156.
Engeström, Y. (2005). *Developmental work research: Expanding activity theory in practice*. Berlin, Germany: Lehmanns Media.
Engeström, Y. (2011). From design experiments to formative interventions. *Theory & Psychology, 21*, 598–628.
Engeström, Y., & Sannino, A. (2010). Studies of expansive learning: Foundations, findings and future challenges. *Educational Research Review, 5*(1), 1–24.
Fisher, C., & Amabile, T. M. (2009). Creativity, improvisation and organizations. In T. Rickards, M. Runco, & S. Moger (Eds.), *The Routledge companion to creativity* (pp. 13–24). Abingdon, VA: Routledge.
Heracleous, L., & Jacobs, C. (2011). *Crafting strategy: Embodied metaphors in practice*. Cambridge, England: Cambridge University Press.
Jensen, E. (2005). Teaching with the brain in mind (2nd ed.). Alexandria, VA: ASCD.
John-Steiner, V., Connery, M. C., & Marjanovic-Shane, A. (2010). Dancing with the muses: A cultural-historical approach to play, meaning making and creativity.

In M. C. Connery, V. John-Steiner, & A. Marjanovic-Shane (Eds.), *Vygotsky and creativity: A cultural-historical approach to play, meaning and the arts* (pp. 3–15). New York, NY: Lang.

Lee, Y. (2008). Design participation tactics: The challenges and new roles for designers in the co-design process. *CoDesign, 4*(1), 31–50.

Lektorsky, V. A. (2009). Mediation as a mean of collective activity. In A. Sannino, H. Daniels, & K. D. Gutièrrez (Eds.), *Learning and expanding with activity theory* (pp. 75–87). Cambridge, England: Cambridge University Press.

Lompscher, J. (1999). Learning activity, and its formation: Ascending from the abstract to the concrete. In J. Lompscher & M. Hedegaard (Eds.), *Learning activity and development* (pp. 139–166). Aarhus, Denmark: Aarhus University Press.

Lompscher, J. (2004). *Lernkultur Kompetenzentwicklung aus kulturhistorischer Sicht. Lernen Erwachsener im Arbeitsprozess* [Learning culture and competence development out of a cultural-historical perspective. Adult learning in work processes]. Berlin, Germany: Lehmanns Media.

Orr, J. E. (1996). *Talking about machines: An ethnography of a modern job.* Ithaca, NY: Cornell University Press.

Orr, J. E. (2006). Ten years of talking about machines. *Organization Studies, 27*(12), 1805–1820.

Papert, S., & Harel, I. (1991). *Constructionism.* New York, NY: Ablex Publishing Corporation.

Polanyi, M. (1969). *Knowing and being.* London, England: Routledge.

Reed, R., Storrud-Barnes, S., & Jessup, L. (2012). How open innovation affects the drivers of competitive advantage: Trading the benefits of IP creation and ownership for free invention. *Management Decision, 50*(1), 58–73.

Resnick, M., Myers, B., Nakakoji, K., Shneiderman, B., Pausch, R., Selker, T., & Eisenberg, M. (2005). *Design principles for tools to support creative thinking.* Retrieved from http://repository.cmu.edu/isr/816

Roos, J., & Victor, B. (1999). Towards a new model of strategy-making as serious play. *European Management Journal, 17*(4), 348–355.

Roos, J., Victor, B., & Statler, M. (2004). Playing seriously with strategy. *Long Range Planning, 37*, 549–568.

Sanders, E., & Stappers, P. (2008). Co-creation and the new landscapes of design. *CoDesign, 4*(1), 5–18.

Sannino, A. (2011). Activity theory as an activist and interventionist theory. *Theory & Psychology, 21*(5), 571–597.

Sannino, A., Daniels, H., & Gutiérrez, K. D. (2009). Activity theory between historical engagement and future-making practice. In A. Sannino, H. Daniels, & K. D. Gutièrrez (Eds.), *Learning and expanding with activity theory* (pp. 1–15). Cambridge, England: Cambridge University Press.

Sanoff, H. (2000). *Community participation methods in design and planning.* New York, NY: Wiley.

Schulz, K.-P. (2008). Shared knowledge and understandings in organizations: Its development and impact in organizational learning processes. *Management Learning, 39*(4), 457–473.

Sleeswijk Visser, F., Van der Lugt, R., & Stappers, P. J. (2007). Sharing user experiences in the product innovation process: Participatory design needs participatory communication. *Creativity & Inn Man, 16*(1), 35–45.

Statler, M., Heracleous, L., & Jacobs, C. (2011). Serious play as a practice of paradox. *Journal of Applied Behavioral Science, 47*(2), 236–256.

Statler, M., Roos, J., & Victor, B. (2009). Ain't misbehavin': Taking play seriously in organizations. *Journal of Change Management, 9*(1), 87–107.

Vera, D., & Crossan, M. (2005). Improvisation and innovative performance in teams. *Organization Science, 16*, 203–224.

Von Held, F. (2012). *Collective creativity: Exploring creativity in social network development as part of organizational learning.* Berlin, Germany: Springer.

Von Hippel, E. (2006). *Democratizing innovation.* Cambridge, MA: MIT Press.

Vygotsky, L. S. (1971). *The psychology of art.* Cambridge, MA: MIT Press.

Vygotsky, L. S. (1976). Play and its role in the mental development of the child. In J. S. Bruner, A. Jolly, & K. Sylva (Eds.), *Play: Its role in development and evolution* (pp. 537–554). New York, NY: Penguin Books.

Vygotsky, L. S. (1978). *Mind in society: The development of higher psychological processes.* Cambridge, MA: Harvard University Press.

Vygotsky, L. S. (1997). The history of the development of higher mental functions. In R. W. Rieber (Ed.), *The collected works of L. S. Vygotsky: The history of the development of higher mental functions* (Vol. 4, pp. 1–251). New York, NY: Plenum.

Vygotsky, L. S. (2004). Imagination and creativity in childhood. *Journal of Russian and Eastern European Psychology, 42*(1), 7–97.

West, M. (2002). Sparkling fountains or stagnant ponds: An integrative model of creativity and innovation implementation in work groups. *Applied Psychology: An International Review, 51*(3), 355–424.

West, M., & Farr, J. (1990). *Innovation and creativity at work: Psychological and organizational strategies.* Chichester, England: Wiley.

10 Learning, Social Creativity, and Cultures of Participation

Gerhard Fischer

Most interesting design problems are systemic, ill-defined, and unique. Systemic problems require stakeholders from different disciplines; ill-defined problems require that the owners of problems are involved, because these problems can not be delegated, and unique problems require learning and the construction of new knowledge.

Over the last two decades, the research and education activities in our Center for Lifelong Learning and Design at the University of Colorado, Boulder have been focused on three major objectives: (1) to make learning a part of life; (2) to engage in design of sociotechnical environments in different application areas; and (3) to explore and exploit the power of new media in these contexts. Our methodology was grounded in the aspiration to do "basic research on real problems." Learning and creativity research in such contexts is fundamentally different from traditional research in these areas. Traditionally learning is focused on schools and formal learning environments, conceptualized by a transmission model in which the students learn what the teacher knows (Engeström, 2001). Traditionally, creativity is analyzed in the context of well-defined problems that may require nonstandard and nonobvious solution methods, a prominent example being the nine-dot problems (Sternberg, 1999).

This article first describes components of our evolving conceptual framework relating learning, creativity, and cultures of participation. It then describes *sociotechnical environments* addressing different societal challenges grounded in the conceptual framework. It concludes by articulating implications for future developments by exploring the unique synergy between learning, creativity, and cultures of participation.

A CONCEPTUAL FRAMEWORK FOR EXPLORING RELATIONSHIPS BETWEEN LEARNING, SOCIAL CREATIVITY, AND CULTURES OF PARTICIPATION

Most interesting and important societal problems of today are complex systemic problems that require more knowledge than any single person can possess (Arias, Eden, Fischer, Gorman, & Scharff, 2000). In addition, design problems are unique, requiring new aspects to be explored. Social creativity and cultures of participation offer important and interesting possibilities to cope with major problems our societies are facing today. These problems include the following:

1. Problems for which expertise and knowledge is widely distributed (e.g., synthesizing the knowledge about the topic, Creativity and Information Technology, in the CreativeIT Wiki).
2. Problems of a *magnitude* such that individuals and even large teams cannot solve (e.g., modeling all buildings in the world in three-dimensional as addressed by Google SketchUp and 3D Warehouse).
3. Problems of a *systemic nature* requiring the collaboration of many different minds from a variety of backgrounds (e.g., urban planning problems as addressed by the Envisionment and Discovery Collaboratory).
4. Problems supporting participation as a *community of learners* (e.g., courses-as-seeds engaging learners to become active contributors).

Most current practices and research activities about learning are focused on formal learning environments (schools and universities), and they are dominated by a transmission model in which the teacher "knows the answer," and the students should learn what the teacher knows. But in the problem domain explored by our research, these assumptions do not hold, and the fundamental challenges can be characterized as follows:

In important transformations of our personal lives and organizational practices, we must learn new forms of activity which are not there yet. They are literally learned as they are being created. There is no competent teacher. Standard learning theories have little to offer if one wants to understand these processes. (Engeström, 2001, p. 138)

Coping with problems where the answer is not known requires learning from each other and synthesizing new knowledge creatively by bringing different views and experiences together and exploiting the "symmetry of ignorance" as a source of creativity (Fischer, Ehn, Engeström, & Virkkunen, 2002).

Creativity is often associated with ideas and discoveries that are fundamentally novel with respect to the whole of human history (*historical creativity*). Creativity, however, also happens daily in real problem-solving activities, and not only in research labs or art studios as exceptional events. We are primarily concerned here with ideas and discoveries in everyday work practices that are novel with respect to an individual human mind or social community (*psychological creativity*; Boden, 1991)—a capacity inherent to varying degrees in all people and needed in most problem-solving situations.

Analyzing the contributions of outstanding creative people (Gardner, 1993) helps to establish a framework for creativity, but understanding creativity in the context of everyday activities is equally important for people to create better work products. The analysis of everyday design practices (Rogoff & Lave, 1984) has shown that knowledge workers and designers have to engage in creative activities to cope with the unforeseen complexities of real-world tasks.

The power of the unaided individual mind is highly overrated (John-Steiner, 2000; Salomon, 1993). As argued above, although creative individuals (Gardner, 1995; Sternberg, 1988) are often thought of as working in isolation, much of our intelligence and creativity results from interaction and collaboration with other individuals (Csikszentmihalyi & Sawyer, 1995). Creative activity grows out of the relationship between an individual and the world of his or her work, as well as from the ties between an individual and other human beings (Fischer, Nakakoji, Ostwald, Stahl, & Sumner, 1998; Gardner, 1995). Much human creativity arises from activities that take place in a social context in which interactions with other people and the artifacts that embody group knowledge are important contributors to the process. Creativity does not happen inside a person's head but in the interaction between a person's thoughts and a sociocultural context (Engeström, 2001).

To support social creativity, situations need to be sufficiently open-ended and complex that users will encounter new, unpredictable conditions and will eventually experience breakdowns (Schön, 1983). As any professional designer knows, breakdowns—although at times costly and painful—offer unique opportunities for reflection and learning, underscoring the importance of the back-talk of situations (Fischer et al., 1998).

Cultures are defined in part by their media and their tools for thinking, working, learning, and collaborating. In the past, the design of most media emphasized a clear distinction between producers and consumers (Benkler, 2006). Television is the medium that most obviously exhibits this orientation and has contributed to the degeneration of humans into *couch potatoes* (Fischer, 2002) for whom remote controls are the most important instruments of their cognitive activities. In a similar manner, our current educational institutions often treat learners as consumers, fostering a mind-set in students of consumerism rather than ownership of problems for the rest of their lives. As a result, learners, workers, and citizens often feel left out of decisions by teachers, managers, and policymakers, denying them opportunities to take active roles.

The rise in *social computing* represents unique and fundamental opportunities, challenges, and transformative changes for innovative research and practice in supporting *cultures of participation* (Fischer, 2011; Jenkins, 2009) as we move away from a world in which a small number of people define rules, create artifacts, and make decisions for many consumers toward a world in which everyone has interests and possibilities to actively participate. In cultures of participation, not every participant must contribute, but all participants must have opportunities to contribute when they want to. For cultures of participation to become viable and be successful, it is critical that a sufficient number of participants take on the more active and more demanding roles. To encourage and support *migration paths toward more demanding roles,* mechanisms are needed that lead to more involvement and motivation, and facilitate the acquisition of the additional knowledge required by the more demanding and involved roles (Porter, 2008; Preece & Shneiderman, 2009).

Where do new ideas come from in cultures of participation? The creativity potential is grounded in user-driven innovations supported by *metadesign environments,* in taking advantage of *breakdowns* as sources for creativity and in exploiting the *symmetry of ignorance*-meaning that all stakeholders are knowledgeable in some domains and ignorant in others (Arias et al., 2000). To increase the creativity potential, cultures of participation requires *diversity, independence, decentralization,* and *aggregation.* Each participant should have some unique information or perspective (*diversity*). Participants' opinions are not determined by the opinions of those around them (*independence*). Participants are able to specialize and draw on local knowledge (*decentralization*). Mechanisms exist for turning individual contributions into collections and private judgments into collective decisions (*aggregation*). In addition, participants must be able to express themselves, requiring technical knowledge how to contribute; they must be willing to contribute and must be allowed to have their voices heard.

Cultures of participation are related to other conceptual frameworks, specifically to *communities of practice* (Lave, 1991; Wenger, 1998) and *expansive learning* (Engeström, 2001; Engeström & Sannino, 2010). Cultures of participation complement and transcend communities of practice with their focus to exploit the creativity potential of communities of interest (Fischer, 2001) by supporting the integration of multidimensional expertise. They address new frontiers for expansive learning as postulated by Engeström:

> Perhaps the biggest challenge for future studies and theorizing in expansive learning comes from the emergence of what is commonly characterized as social production or peer production. . . . In social production or peer production, activities take the shape of expansive swarming and multidirectional pulsation, with emphasis on sideways transitions and boundary-crossing. (Engeström & Sannino, 2010, p. 21)

Social creativity and cultures of participation require *active contributors*—people acting as designers in personally meaningful activities—not just consumers (Fischer, 2002). The necessity of involving and empowering users and allowing them to act as designers requires the expansion of the creative process from the individual to the group (National Research

Council, 2003). The sharing of products of individual creativity enables other people to work on them as a continuous activity without repeating unnecessary work. For example, the open source movement (Raymond & Young, 2001) demonstrates that the sharing of source code makes it possible for others to go forward when the original developers stop for various reasons, such as loss of interest or lack of time or new ideas.

Metadesign (Fischer & Giaccardi, 2006) is focused on "design for designers." Metadesigners create the social and technical prerequisites for cultures of participation by sharing control over the design process among all stakeholders. Users are empowered with opportunities, tools, and social rewards to extend a system to fit their needs, rather than being forced to use closed systems designed beforehand by software engineers. As owners of problems, users can be active contributors engaged in creating knowledge rather than passive consumers restricted to the consumption of existing knowledge.

Existing design methodologies are insufficient to cope with the emergence of situated and unintended requirements (Suchman, 1987; Winograd & Flores, 1986). Sociotechnical environments for which the design does not end at the time of deployment and whose success hinges on continued user participation (Henderson & Kyng, 1991) are needed. Metadesign (1) *extends boundaries* by supporting users as active contributors who can transcend the functionality and content of existing systems in *personally meaningful activities*; (2) creates artifacts that can be subjected to critical reflection and open to adjustment and tweaking; (3) supports unintended and subversive uses (not just anticipated ones); (4) allows learners to engage in personally meaningful activities; and (5) distributes *control* among all stakeholders in design processes.

Social creativity and cultures of participation thrives on the diversity of perspectives by making all voices heard. They require constructive dialogs between individuals negotiating their differences while creating their shared voice and vision. In the following, I shall describe the need for multiple voices by exploring different dimensions of diversity and distances (Fischer, 2005).

Voices from different places: Spatial distance. Bringing spatially distributed people together with the support of computer-mediated communication allows the prominent defining feature of a group of people interacting with each other to become shared concerns rather than shared location. It further allows more people to be included, thus exploiting local knowledge. Whereas communication technologies enable profoundly new forms of collaborative work, research has found that closely coupled work can still be difficult to support at a distance (Olson & Olson, 2001). In addition, critical stages of collaborative work, such as establishing mutual trust, appear to require some level of face-to-face interaction. Brown and Duguid (2000) present a similar argument: "Digital technologies are adept at maintaining communities already formed. They are less good at making them" (p. 226).

Voices from the past: Temporal distance. Design processes often take place over many years, with initial design followed by extended periods of evolution and redesign. The idea of exploiting and building on the voices of the past to enhance social creativity is important not only for software reuse but for our overall cultural heritage. In cultural evolution, there are no mechanisms equivalent to genes and chromosomes (Csikszentmihalyi, 1996). Therefore, new ideas or inventions are not automatically passed on to the next generation, and education becomes a critical challenge to learn from the past (Bruner, 1996). Many creativity researchers have pointed out that the discoveries of many famous people (e.g., Einstein, who could build on the work of Newton) would have been inconceivable without the prior knowledge, without the intellectual and social network that simulated their thinking and without the social mechanisms that recognized and spread their innovations.

Voices from different communities: Conceptual distances. Design communities are social structures that enable groups of people to share knowledge and resources in support of collaborative design. Different communities grow around different types of design practice. Each design community is unique, but for the purposes of this discussion, *communities of practice* and *communities of interest* are differentiated. Communities of practice (Wenger, 1998) consist of practitioners who work as a community in a certain domain undertaking similar work. Examples of communities of practice are architects, urban planners, research groups, software developers, and end users. Communities of practice gain their strength from shared knowledge and experience. However, they face the danger of *group-think* (Janis, 1972): The boundaries of domain-specific ontologies and tools that are empowering to insiders are often barriers for outsiders and newcomers. Communities of interest (Fischer, 2001) bring together stakeholders from different communities of practice to solve a particular (design) problem of common concern. They can be thought of as "communities-of-communities" (Brown & Duguid, 2000). Examples of communities of interest are described in the following section. Fundamental challenges facing communities of interest are found in building a shared understanding (Resnick, Levine, & Teasley, 1991) of the task at hand, which often does not exist at the beginning but is evolved incrementally and collaboratively and emerges in people's minds and in external artifacts. Members of communities of interest must learn to communicate with and learn from others (Engeström, 2001) who have different perspectives and perhaps different vocabularies to describe their ideas and to establish a common ground (Clark & Brennan, 1991).

In a world in which solutions are neither given nor confined in one single mind (Bennis & Biederman, 1997), we need not only new models of collaboration but also effective creativity support tools (Shneiderman, 2007). These tools have the potential (1) to provide time on task by eliminating prerequisite skills and by automating low-level skills (e.g., the use of spelling correctors, compilers, spreadsheets, etc.); (2) to make information relevant to the task at hand (by employing task and user models); (3) to support emerging insights by synthesizing, visualizing, and simulating information from different sources; and (4) to make all voices heard by exploiting the symmetry of ignorance and conceptual collisions.

FOSTERING LEARNING AND SOCIAL CREATIVITY WITH SOCIOTECHNICAL ENVIRONMENTS

Grounded in our conceptual framework described in the previous section, we have developed over the last two decades a variety of sociotechnical environments that are briefly described in this section indicating their contribution to learning, social creativity, and cultures of participation (Shneiderman, 2002). Table 10.1 provides on overview of the sociotechnical environments described in this section.

Table 10.1   Overview of Sociotechnical Environments

Sociotechnical Environment	*Application Domain*	*Creativity Dimension*	*Cultures of Participation*
CreativeIT Wiki	Research community in creativity	Supporting the creations of mind maps, videos, anecdotes, and stories	Engaging the community by supporting processes and activities surrounding the creation of content
SketchUp + 3D-Warehouse + Google Earth	Three-dimensional modeling	Creating unique artifacts and collections	Engaging the talent pool of the whole world
Envisionment and Discovery Collaboratory (EDC)	Urban planning	Supporting communities of interest	Putting owners of problems in charge
Courses-as-Seeds	Communities of learners	Knowledge creating and sharing by learners	Supporting the community of learners

CreativeIT Wiki

Conventional wikis (Tapscott & Williams, 2006) have proven to be usable and useful to support communities, but one of their main limitations is their *lack* of support for different media types as they are applied to research in Creativity and Information Technology as explored and supported by the NSF program CreativeIT (www.nsf.gov/pubs/2007/nsf07562/nsf 07562. htm). A consequence of this limitation is that communities (particularly those not focused on text) have only limited means to describe the research contributions. In our NSF supported research projects (Dick, Eden, & Fischer, 2009), we have explored the following factors in understanding and designing new wikis that can be used to support collaborative design and social creativity:

(1) Wikis have always had the goal of being *open, simple, and low-threshold environments*; this creates the challenge of increasing the expressiveness (the "high ceiling") required for creative activities in a wiki while retaining the low threshold.
(2) Most wikis have been used as *content management systems* in which individual contributions are accumulated; this raises the demand to improve support for dialogue, interpretation, interactions, and reflection.
(3) Current wikis present only the current versions of content, and minority opinions are often lost in the rewriting of wiki items; this creates the challenge of making *minority voices heard* to avoid the pitfall of average mediocre products and ideas (Lanier, 2006).
(4) Many wikis suffer from a lack of participation; they are "systems built but users never come."

We have investigated these requirements in the CreativeIT Wiki (http://swiki.cs.colorado. edu/CreativeIT) serving as a sociotechnical environment supporting the diverse communities interested in creativity and information technology (National Research Council, 2003). Our *assessment studies* have provided indications for the following challenges: (1) current wiki-like environments are limited (we need to analyze and create additional objects such as mind maps, videos, anecdotes, and stories); (2) different modes of interacting with wikis need to be supported (including: face-to-face, virtual, synchronous, and asynchronous activities); and (3) the right balance between supporting more complex interactions and more varied objects and avoiding the loss of a low threshold for participation needs to be found.

A research team at Google in Boulder, CO is working on the objective of having all buildings in the world modeled in three dimensions. Google Earth is being used to explore this virtual three-dimensional world. This desirable objective cannot be achieved solely by a development team at Google due to the sheer amount of work it requires. The team at Google has chosen to create a sociotechnical environment (supporting metadesign and wiki-style environments for sharing artifacts) by integrating SketchUp, 3D Warehouse, and Google Earth to support everyone motivated enough to participate in this effort. This project represents a unique, large-scale example in evaluating the conceptual framework for social creativity and collaborative design.

SketchUp (http://sketchup.google.com/) is an interactive, three-dimensional modeling environment. Although SketchUp is a high-functionality environment with a reasonably low threshold and a high ceiling, developing sophisticated models with SketchUp requires a *nontrivial learning effort*. In order to motivate enough people and make them independent of "high-tech scribes," powerful learning mechanisms for SketchUp are critical to allow everyone who wants to contribute to learn how to do so.

The 3D Warehouse (http://sketchup.google.com/3dwarehouse/) is an information repository for the collection of models created by all users who are willing to share the models they created with SketchUp. The 3D Warehouse contains thousands of models from different domains, including buildings, houses, bridges, sculptures, cars, and people. It supports collection mechanisms to organize models and supports ratings and reviews from community members.

Google Earth has the capability to show three-dimensional objects consisting of users' submissions that were developed using SketchUp. Figure 10.1 shows downtown Denver modeled in three-dimensional and displayed in Google Earth.

Figure 10.1   Downtown Denver modeled in Google Earth using SketchUp.

The assessment of this large-scale effort has shown that extensive support for learning to become a contributor (in this case, to be able to develop models with SketchUp) is critically important to foster a culture of participation. As the 3D Warehouse grows, support is not only needed for the contribution of additional three-dimensional models, but the rich information stores needs to be organized and *new curatorial mechanisms* need to be explored, designed, and implemented.

The Envisionment and Discovery Collaboratory

The Envisionment and Discovery Collaboratory (EDC; Arias et al., 2000) is a long-term research platform exploring conceptual frameworks for collaborative design and social creativity in the context of complex design problems. It brings together participants from various backgrounds to frame and solve ill-defined, open-ended design problems. The knowledge to understand, frame, and solve these problems does not already exist (Engeström, 2001) but is constructed and evolves during the solution process—an ideal environment to study social creativity. The EDC represents a *sociotechnical environment* incorporating a number of technologies, including tabletop computing, the integration of physical and computational components supporting new interaction techniques, and an open architecture supporting metadesign activities. The vision of the EDC is to provide contextualized support for *reflection-in-action* (Schön, 1983) within collaborative design activities.

Figure 10.2 A community of interest using the EDC for a design session.

Figure 10.2 shows a design session exploring urban planning problems involving different stakeholders. The EDC supports face-to-face problem-solving activities by allowing the participants to discuss and explore problems while taking advantage of a shared construction space facilitated by a tabletop computing environment. As participants interact with physical objects that are used to represent the situation currently being discussed and create design situations by sketching, corresponding computational representations are created and incrementally updated by using technologies that recognize these actions. Computer-generated information is projected back onto the horizontal physical construction area, creating an augmented reality environment. This physical construction is coupled with information relevant to the problem currently being discussed.

Grounded in a metadesign perspective, we have included mechanisms within the EDC to allow participants to inject content into the simulations and adapt the environment to new scenarios. Also, we have created ways to link to existing data and tools so that participants can draw on information from their own areas of expertise to contribute to the emerging, shared model. By exploring and supporting these activities, the EDC has given us insights into collaborative design that draw on both individual and social aspects of creativity.

Evaluations showed (Warr, 2007) that the EDC empowers users in personally meaningful tasks to engage as active contributors, externalizing ideas and thereby allowing knowledge to be created, integrated, and disseminated. It supports users to interact and communicate with boundary objects leading to the generation of new ideas through the combination and improvement of existing ideas (e.g., participants considered the sketching function allowing the creation of external representations to be crucial for the generation of objects "to-think-with" and "to-negotiate-about.")

More specific, we have observed that more creative solutions to urban planning problems can emerge from the collective interactions with the environment by *heterogeneous communities of interests* compared with *homogeneous communities of practice* (Fischer, 2001). We have observed also that participants are more readily engaged if they perceive the design activities as *personally meaningful* by associating a purpose with their involvement (Fischer, 2002), and participants must be able to *naturally express* what they want to say (Eden, 2002).

Courses-as-Seeds

Courses-as-seeds (DePaula, Fischer, & Ostwald, 2001) is an educational model that explores metadesign and social creativity in the context of fundamentally changing the nature of courses taught in universities. Its goal is to create a culture of informed participation (Fischer & Ostwald, 2005) that is situated in the context of university courses transcending the temporal boundaries of semester-based classes. The major role for new media and new technologies from a culture-of-participation perspective is not to deliver predigested information and nonchangeable artifacts and tools to individuals but rather to provide the opportunity and resources for engaging them in authentic activities, for participating in social debates and discussions, for creating shared understanding among diverse stakeholders, and for framing and solving personally meaningful problems.

Over the last decade, our teaching objectives and practices have increasingly tried to reconceptualize learning in courses from a cultures-of-participation perspective. Our courses are using wikis as course information environments. Traditionally, the content of a course is defined by the resources provided by instructors (such as lectures, readings, and assignments), but, in courses-as-seeds, the instructor provides the initial seed rather than a finished product. By involving students as active contributors, courses do not have to rely only on the intellectual capital provided by the instructors, but they are enriched on an ongoing basis by the contribution of all participants.

Courses-as-seeds represent a *community-of-learners* model (Rogoff, Matsuov, & White, 1998) and explores new middle ground between *adult-run* and *children-run* education. All participants are active, and the more skilled partners (experienced teachers and coaches) can provide leadership and guidance. The learners have opportunities to become responsible and organize their own learning, exploit their previous interests, and sustain their motivation to learn by having some control over their contributions.

The courses-as-seeds model represents a system of values, attitudes, and behaviors that differ radically from the traditional educational culture in which courses are conceived as finished products, and students are viewed as consumers. Courses-as-seeds create a culture based on a *designer mindset* that emphasizes habits and tools that empower students to actively contribute to the design of their education (and eventually to the design of their lives and communities).

IMPLICATIONS: LESSONS LEARNED AND CHALLENGES AHEAD

The developments of the sociotechnical environments described briefly in the previous section have explored our basic assumptions that learning, social creativity, and cultures of participation can be enhanced by making all voices heard, harnessing diversity, and enabling people to be aware of and to access each other's work and ideas, relate them to their own, and contribute the results back to the community. Whereas social creativity seen from this perspective is essential for framing and solving complex design problems, it contributes also to the invention and transformation of our social and cultural environments. With modern decentralization of knowledge into highly specialized niches, no single person is likely to have sufficient knowledge to solve a complex problem in any given field, and collaboration is therefore necessary.

Our studies have provided evidence for our basic assumption that innovative sociotechnical environments create feasibility spaces for new social practice. We have articulated some initial success factors from our research including *promises*-new perspectives with potential that should be pursued, *pitfalls*-problematic insights that should not be overlooked, and misconceptions that must be exposed and examined. These factors were derived from the assessment studies of the specific application contexts but are more broadly applicable to study design creativity, and they contribute to an enrichment of the conceptual framework articulated in this chapter.

Our basic assumption is that collaborative design and social creativity are necessities rather than luxuries for most interesting and important design problems in today's world. But there is ample evidence that there should be a *and* and not a *versus* relationship between individual and social creativity as aptly expressed by Rudyard Kipling "The strength of the pack is in the wolf, and the strength of the wolf is in the pack." This claim is strongly supported by other studies (Bennis & Biederman, 1997; Csikszentmihalyi, 1996) and other conceptual frameworks such as the fish-scale model (Campbell, 2005), which postulates that we should achieve "collective comprehensiveness through overlapping patterns of unique narrowness" (p. 3). Metadesign supports social creativity by democratizing design allowing all users to become participants in personally meaningful problems.

An important objective of metadesign is to create important foundations for collaborative design and social creativity by encouraging and supporting owners of problems to contribute user-generated content. Underdesign (Brand, 1995), which is negotiated rather than planned in advance, allows owners of problems to adapt a system to local contingencies and conditions.

Underdesign is a defining activity for metadesign aimed at creating design spaces for others. It assumes that the meaning, functionality, and content of a system are not fully defined by designers and user-representatives alone at design time but are socially constructed throughout the entire design, deployment, and use cycles of the system. Emphasizing underdesign as an important objective of metadesign creates important foundations for social creativity and cultures of participation by encouraging and supporting owners of problems in contributing user-generated content in Web 2.0 environments such as Wikipedia, Second Life, Flickr, YouTube, and open source (Benkler, 2006; Tapscott & Williams, 2006; Von Hippel, 2005).

In cultures of participation, there is no clear distinction between developers and users: All users are potential developers. Being a consumer or being a designer is a not binary choice: It is rather a continuum ranging from passive consumer, to well-informed consumer, to end user, to power user, to domain designer all the way to metadesigner (Preece & Shneiderman, 2009).

People will decide on the worthiness of doing something by relating the perceived value of an activity to the perceived effort of doing it (Fischer & Giaccardi, 2006). Experiences with systems developed by cultures of participation have exposed the following barriers: Individuals must perceive a value in contributing to an activity that is large enough to outweigh the effort, and the effort required to contribute to this activity must be low enough to avoid interfering with the work at hand. From a metadesign perspective, major efforts at design time are needed to create the structures that will empower users at use time and greatly reduce their cost of participation. *Value considerations* can be influenced by allowing people to engage in personally meaningful tasks. People are willing to spend considerable effort on things that are important to them. The *effort* can be reduced by lowering the threshold required to learn and make a contribution and by taking advantage of derived information from the actions of participants (e.g., personalizing environments by creating task and user models of their behavior).

Without active contributions and participation from motivated users, learning and social creativity will not succeed. Important motivational dimensions (Csikszentmihalyi, 1996) to be considered are: *generalized reciprocity, social recognition, rewards, and social capital.* Although participants in community-based efforts, as exemplified by our application contexts, typically do not get paid for their contribution, there are other forms of external compensation contributing to extrinsic motivation. Reputation in these communities is an external motivator governed by what you contribute to the community (Raymond & Young, 2001). More important and more interesting than extrinsic motivation is intrinsic motivation that is positively influenced by the fact that participants find their engagement intellectually stimulating and personally enriching. Participating in these projects may be a way to learn about a new technology that may be useful to further professional development of technically inclined participants.

The theory of the Long Tail (Anderson, 2006) conveys that our culture and economy is increasingly shifting away from a focus on a relatively small number of "hits" (mainstream products and markets) at the head of the demand curve and toward a huge number of niches in the tail. As the costs of production and distribution fall, especially online, there is now less need to lump products and consumers into one-size-fits-all containers.

Although the Long Tail is most often discussed as a phenomenon of interest for web-based businesses, it has implications for learning and social creativity. By empowering stakeholders with unique interest and knowledge to be active contributors, the networked information economy has unleashed a flowering of creativity across all fields of human endeavor and has created a Long Tail of niche communities engaging in a very large number of idiosyncratic topics in learning and social creativity (Collins, Fischer, Barron, Liu, & Spada, 2009).

Learning and social creativity require the codesign of social and technical systems. They need to use models and concepts that not only focus on the artifact but exploit the social context in which the systems will be used. Creativity flourishes best in a unique kind of social environment: One that is stable enough to allow continuity of effort, yet diverse and broad-minded enough to nourish creativity in all its subversive forms. Practice without process becomes unmanageable, but process without practice damps out the creativity required for innovation; the two sides exist in perpetual tension.

By studying design activities in specific application contexts addressing specific societal challenges of our world, our research lays the groundwork for an enriched conceptual framework for social creativity and cultures of participation. Achieving these objectives is not only a technical problem; it requires new cultures, new mind-sets, and innovative sociotechnical environments that provide people with powerful media to express themselves and engage in personally meaningful activities. Research activities have only scratched the surface of exploiting the power of collective minds equipped with new media. The challenges of the complex problems that we all face make this approach not a luxury, but a necessity.

ACKNOWLEDGMENTS

The author thanks the members of the Center for LifeLong Learning and Design who have made major contributions to the frameworks and systems described in this chapter. The research was supported in part by the following grants from the National Science Foundation: (1) REC-0106976 "Social Creativity and Meta-Design in Lifelong Learning Communities," (2) IIS-0613638 "A Meta-Design Framework for Participative Software Systems," (3) IIS-0709304 "A New Generation Wiki for Supporting a Research Community in Creativity and IT," (4) OCI-1028017 "CDI-Type I: Transformative Models of Learning and Discovery in Cultures of Participation." A major reformulation of the chapter was facilitated by the support of a Chair of Excellence fellowship granted to the author by the University Carlos III of Madrid.

REFERENCES

Anderson, C. (2006). *The long tail: Why the future of business is selling less of more.* New York, NY: Hyperion.

Arias, E. G., Eden, H., Fischer, G., Gorman, A., & Scharff, E. (2000). Transcending the individual human mind: Creating shared understanding through collaborative design. *ACM Transactions on Computer Human-Interaction, 7*(1), 84–113.

Benkler, Y. (2006). *The wealth of networks: How social production transforms markets and freedom.* New Haven, CT: Yale University Press.

Bennis, W., & Biederman, P. W. (1997). *Organizing genius: The secrets of creative collaboration.* Cambridge, MA: Perseus Books.

Boden, M. (1991). *The creative mind: Myths & mechanisms.* New York, NY: Basic Books.

Brand, S. (1995). *How buildings learn: What happens after they're built.* New York, NY: Penguin Books.

Brown, J. S., & Duguid, P. (2000). *The social life of information.* Boston, MA: Harvard Business School Press.

Bruner, J. (1996). *The culture of education.* Cambridge, MA: Harvard University Press.

Campbell, D. T. (2005). *Ethnocentrism of disciplines and the fish-scale model of omniscience.* In S. J. Derry, C. D. Schunn, & M. A. Gernsbacher (Eds.), *Interdisciplinary collaboration: An emerging cognitive science* (pp. 3–21). Mahwah, NJ: Erlbaum.

Clark, H. H., & Brennan, S. E. (1991). Grounding in communication. In L. B. Resnick, J. M. Levine, & S. D. Teasley (Eds.), *Perspectives on socially shared cognition* (pp. 127–149). Hyattsville, MD: American Psychological Association.

Collins, A., Fischer, G., Barron, B., Liu, C., & Spada, H. (2009). Long-tail learning: A unique opportunity for CSCL? In A. Dimitracopoulou, C. O'Malley, D. Suthers, & P. Reimann (Eds.), *Proceedings of the 8th international conference on computer supported collaborative learning, CSCL'09* (Vol. 2, pp. 22–24). Rhodes, Greece: University of Aegean.

Csikszentmihalyi, M. (1996). *Creativity: Flow and the psychology of discovery and invention.* New York, NY: HarperCollins.

Csikszentmihalyi, M., & Sawyer, R. K. (1995). Creative insight: The social dimension of a solitary moment. In R. J. Sternberg & J. E. Davidson (Eds.), *The nature of insight* (pp. 329–364). Cambridge, MA: MIT Press.

DePaula, R., Fischer, G., & Ostwald, J. (2001). Courses as seeds: Expectations and realities. In P. Dillenbourg, A. Eurelings, & K. Hakkarainen (Eds.), *Proceedings of the European conference on computer-supported collaborative learning* (pp. 494–501). Maastricht, The Netherlands: McLuhan Institute.

Dick, H., Eden, H., & Fischer, G. (2009). Increasing and sustaining participation to support and foster social creativity. *Proceedings of the international conference on creativity and cognition, C&C'2009* (pp. 363–364). Berkeley, CA: ACM Press.

Eden, H. (2002). Getting in on the (inter)action: Exploring affordances for collaborative learning in a context of informed participation. In G. Stahl (Ed.), *Proceedings of the computer supported collaborative learning, CSCL'2002 conference* (pp. 399–407). Hillsday, NJ: Erlbaum.

Engeström, Y. (2001). Expansive learning at work: Toward an activity-theoretical reconceptualization. *Journal of Education and Work, 14*(1), 133–156.

Engeström, Y., & Sannino, A. (2010). Studies of expansive learning: Foundations, findings and future challenges. *Educational Research Review, 5*(1), 1–24.

Fischer, G. (2001). Communities of interest: Learning through the interaction of multiple knowledge systems. In *24th annual information systems research seminar in Scandinavia, IRIS'24* (pp. 1–14). Ulvik, Norway: University of Oslo.

Fischer, G. (2002). Beyond "couch potatoes": From consumers to designers and active contributors. *FirstMonday Peer-Reviewed Journal, 7*(12). Retrieved from http://firstmonday.org/htbin/cgiwrap/bin/ojs/index.php/fm/article/view/1010/931

Fischer, G. (2005). Distances and diversity: Sources for social creativity. *Proceedings of Creativity & Cognition* (pp. 128–136). London, England: ACM Press.

Fischer, G. (2011). Understanding, fostering, and supporting cultures of participation. *Interactions, 18*(3), 42–53.

Fischer, G., Ehn, P., Engeström, Y., & Virkkunen, J. (2002). In T. Binder, J. Gregory, & I. Wagner (Eds.), *Proceedings of the participatory design conference,*

Pdc☐*02* (pp. 426–428). Malmö, Sweden: Computer Professionals for Social Responsibility.

Fischer, G., & Giaccardi, E. (2006). Meta-design: A framework for the future of end user development. In H. Lieberman, F. Paternò, & V. Wulf (Eds.), *End user development* (pp. 427–457). Dordrecht, The Netherlands: Kluwer Academic Publishers.

Fischer, G., Nakakoji, K., Ostwald, J., Stahl, G., & Sumner, T. (1998). Embedding critics in design environments. In M. T. Maybury & W. Wahlster (Eds.), *Readings in intelligent user interfaces* (pp. 537–559). San Francisco, CA: Morgan Kaufmann.

Fischer, G., & Ostwald, J. (2005). Knowledge communication in design communities. In R. Bromme, F. W. Hesse, & H. Spada (Eds.), *Barriers and biases in computer-mediated knowledge communication* (pp. 213–242). New York, NY: Springer.

Gardner, H. (1993). *Creating minds*. New York, NY: Basic Books.

Gardner, H. (1995). *Leading minds: Anatomy of leadership*. New York, NY: Basic Books.

Henderson, A., & Kyng, M. (1991). There's no place like home: Continuing design in use. In J. Greenbaum & M. Kyng (Eds.), *Design at work: Cooperative design of computer systems* (pp. 219–240). Hillsdale, NJ: Erlbaum.

Janis, I. (1972). *Victims of groupthink*. Boston, MA: Houghton Mifflin.

Jenkins, H. (2009). *Confronting the challenges of participatory cultures: Media education for the 21st century*. Cambridge, MA: MIT Press.

John-Steiner, V. (2000). *Creative collaboration*. Oxford, England: Oxford University Press.

Lanier, J. (2006). *Digital maoism: The hazards of the new online collectivism*. Retrieved from http://www.edge.org/3rd_culture/lanier06/lanier06_index.html

Lave, J. (1991). Situated learning in communities of practice. In L. B. Resnick, J. M. Levine, & S. D. Teasley (Eds.), *Perspectives on socially-shared cognition* (pp. 63–82). Washington, DC: American Psychological Association.

National Research Council. (2003). *Beyond productivity: Information technology, innovation, and creativity*. Washington, DC: National Academy Press.

Olson, G. M., & Olson, J. S. (2001). Distance matters. In J. M. Carroll (Ed.), *Human-computer interaction in the new millennium* (pp. 397–417). New York, NY: ACM Press.

Porter, J. (2008). *Designing for the social web*. Berkeley, CA: New Riders.

Preece, J., & Shneiderman, B. (2009). The reader-to-leader framework: Motivating technology-mediated social participation. *AIS Transactions on Human-Computer Interaction, 1*(1), 13–32.

Raymond, E. S., & Young, B. (2001). *The cathedral and the bazaar: Musings on Linux and open source by an accidental revolutionary*. Sebastopol, CA: O'Reilly & Associates.

Resnick, L. B., Levine, J. M., & Teasley, S. D. (Eds.). (1991). *Perspectives on socially shared cognition*. Washington, DC: American Psychological Association.

Rogoff, B., & Lave, J. (Eds.). (1984). *Everyday cognition*. Cambridge, MA: Harvard University Press.

Rogoff, B., Matsuov, E., & White, C. (1998). Models of teaching and learning: Participation in a community of learners. In D. R. Olsen & N. Torrance (Eds.), *The handbook of education and human development: New models of learning, teaching and schooling* (pp. 388–414). Oxford, England: Blackwell.

Salomon, G. (Ed.). (1993). *Distributed cognitions: Psychological and educational considerations*. Cambridge, England: Cambridge University Press.

Schön, D. A. (1983). *The reflective practitioner: How professionals think in action*. New York, NY: Basic Books.

Shneiderman, B. (2002). *Leonardo's laptop: Human needs and the new computing technologies.* Cambridge, MA: MIT Press.

Shneiderman, B. (2007). Creativity support tools: Accelerating discovery and innovation. *Communications of the ACM, 50*(12), 20–32.

Sternberg, R. J. (Ed.). (1988). *The nature of creativity.* Cambridge, England: Cambridge University Press.

Sternberg, R. J. (Ed.). (1999). *Handbook of creativity.* Cambridge, England: Cambridge University Press.

Suchman, L. A. (1987). *Plans and situated actions.* Cambridge, England: Cambridge University Press.

Tapscott, D., & Williams, A. D. (2006). *Wikinomics: How mass collaboration changes everything.* New York, NY: Portofolio, Penguin.

Von Hippel, E. (2005). *Democratizing innovation.* Cambridge, MA: MIT Press.

Warr, A. (2007). *Understanding and supporting creativity in design* (Doctoral dissertation). University of Bath, Bath, England.

Wenger, E. (1998). *Communities of practice: Learning, meaning, and identity.* Cambridge, England: Cambridge University Press.

Winograd, T., & Flores, F. (1986). *Understanding computers and cognition: A new foundation for design.* Norwood, NJ: Ablex Publishing Corporation.

11 Professional Creativity
Toward a Collaborative Community of Teaching

Viv Ellis

The substantive focus of this chapter is school teaching, specifically in England, at a time when conceptions of profession, of teaching as a profession, and of the professional knowledge base of teachers continue to be contested. Teaching is sometimes defined as a "state-mediated" profession (Johnson, 1972) in that teachers mediate the state's educational goals in relation to a state-defined clientele. This definition highlights the bureaucratic and regulatory aspects of professional work such as school teaching. Nonetheless, teaching is a type of profession that in England, as in many parts of the world, has become vulnerable to neoliberalism's push toward the marketization of public services managed through vertical hierarchies of control—in other words, New Public Management (McLaughlin, Osborne, & Ferlie, 2002). Markets and hierarchies are seen as challenges to the traditional notions of professions as autonomous communities. In this chapter, drawing on related theoretical resources derived from Marxian political economy—cultural-historical activity theory, the British tradition of cultural studies, and the critical sociology of professions—I argue that the difficult and contested concept of profession necessarily grows out of the processes of collective creativity and learning that are the focus of this book. Collective creativity is both a condition and defining attribute of professional cultures that make the actions of individual professionals meaningful and societally significant. A profession in its historical sense is recognizable because of its developmental stance toward both its own knowledge base *and* its social relations. Collective creativity and learning are distinguishing features of professionals as occupational groups, even when they are of the state-mediated kind and even when their organizational autonomy is challenged by markets and hierarchies.

The chapter's argument is structured as follows. First, I consider profession as a contested concept and the collective, socially organized dimensions of professional work. I draw particularly on the critical sociology of Adler (Adler & Heckscher, 2006; Adler, Kwon, & Heckscher, 2008) and his theoretical model of a profession as a collaborative community with societally significant, knowledge-creating responsibilities. Then, I consider creativity from the related perspectives of the British tradition of cultural studies and Vygotskian and neo-Vygotskian theory. From these perspectives, the twin emphases on human symbolization and economics in contemporary discourses of creativity are revealed. I also distinguish between my conceptualization and another conceptualization of professional creativity, specifically the category of "Pro-c" creativity of Kaufman and Beghetto (2009) in order to clarify the distinction between collective and individual conceptualizations of creativity. Next, I turn to education and, specifically, to school teaching in England. I note the contradictory pressures on professionals such as teachers in New Public Management regimes to be both compliant and creative at the same time as being constructed as vertically accountable, isolated individuals. It is at this point that I give an example from my own work of a formative intervention designed to stimulate or reenergize teachers' professional, collective creativity. In the final section, I draw together the preceding stages of my argument to propose professional creativity as future-oriented, intellectual interdependence, based on principles of semiotic freedom and democratic engagement with clients and publics, exercised within a collaborative community committed both to the development of new knowledge and to the elaboration of the system of values and ideals that underpin its authority.

It is worth acknowledging at the outset that such an argument risks presenting a very idealistic view of professions, one that perpetuates what might be described as the vested interests and monopoly power of certain occupational groups. My aim is to show that rather than seeking to advance professions and professional status as autonomous, self-serving communities, it is instead necessary under current (and likely future) conditions to see professions as collaborative communities that have relatively open social ties and actively seek public engagement in fulfilling their responsibilities for knowledge creation.

COMMUNITY: THE COLLECTIVITY OF PROFESSIONS

In this section, I build on earlier discussions of professions in the literature and engage with the work of Adler (Adler & Heckscher, 2006; Adler et al., 2008). A principal insight of Adler's critical sociology is that professional knowledge creation is a community-based, collective enterprise situated in cultural-historical context. In its emphasis on knowledge creation within communities of practice—or in joint work on the transformation of the object of activity—Adler's work is relevant to and extends the sociocultural and activity theoretical tradition of research on learning and collectivity.

For many, profession "is an essentially contested concept" (Hoyle & John, 1995, p. 1), associated with changing class relations after industrialization, the expansion of higher education, and the emergence of a twentieth century welfare state. Conventionally, definitions of professionality refer to specialist bodies of knowledge, autonomy in work practices, and high levels of social responsibility. Freidson (2001) defined it as a "third logic," separate and distinct from the ways in which other types of work are organized (under the logics of market and bureaucracy). Etzioni (1969) went so far as to insist that *true* professions are concerned with matters of life and death and cloaked with rights to "privileged communication," criteria that perhaps only law and medicine can claim to meet.

But while all these attempts at definition have specialist knowledge, autonomy, and status at their core, they do not always emphasize the collectivity of profession as a concept, that *profession* represents an occupational group of specialist workers. Nor do they always recognize that the population of workers to whom the term professional might be applied is expanding just as the ways in which professionals work as part of teams and hybrid organizations is increasing. Unlike Etzioni's dismissal of teachers and nurses (among others) as "semi-professionals", others have attempted to distinguish between groups of professional workers on the basis of their relations to the state and public service organizations. Johnson (1972), for example, referred to three types of professional power structure: collegiate, patronage, and mediated. Teachers were in Johnson's category of state-mediated professionals whereby:

> An agency, usually a state organization, acts as mediator between the profession and its clientele in deciding the profession's client population and in broad terms what should be provided for its clientele through a legal framework and the overall allocation of resources. By this means, the state acts as the corporate patron of the professionals who provide services on its behalf, through the state's agencies. . . . The state delegates power to, and in the process, legitimizes the status of the professionals concerned. (White, 2006, p. 207)

State-mediation of professional work such as school teaching is often seen to "threaten[s] the maintenance or inhibit[s] the emergence of the 'complete community' of professionalization" (Johnson, 1972, p. 80). Adler and colleagues (2008; also Adler & Heckscher, 2006), however, rather than basing their discussion of professional work on a comparison with what might be viewed as a singular, anachronistic ideal-type, situate profession within three broad organizing principles—hierarchy, market, and community—and suggest that whereas markets and hierarchy are in the ascendant, they do not reduce the importance of community in understanding professional work. Indeed, the contribution by Adler and colleagues (2008) is an emerging theoretical model of *collaborative community*, one that sustains traditional community priorities of trust and collegiality while promoting more open social ties and the "stronger civic engagement necessary for the welfare of contemporary society" (Adler et al., 2008, p. 359). The model of a collaborative community is also one within which the specialist knowledge from which professional work derives (and gains public status) can be accessed and developed.

Collaborative Community and Professional Knowledge Creation

In proposing collaborative community as a theoretical model of contemporary professional work, Adler rejects two earlier ideal types of community, *Gemeinschaft* (collectivist but insular, akin to craft guilds) and *Gesellschaft* (seen as embodied in modern liberal professions and experts for hire). Neither of these historical types of community are seen as adequate for current and future conditions in that they both have limited capacity to support the creation and diffusion of new knowledge. So, the "functional pressures" of market and hierarchy/bureaucratization "are encouraging the emergence of the collaborative form' of community" (Adler et al., 2008, p. 364). And an important focus of these functional pressures is the capacity of professional groups to respond to new problems of practice with new ideas—that is, the knowledge-creating capacities of professions. Indeed, the knowledge-creating capacities of the three different organizing principles (market, hierarchy, and community) of professional work are absolutely fundamental to Adler and colleagues' general argument. Table 11.1 summarizes the different strengths and weaknesses of these organizing principles for professional knowledge creation (after Adler et al., 2008).

Table 11.1   The Strengths and Weaknesses of Three Different Organizing Principles of Professional Work for Knowledge Creation (Generated from the discussion in Adler et al., 2008.)

Organizing principle	*Strength*	*Weakness*
Community	High levels of trust facilitate access to tacit knowledge held in shared practices and promote local knowledge creation.	There is a risk of insularity within communities as "silos" and the closure of outward-looking innovation.
Market	Flexibility and responsiveness to new problems of practice are encouraged.	Knowledge creation tends toward short-term "solutions" that lead only to individual capitalization.
Hierarchy	Managerial techniques of control can effectively disseminate codified knowledge.	Bureaucratic hierarchies provide weak incentives to create new knowledge and lack sensitivity to tacit knowledge.

Adler and colleagues (2008) claim that their theoretical model of collaborative community integrates these three organizing principles rather than rejecting one or the other. Collaborative community as a new model addresses hierarchical forms of management, market pressures, and competition whereas simultaneously transforming traditional community principles. It does this by encouraging responsiveness to new work situations and by challenging local knowledge creation to have wider, systemic impact. Collaborative community as a theoretical model of the organization of professions is, therefore, interesting rhetorically as well as offering a challenging sociological analysis. As a concept, however, it is useful to my argument in this chapter in three ways. First, it emphasizes "value-rationality" as the basis of professional authority—the means by which professionals "coordinate their activity through a set of shared commitment to ultimate goals" (Adler et al., 2008, p. 366). Value-rationality in terms of school teaching reflects both the moral and ethical interests involved as well as the position of teachers as professionals in relation to the state but also to the wider publics. Second, collaborative community acknowledges the often hierarchical nature of organizations such as schools rather than sentimentally smoothing this out of the picture. And third, most important, collaborative community, in Adler's formulation, sets a challenge to develop a "more outward-looking, civic kind of professionalism" (Adler et al., 2008, p. 369), not just in terms of interprofessional working (teachers, social workers, psychologists, health care workers, etc., working together) but in terms of public engagement with and beyond the client group of children and families.

CREATIVITY: SYMBOLIZATION AND ECONOMICS AS TWIN ACCENTS IN THE DISCOURSE

In this section, I show how the twin perspectives of cultural studies and Vygotskian and neo-Vygotskian theory reveal the contradictory emphases in contemporary discourses of creativity, contradictions that set the human capacity to symbolize and make meaning against economic conceptualizations of innovation and capitalization.

The British tradition of cultural studies, especially in the work of Raymond Williams (1958, 1965) and that associated with the Birmingham Centre for Contemporary Cultural Studies (Hall, 1980; Hoggart, 1957; Thompson, 1963; Willis, 1977; Willis, Jones, Canaan, & Hurd, 1990), made a significant contribution to understanding creativity during the late twentieth century. Arising from a range of intellectual heritages, especially those derived from Marx and critical theory of the Frankfurt School, cultural studies sought to recover creativity from elitist, individualistic accomplishments in the arts and instead assert it as a general human capacity. This capacity arose from a species desire to symbolize; the development of the individual and the development of the culture through symbolic activity were posited as reciprocal processes:

> We insist that there is a vibrant symbolic life and symbolic creativity in everyday life, everyday activity and expression—even if it is sometimes invisible, looked down on or spurned. We don't want to invent it or propose it. We want to recognize it—literally re-cognize it. (Willis et al., 1990, p. 1)

The significance of Raymond Williams's early writing on culture and creativity cannot be underestimated as a contribution to the intellectual context in which Vygotskian and later cultural-historical ideas were understood in the United Kingdom. His careful analysis of the cultural shifts of meaning—creativity as divinely inspired, to creativity as the exceptional revelation of human experience by the artist, to creativity as ubiquitous (Williams, 1965)—anticipate many of the later developments, particularly in the educational discourse.[1] Faced with the criticism that his analysis of creativity as an everyday capacity detracted from the evaluations of "high culture," his response cut across later distinctions that were to be made between "little c" ("mundane") and "big C" (elite or "high") creativity (Amabile, 1983; Craft, 2005; Kaufman & Beghetto, 2009):

> The solution is not to pull art down to the level of other social activity as this is habitually conceived. The emphasis that matters is that there are, essentially, no "ordinary" activities, if by "ordinary" we mean the absence of creative interpretation and effort. Art is ratified, in the end, by the fact of creativity in all our living. Everything we see and do, the whole structure of our relationships and institutions, depends, finally, on an effort of learning, description and communication. (Williams, 1965, p. 34)

Jones (2011) distinguishes two main accents in the contemporary discourses of creativity in England. The first is a mid-twentieth century emphasis on symbolization and self-development: "any human development beyond the stage of elementary mental functioning is dependent on sign-making" (p. 21). He connects this accent with "Marx's stress on human creative powers . . . given a linguistic inflection, specific individual actions coalesce into a general, collective creativity, which is a defining and sustaining property of humanity" (Jones, 2011, p. 21). The second accent in the discourse, according to Jones (2011), has its source in "economic production and enterprise" (p. 23). Proponents of this second accent assert a changed "post-industrial" or "post-bureaucratic" order in which educational structures and institutions are seen to lag behind the transformed economic structures of global capitalism. From this perspective, the aims of education should be to unlock creativity just as post-industrial workplaces have done. Creativity, under this analysis, becomes a set of "thinking skills" necessary for the individual's prosperity and the global economic competitiveness of their employers (and nations). Creativity is a "set of dispositions involving qualities such as initiative, innovativeness, commitment, patience and concentration, whose stimulus and justification lay primarily in economic life" (Jones, 2011, p. 24). The second accent has been completely "severed" from the first and its emphasis on human symbolization and individual and cultural development. For Jones, the economic stimulus and justification has been in the ascendant in discourses of creativity in England over the last decade.

Wheeler (2006) extends the cultural studies emphasis on "symbolic creativity" by drawing on recent biosemiotic theory. Scientific studies of species-specific characteristics such as symbolization have become the focus of Wheeler's research and lead her to question contemporary economic inflections of creativity, limited in terms of their capacity to explain cultural development and limited also because of their emphasis on the present:

> In particular, because creative freedom and innovation in modernity come to be conceived mainly in terms of economic freedom and market innovation—which are very partial ways of conceiving human creativity—we need a more comprehensive account of cultural creativity than that afforded solely by the idea of economic innovation and individual capital accumulation. Creativity—the means by which human cultures evolve—is a *social* affair. Its contraction to the sphere of economic self-interest, especially as that is conceived of only in terms of the greedy present of an individual lifetime, is quite simply a historical category mistake: Creativity is not simply about either profit or the present. For the brilliance of human creativity lies also in its intuition of things as yet unseen that will be revealed "in later days to other eyes" (Wheeler, 2006, p. 141, quoting M. Polanyi).

Wheeler's critique of individualistic, ahistorical conceptualizations of creativity—memorably phrased as "the greedy present of an individual life-time"—has much in common with the Vygotskian and neo-Vygotskian perspectives on creativity.

IMAGINATION, TRANSFORMATION, AND INTELLECTUAL INTERDEPENDENCE

Vygotsky's papers on creativity distinguish between childhood, adolescent, and adult creativity but together build a general argument for the importance of the imagination in all forms of intellectual activity. For Vygotsky, "imagination was conscious, concrete, and—especially after childhood—interdependent with thinking in concepts and reasoning" (Ayman-Nolley, 1992, p. 82).

Smolucha, a translator of these papers, has shown how the creative imagination, although evident in childhood play, "becomes a higher mental function" (Smolucha, 1992) when, during adolescence, it is integrated with thinking in concepts. The "maturity" of this higher mental function is found in artistic and scientific creativity. But, overall, Vygotsky emphasized the "combinatory imagination" (the creative synthesis of previous experience in new situations) as an aspect of all cultural life. As such, creativity could only be identified or "labeled" in relation to existing domains of concepts or discourses or ways of reasoning. Indeed, Vygotsky suggested that it was the growth of conceptual understanding through adolescence that set the ground for mature creativity: "For the first time the formation of concepts brings with it a release from the concrete situation and a likelihood of a creative reworking and transformation of its elements" (Vygotsky, 1994, p. 276).

The reworking and transformation made possible by the combinatory imagination is at the core of Vygotsky's ideas about creativity, according to John-Steiner and Meehan (2000). For Van der Veer and Valsiner (1991, 2000), underpinning the combinatory imagination is "intellectual interdependence." Basing this idea on the dialectic between internalization and externalization in Vygotskian theory, Van der Veer and Valsiner (1991) argue that the meanings of cultural tools aren't simply internalized by the individual "but, rather, they are analyzed and reassembled in novel ways. Hence the individual is a co-constructor of culture, rather than a mere follower of the enculturation efforts of others" (p. 395). Externalization based on the reflective perception and internalization or transformation of signs and symbols together form the general human capacity referred to as creativity. Later, in their examination of the development of ideas in science, Valsiner and Van der Veer (2000) develop this idea of intellectual interdependency as a way of understanding the relationship between institutions, individuals, and "nature." Intellectual interdependency is the process by which new understandings of phenomena are:

> actively constructed by intentional persons, who are involved in a field of mutually communicable meanings, or ideas. Within this field, persons act in a goal-oriented manner: Communication is directed towards personally desirable possible future state of affairs [*sic*]. (Valsiner & Van der Veer, 2000, p. 10)

Valsiner and Van der Veer's concept of intellectual interdependency, based as it is on Vygotsky's sociogenetic epistemology, is a useful contribution to the elaboration of professional creativity. It suggests that the collectivity of a profession is not based on an accumulation or aggregation of individual mental processing but on a dialogic and expansive transformation of shared social arrangements arising out of disruptions, breakdowns, or contradictions that emerge when intellectual heritages come into contact with one another over time. Intellectual interdependency, in Van der Veer and Valsiner's formulation, therefore also captures some of the historicity of creativity and the nature of creativity as a general human capacity evident in individuals that is nonetheless developed socially. Intellectual interdependency builds on Vygotsky's dialectical emphasis on continuity and change, reproduction, and transformation:

> If human activity were limited to reproduction of the old, a person would, in essence, be attending only to the past. The creative activity of an individual does this, essentially: It attends to the future, creating it, and changing the view of the present. (Vygotsky, 2004, 50)

This cultural and historical view of creativity—whether derived from the resources of cultural studies or Vygotsky's radical psychology—is strikingly different from dominant views of creativity and learning or teaching in much of the educational research, as I show in the next section. Centrally relevant to the idea of professional creativity is the concept of intellectual interdependence, "the process of construction of new ideas through the transformation of old ones in a communicative process" (Valsiner & Van der Veer, 2000, p. 12) and the contribution of these new and transformed ideas to the knowledge base of a collaborative community that is evolving historically. As such, professional creativity as I am conceptualizing it in this chapter is profoundly different from another conceptualization of professional creativity—the category of "Pro-c creativity" proposed by Kaufman and Beghetto (2009). "Pro-C," according to Kaufman and Beghetto (also Kaufman, Beghetto, Baer, & Ivcevic, 2010), is an individual characteristic of "professional level creators who have not yet achieved legendary status" (Kaufman et al., 2010, p. 381) but who have nonetheless received the approval of their peers and "prizes/honors" (p. 382). Professional creativity as defined by Kaufman and Beghetto is a social marker of individual expertise in a particular craft—and a specific (pre-"legendary") stage in the development of that expertise at that. Professional creativity, as I have been conceptualizing it, is both a criterion and a precondition for a kind of relational work in the public sphere that leads to the collective creation of new and transformed knowledge on the basis of authority bestowed by a system of shared values and ideals.

SCHOOL TEACHING IN ENGLAND: COMPLIANCE AND CREATIVITY

In this section, I turn to education and specifically to school teaching in England. Following a selective review of some of the literature on creativity and teaching and learning, I discuss the contradictory pressures on teachers in England's New Public Management policy regime to be both compliant and creative at the same time as being regulated through vertical forms of accountability and audit. I then briefly discuss an example from my work of a formative intervention designed to stimulate teachers' professional creativity.

Craft (2005) offers a broad survey of the international research literature on creativity and learning, focused particularly on the institution of schooling. She notices a shift away from twentieth-century interests in psychological measurement toward an early twentieth-century focus on knowledge production and innovation, reflecting what others have seen as increasingly economic accents in the discourse. While noting the unhelpfulness of false dichotomies, Craft nonetheless organizes part of her discussion around the distinction between creative learning and learning creativity. The former, she suggests, is associated with making learning "more interesting and effective" (Craft, 2005, p. 22); the latter is designed to foster young people's creative capacities. What underlies both approaches, however, in Craft's analysis—even when overlaid with the field evaluation or systems theories of creativity derived from Sternberg (1988) and Csikszentmihalyi (1988)—is an individualistic conception of the learner, creative or otherwise. Craft's proposal for creativity as "possibility thinking" (Cremin, Burnard, & Craft, 2006) grows out of developments in "thinking skills," where creativity can become an individual, teachable, metacognitive skill useful for achieving already valued ends. Likewise, Sawyer (2012), while rejecting the false dichotomy of "structure" and "improvisation" in his discussion of expert teaching, nonetheless maintains the binary terms of the relationship between individual autonomy and scripted instruction. Expertise in classroom teaching is conceptualized as individual, disciplined, improvisational performance (Sawyer, 2012, p. 5), consequently underdeveloping the collective and intellectually interdependent nature of disciplinary work.[2] From both perspectives, there is an underemphasis on the collective nature of expert teaching as professional work.

In England, from 1997, the New Labour government of Tony Blair enacted a series of educational reforms designed to change the economic, institutional, and pedagogic structures of schooling, in part by changing the way that teaching as professional work was understood. Although the degree to which the reforms were successful is questionable, the scale and pace of change was ambitious and the levels of funding likely to be unrepeatable for generations: More than £3.8 billion was invested in just one strand of these reforms alone, the National Strategies (Department for Education and Employment, 2001; Department for Education and Skills, 1998; Ellis, 2011b). The National Strategies specified, school term by school term, year by year, *what* and *how* every child should be taught in great detail, often with teacher plans and resources that amounted to scripted instruction. The unprecedentedly high levels of funding for the Strategies (initially focused on literacy and numeracy as "basic skills") led, amongst other things, to literally thousands of lesson plans and other resources becoming available on government websites and hundreds of new textbooks for schools, sold to them as "Strategy-compliant." A national system of heavily scripted training for teachers was complemented by a statutory requirement on university education departments to base their teacher education programs on the Strategy materials. Schools and university education departments were inspected by the government's Office for Standards in Education to assess their degree of compliance with Strategy routines, and penalties (in the form of intensive monitoring, the downgrading of public rankings, the withdrawal of funding and, ultimately, closure) were applied.

From the outset, an integral part of the New Labour reforms to public services such as education was to change what it meant to be a professional—to "transform" professionalism, as Tony Blair's "delivery expert" Michael Barber put it (Barber, 2005, 2007).

From Barber's perspective, throughout the 1970s and 1980s, teachers particularly were "uninformed" occupational groups—professional work in the public services was founded on a poor knowledge base and was inflexible and unresponsive to client (and state) demand (the state-mediated nature of teachers as professionals becoming acutely obvious during the reform period). In his retrospective analysis of the New Labour reforms with which he was so closely associated, Barber (2005, 2007) divided the period into two phases: the first, of "informed prescription" where teachers were unapologetically told what to do in minute detail and punished for noncompliance. Barber referred to this phase of reform as aiming to change teachers' behaviors, not their minds (Stannard & Huxford, 2007): "Hearts and minds" were unimportant considerations when reform was urgent. The first phase included the introduction of the National Strategies in primary and secondary schools. The second phase was to be one of "informed professionalism" where teachers were to be able to exercise their judgment on the basis of lessons learned. This phase corresponded, roughly, to the period when the initial gains in test scores in literacy and numeracy leveled off and teacher morale plummeted, something noted in the government-commissioned evaluation of the Strategies (Earl et al., 2003). It was during this phase that creativity gained a higher profile in the evolving policy framework.

Between 2002 and 2010 (ending with the election of a Conservative-Liberal coalition government), almost one-third of schools in England had contact with a scheme known as Creative Partnerships, a joint enterprise between the Department for Education and the Department of Culture, Media, and Sport (Hatcher, 2011). Creative Partnerships claimed to have worked with over 50,000 teachers and to have provided specific training in "creative teaching and learning" for over 32,000 (Sefton-Green, Thomson, Jones, & Breslin, 2011). It was in receipt of over £160 million of public funds, a fraction of the budget of the National Strategies but a significant sum nonetheless. Creative Partnerships was founded on a belief that teachers, by working alongside a "creative practitioner" (artist, musician, actor, etc.) would encourage "creative learning" across the school curriculum, regardless of subject. Money was invested in local projects and, framed as action research, aimed to improve children's attainment by encouraging "creative learning."[3]

In researching the interventions of Creative Partnerships in schools, Hatcher (2011) and others (e.g., Hall, Thomson, & Russell, 2007) noted a "culture clash" between school teachers and creative practitioners. Creative practitioners sought to enact "competence pedagogies" where collaboration with teachers and students was directed at developing underlying knowledge and specific skills; teachers tended to enact "performance pedagogies," where their interest was in imitating what the creative practitioner did so that the task could be repeated.[4] A superficial appropriation of creative practitioners' cultural tools on the part of school teachers was, as Hatcher noted, hardly surprising given the context of New Labour's educational reforms. Not only had the tight prescription of teaching routines and public measurement of standards produced a situation where teachers' work was focused on "measurable outcomes rather than on the processes of learning" (Hatcher, 2011, p. 407), but associated reforms of economic and institutional structures such as the Academies program were leading to reduced opportunities for collaboration between teachers and schools as market competition was encouraged. The Academies program—loosely based on the American charter school movement—encouraged or coerced schools to opt out of school districts, partner up with commercial or charitable organizations, and sign contracts for the provision of services directly with Secretary of State for Education.

A review by England's National College for School Leadership (NCSL) noted that one of the (in their words "unintended") consequences of the Academies program was that it reduced opportunities for collaboration with teachers outside of their academy (or chain of academies—partnered with the same sponsor) and was also underpinned by a conviction that their particular approach was "always right" (Hill, 2010). Chains of academies, the NCSL report noted, tended to impose a standardized model of teaching. Indeed, sometimes these standardized approaches were branded and sold or traded with "delivery" of teaching on the standardized model being used as a key performance indicator. Lack of student progress was regarded as indicative of low levels of fidelity to the model rather than any deficiency in the model itself. And as the Academies program grew and new schools have been built, architectural designs have increasingly excluded any kind of communal area or meeting place for teachers. Following a recent decision by the Secretary for Education, schools in England no longer have to provide staff-rooms ("for use by the teachers, for the purpose of work and for social purposes") that were once a legal requirement (Bloom, 2012).

Many of the educational reforms in England over the last 15 years have sought to produce teachers as isolated professionals—isolated within their schools, in turn isolated from other schools—and subject to strong vertical accountability. Market competitions between schools (for client parents and their offspring) based on test scores and other quantifiable measures has been encouraged. Hierarchical control and tight prescription of central-ized routines and resources has partly given way in a "second phase" of reform, and creativity has been appropriated as a mode of delivery. The dis-course of delivery—of scripted instruction in order to deliver "results"—is now accented with creativity, but creativity of a very odd kind: a backward-looking creativity where the outcomes are already known (a particular per-centage of the student population achieving the benchmark test score), so that the teacher's challenge is to reverse-engineer their interactions with students to achieve that result.

STIMULATING PROFESSIONAL CREATIVITY

In the context of these reforms, between 2005 and 2008, I was engaged in a formative intervention in the teacher education setting, an interven-tion involving a collaboration between groups of English language and literature teachers in four schools and the students from one teacher educa-tion program (my own). The project was framed as a variation of Devel-opmental Work Research (Engeström, 2007), a methodology designed to stimulate "critical design agency" among participants, a form of agency synonymous with the conception of creativity being developed in this chapter.[5] My intention was to stimulate—or reenergize—the professional creativity of teachers by promoting a collaborative community within the social space of the Developmental Work Research participatory data anal-ysis workshops known as Change Laboratories (Ellis, 2010, 2011a). At a fundamental level, the teachers' participation and my own was sustained by a commitment to the ideas that creativity can be developed relational-ly—through an openness to the new, a willingness to examine the present, and to mutual communication.

In previous reporting of the outcomes of this project, I have emphasized the ways in which joint analysis of the ethnographically generated represen-tations of current practices ("mirror data") surfaced relatively superficial appropriations of key conceptual tools (for language and literacy teach-ers) such as genre. Compliance with the National Strategy reform routines produced genre as a set of rules that needed to be followed in the teaching of writing. New ways of organizing the teaching and learning of writing emerged in the social space of the Change Laboratories arising out of a recovery of a deeper appropriation of genre (on the part of teachers and student teachers) as a recognizable patterns of interaction rather than a "tickable" list of features, and this recovery was then put into an articula-tion with future actions, new ways of organizing the teaching of writing under current conditions. What has been underemphasized in my accounts of the project has been the time taken in the preliminary stages to work with teachers to find a genuine problem of practice, to perceive a problem, or to frame a question before even reaching the stage of reflecting on data that mirrors the problem or question. And this, for me, was the essential preliminary to generating new ideas, preliminary to the possible articulation of an object of activity. The story as I have told it has underemphasized this major shift in perception required on the part of the participating teachers, a shift that required seeing the *possibility* of a shared object, when object is understood as something desirable, motivating, and sense-making. Reaching the point when good intentions (agreeing to engage in development work with me) became what might be called a "need state" (Bratus & Lishin, 1983) was a reciprocal part of the process whereby a potentially shared object might emerge, and the subsequent analysis of contradictions might become productive. The gradual process by which an intentional, future-orientation might emerge—a state some, after Fogel (1993, p. 125), refer to as "anticipatory directionality" (Engeström, 2005)—was *the* essential preliminary stage through which the professional creativity of the teachers was eventually to be realized. And in a context at a time when teachers were not only not required but actively discouraged from engaging in this sort of activity (when fidelity to the standardized model is the sole criterion for professional authority), the time taken for new possibilities to become visible was considerable. In such a context, formative interventions are disruptive at many different levels.

In a discussion of the limits on creativity from a cultural studies and biosemiotic perspective, Wheeler points to the need for institutional and bureaucratic power structures to be continually disrupted:

> As human societies grow into ever more complex forms, they also produce accretions of power—first in institutionalized religion, and then in institutionalized secular bureaucracies and other blocs—whose general effects of vested interests tends towards limitations (first mythic and then rationalized) upon the creativity which all humans are inclined to bring, if at all possible, to their expansive labor on, or in, the world of the human *Umwelt*. (Wheeler, 2006, p. 137)

The methodology for stimulating professional creativity I have been discussing in this section could be described as a disciplined attempt to disrupt existing practices on the basis of a shared commitment to transform the object of activity. In this way, professional creativity in the way I have been conceptualizing it, far from being an idealistic device to reproduce the power and authority of (professional) vested interests and self-serving monopolies, is rather an indication of the responsibility of professions to engage in the "more outward-looking, civic kind of professionalism" Adler et al. (2008, p. 369) has proposed. My discussion of the methodology in this section has not sought to present a simple *panacea* or to recount a victory narrative. Rather, I have tried to indicate the long timescales and close relationships necessary to reach even the preliminary stage in stimulating professional creativity under conditions of New Public Management.

TOWARD A COLLABORATIVE COMMUNITY
OF TEACHING: THE CHALLENGE

In this chapter, and the attempt to elaborate professional creativity as a useful idea, a future-oriented intellectual interdependence has been advanced as intrinsic to professional work. A profession, as a type of collaborative community, must manage at least two directions of activity simultaneously—one that encourages disputation and deliberation among the particular community, a sharing and transformation of intellectual heritages, learning; the other direction, outward, open to peers in other communities and also the wider publics, an expanded collectivity. The "outward-looking, civic kind of professionalism" proposed by Adler et al. (2008, p. 369) is one that might more fully realize the "collaborative ideal" in a context in which the functional pressures of markets and hierarchies have to be addressed. A yearning for a time when professional work meant disciplined performance by autonomous individuals is no longer good enough, if indeed it ever was. At the same time, it is important to recognize that, historically, neither the highest levels of creativity nor the highest levels of professionality have been associated with scientific rationalism, so assertions of future-orientations need to be carefully qualified. As Lektorsky (1999) pointed out, creativity isn't merely an advanced form of scientific rationality that can simply be expressed as modernizing "progress." A great challenge for modernizing states and reform-minded professions is, therefore, one of encouraging democratic debate within and about the goals and purposes of professional activities such as school-teaching rather than defaulting to technical-rationality and the reformist modalities of New Public Management. For the *transformation* of teaching and learning in schools, a consideration of what Lektorsky called "a new type of rationality" would be necessary, the main feature being its "attitude of profound value" (p. 69). Proposing, after Adler and others, value-rationality as the basis of authority for a profession such as teaching requires an acceptance of necessary indeterminacy and openness, of prolonged and expansive cycles of activity time, and of attending to the future rather than continually seeking to measure the present. Therein lies the challenge—and it is a political one.

At a time when university involvement in the professional education of teachers is under threat in some parts of the world (Zeichner & Bier, in press), professional creativity as a concept also suggests both a more engaged and a more critical role for higher education than may be the case at present. Conceiving of the work of university faculty such as teacher educators as stimulating the recognition of breakdowns, contradictions, and disruptions in professional practices, encouraging intellectual interdependence, and facilitating the creation of new ideas and social arrangements that respond to these problems of practice, offers a rather different prospect to the endless production and quality assurance of individual autonomous professionals. Teacher education as a field might, therefore, have a much more significant role than it does at present in producing the conditions for a future-oriented, intellectual interdependence that permits the exercise of professional creativity in school teaching.

NOTES

1. Williams's path-breaking studies of culture were published at the same time as the first English translation of Vygotsky's *Thought and Language* became available. The experimental, school-based pre-service teacher education course that was offered by the London University Institute of Education during the 1970s prescribed *Thought and Language* and Williams's *The Long Revolution* as core texts.
2. Although I believe the criticism of Sawyer's inherent individualism in his discussion of teaching, it is important to acknowledge Sawyer's other efforts to elaborate "group creativity" (Sawyer, 2003) and "group genius" (Sawyer, 2007).
3. For a more detailed enumeration of creativity initiatives in educational policy in England throughout this period, see Craft (2005, pp. 12–14).
4. The contrast might perhaps also be described as one between disciplinary or discipline-specific pedagogies on the part of the creative practitioners or artists and performative pedagogies on the part of the teachers.
5. The project was termed a variation of DWR principally because I was a participant in the activity systems under examination as well as the researcher-facilitator.

REFERENCES

Adler, P. S., & Heckscher, C. (2006). Towards collaborative community. In C. Heckscher & P. S. Adler (Eds.), *The firm as a collaborative community: Reconstructing trust in the knowledge economy* (pp. 11–105). Oxford, England: Oxford University Press.

Adler, P. S., Kwon, S.-W., & Heckscher, C. (2008). Professional work: The emergence of collaborative community. *Organization Science 19*(2), 359–376.

Amabile, T. (1983). A social psychology of creativity: A componential conceptualization. *Journal of Personality and Social Psychology, 45*(2), 357–376.

Ayman-Nolley, S. (1992). Vygotsky's perspective on the development of imagination and creativity. *Creativity Research Journal, 5*(1), 77–85.

Barber, M. (2005). *Informed professionalism: Realising the potential.* Presentation to the Conference of the Association of Teachers and Lecturers. London, England.

Barber, M. (2007). *An instruction to deliver: Tony Blair, the public services and the challenge of delivery.* London, England: Methuen.

Bloom, A. (2012). No more rooms of their own? *Times Educational Supplement, 27 July,* 22–25.

Bratus, B. S., & Lishin, O. V. (1983). Laws of the development of activity and the problems of psychological and pedagogical shaping of personality. *Soviet Psychology, XXV*(2), 91–103.

Craft, A. (2005). *Creativity in schools: Tensions and dilemmas.* London, England: Routledge.

Cremin, T., Burnard, P., & Craft, A. (2006). Pedagogy and possibility thinking in the early years. *Thinking Skills and Creativity, 1*(2), 108–119.

Csikszentmihalyi, M. (1988). Society, culture, and person: A systems view of creativity. In R. J. Sternberg (Ed.), *The nature of creativity: Contemporary psychological perspectives* (pp. 325–339). Cambridge, England: Cambridge University Press.

Department for Education and Employment. (2001). *Framework for teaching English in years 7, 8 and 9 (Key stage 3 national strategy).* London, England: Author.

Department for Education and Skills. (1998). *The national literacy strategy: Framework for teaching.* London, England: Author.

Earl, L., Watson, N., Levin, B., Leithwood, K., Fullan, M., & Torrance, N. (2003). *Watching and learning 3: Final report of the OISE/UT evaluation of the implementation of the National Literacy and Numeracy Strategies.* Prepared for the Department for Education and Skills, England. Toronto: OISE/University of Toronto.

Ellis, V. (2010). Impoverishing experience: The problem of teacher education in England. *Journal of Education for Teaching, 36*(1), 105–120.

Ellis, V. (2011a). Re-energising professional creativity from a CHAT perspective: Seeing knowledge and history in practice. *Mind, Culture and Activity, 18*(2), 181–193.

Ellis, V. (2011b). What happened to teachers' knowledge when they played the literacy game? In A. Goodwyn & C. Fuller (Eds.), *The great literacy debate: A critical response to the literacy strategy and the framework for English* (pp. 27–44). London, England: Routledge.

Engeström, Y. (2005). Knotworking to create collaborative intentionality capital in fluid organizational fields. In M. Beyerlein, S. Beyerlein, & F. Kennedy (Eds.), *Collaborative capital: Creating intangible value: Advances in interdisciplinary studies of work teams* (Vol. 11, pp. 307–336). Bingley, England: Emerald.

Engeström, Y. (2007). Putting activity theory to work: The change laboratory as an application of double stimulation. In H. Daniels, M. Cole, & J. V. Wertsch (Eds.), *The Cambridge companion to Vygotsky* (pp. 363–382). Cambridge, England: Cambridge University Press.

Etzioni, A. (Ed.). (1969). *The semi-professions and their organization: Teachers, nurses, social workers.* New York, NY: The Free Press.

Fogel, A. (1993). *Developing through relationships: Origins of communication, self, and culture.* Chicago, IL: University of Chicago Press.

Freidson, E. (2001). *Professionalism: The third logic.* Cambridge, England: Polity Press.

Hall, S. (1980). Cultural studies: Two paradigms. *Media, Culture and Society, 2,* 57–72.

Hall, C., Thomson, P., & Russell, L. (2007). Teaching like an artist: The pedagogic identities and practices of artists in schools. *British Journal of the Sociology of Education, 28*(5), 605–619.

Hatcher, R. (2011). Professional learning for creative teaching and learning. In J. Sefton-Green, P. Thomson, K. Jones, & L. Breslin (Eds.), *The Routledge international handbook of creative learning* (pp. 404–414). London, England: Routledge.

Hill, R. (2010). *Chain reactions: A thinkpiece on the development of chains of schools in the English school system.* Nottingham, England: National College for School Leadership.

Hoggart, R. (1957). *The uses of literacy: Aspects of working class life.* London, England: Chatto & Windus.

Hoyle, E. & John, P. (1995). *Professional Knowledge and Professional Practice.* London, England: Cassell.

Johnson, T. (1972). *Professions and power.* Basingstoke, England: Macmillan.

John-Steiner, V. P., & Meehan, T. M. (2000). Creativity and collaboration in knowledge construction. In C. D. Lee & P. Smagorinsky (Eds.), *Vygotskian perspectives on literacy research* (pp. 31–50). Cambridge, England: Cambridge University Press.

Jones, K. (2011). Capitalism, creativity and learning: Some chapters in a relationship. In J. Sefton-Green, P. Thomson, K. Jones, & L. Breslin (Eds.), *The Routledge international handbook of creative learning* (pp. 15–26). London, England: Routledge.

Kaufman, J. C., & Beghetto, R. A. (2009). Beyond big and little: The four C model of creativity. *Review of General Psychology, 13*(1), 1–12.

Kaufman, J. C., Beghetto, R. A., Baer, J., & Ivcevic, Z. (2010). Creative polymathy: What Benjamin Franklin can teach your kindergartener. *Learning and Individual Differences, 20,* 380–387.

Lektorsky, V. A. (1999). Activity theory in a new era. In Y. Engeström, R. Miettinen, & R.-L. Punamaki (Eds.), *Perspectives on activity theory* (pp. 65–79). Cambridge, England: Cambridge University Press.

McLaughlin, K., Osborne, S. P., & Ferlie, W. (2002). *New public management: Current trends and future prospects.* London, England: Routledge.

Sawyer, R. K. (2003). *Group creativity: Music, theatre, collaboration.* Mahwah, NJ: Erlbaum.

Sawyer, R. K. (2007). *Group genius: The creative power of collaboration.* New York, NY: Basic Books.

Sawyer, R. K. (2012). *Explaining creativity: The science of human innovation.* Oxford, England: Oxford University Press.

Sefton-Green, J., Thomson, P., Jones, K., & Breslin, L. (2011). Introduction. In J. Sefton-Green, P. Thomson, K. Jones, & L. Breslin (Eds.), *The Routledge international handbook of creative learning* (pp. 1–8). London, England: Routledge.

Smolucha, F. (1992). A reconstruction of Vygotsky's theory of creativity. *Creativity Research Journal, 5*(1), 49–67.

Stannard, J. & Huxford, L. (2007). *The Literacy Game: The story of the National Literacy Strategy.* London, England: Routledge.

Sternberg, R. J. (Ed.). (1988). *The nature of creativity: Contemporary psychological perspectives.* Cambridge, England: Cambridge University Press.

Thompson, E. P. (1963). *The making of the English working class.* London, England: Victor Gollancz.

Valsiner, J., & Van der Veer, R. (2000). *The social mind: Construction of the idea.* Cambridge, England: Cambridge University Press.

Van der Veer, R., & Valsiner, J. (1991). *Understanding Vygotsky: A quest for synthesis.* Oxford, England: Blackwell.

Vygotsky, L. S. (1994). Imagination and the creativity of the adolescent. In R. Van der Veer & J. Valsiner (Eds.), *The Vygotsky reader* (pp. 266–288). Oxford, England: Blackwell.

Vygotsky, L. S. (2004). Imagination and creativity in childhood. *Journal of Russian and East European Psychology, 42*(1), 7–97.

Wheeler, W. (2006). *The whole creature: Complexity, biosemiotics and the evolution of culture.* London, England: Lawrence & Wishart.

White, V. (2006). *The state of feminist social work.* Abingdon, England: Routledge.

Williams, R. (1958). *Culture and society 1780–1950.* London, England: Pelican Books.

Williams, R. (1965). *The long revolution.* London, England: Pelican Books.

Willis, P. (1977). *Learning to labour: How working class kids get working class jobs.* New York, NY: Columbia University Press.

Willis, P., Jones, S., Canaan, J., & Hurd, G. (1990). *Common culture: Symbolic work at play in the everyday cultures of the young.* Buckingham, England: Open University Press.

Zeichner, K., & Bier, M. (in press). The turn towards practice and clinical experience in US teacher education. *Swiss Journal of Teacher Education.*

12 Collective Concept Formation as Creation at Work

Yrjö Engeström

"I would like to buy a bag of spink," said Pippi. "But I want it nice and crunchy."

"Spink," said the pretty lady behind the counter, trying to think. "I don't believe we have that."

"You must have it," said Pippi. "All well-stocked stores carry it."

"Yes, but we've just run out of it," said the lady, who had never even heard of spink but didn't want to admit that her shop wasn't as well-stocked as any other.

"Oh, but then you did have it yesterday!" cried Pippi eagerly. "Please tell me how it looked. I've never seen spink in all my life. Was it red striped?"

Then the nice lady blushed prettily and said, "No, I really don't know what it is. In any case, we don't have it here."

(Lindgren, 1997, p. 216)

"The realized activity is richer and truer than the consciousness that precedes it."

(Leont'ev, 1978, p. 78)

Concept formation and conceptual change are classic topics in studies of cognition and learning. They are traditionally approached within the framework of what Greeno (2012, p. 311) calls "formal concepts," referring to "a cognitive entity that has a reference class that is determined by an explicit definition and that is used in a system of formal deductive reasoning—that is, a system that uses formal logic or mathematics to derive implications of assertions."

Perhaps because of this particular framework, the relationship between concept formation and creativity (or creation) has seldom been addressed. Prominent texts on concepts and concept formation (e.g., Carey, 2009; Mareschal, Quinn, & Lea, 2010; Murphy, 2004) typically do not have the terms *creativity* or *creation* in their indices.

On the other hand, in his *Explaining Creativity,* Sawyer (2012) does take up concepts, specifically conceptual combination. "It's creative to combine two concepts to make a single new one; for example, a 'boomerang flu' is a flu that goes away and then returns." (Sawyer, 2012, p. 116) Combining concepts may indeed be creative. However, in many cases, including that of "boomerang flu," the combination seems mainly to serve the clarification and communication of an already created idea or concept to a wider audience. In this chapter, I argue that the creative potential of concepts and concept formation is radically greater than that depicted by accounts of conceptual combination.

Studies of concept formation may be mapped with the help of the diagram presented in Figure 12.1. The "formal concepts" characterized by Greeno (2012) belong largely to the lower left-hand quadrant of the diagram. Concepts formed within and between complex activities (Engeström & Sannino, 2012), or "functional concepts" (Greeno, 2012), are typically collective. Such a concept "contributes to the way the participants organize their understanding of what they are doing" (Greeno, 2012, p. 311). This chapter focuses on the formation of such collective functional concepts, specifically ones that have a high degree of cultural novelty.

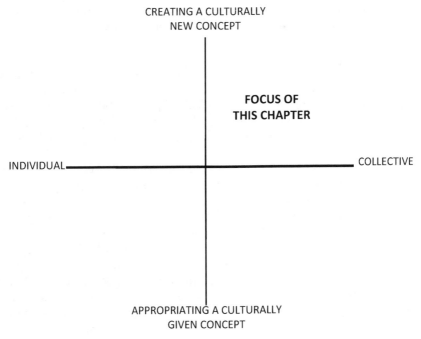

Figure 12.1 Mapping the field of studies of concept formation.

Concept formation in the upper right-hand quadrant of Figure 12.1 may be seen as creation of new worlds, condensed or crystallized in a future-oriented concept. The future-orientation is most vividly seen in *concept cars*, made to showcase new styling and or new technology and shown at motor shows to gauge customer reaction to new and radical designs that may or may not have a chance of being produced (Edsall, 2003). Similarly, a new scientific concept proposed by researchers to capture and explain the essence of a phenomenon is future-oriented in that it calls for further elaboration, testing, extensions, instrumentations, and implementations as well as critiques (e.g., Nersessian, 2012). The Gothic cathedral is another example:

> The building becomes modified in imagination so as to accept topological projections from the theological space. Over generations and generations, theologians elaborate this blend, and those who present the theology use it. The result is a fabulous emergent concept—namely, the Gothic cathedral, a structure that in many complex interacting ways is fused in the blend with Christian theology. (Fauconnier & Turner, 2002, p. 208; also Scott, 2011)

Collective concept formation within and between complex activities is typically a long process in which the concept itself undergoes multiple transformations and partial stabilizations. This type of creation transcends the boundary between the mental and the material. The concept typically radiates outward, finding extensions and practical applications that stretch the boundaries of the concept and make it a constantly moving target.

This chapter deliberately uses the term creation instead of the term creativity. The notion of creation calls for attention to the actions of creating rather than to the possible psychological properties of the subject who creates. Forming new concepts in the way described in this chapter is both an endeavor of collective learning and a creative process of generating something culturally new.

In workplaces, practitioners must increasingly frequently become involved in the reshaping of their work and organizations. Significant transformations in work may be understood as formation and implementation of new collective concepts. In organizational literature, this type of concept formation is often discussed in terms of shifts in organizational archetypes (e.g., Greenwood & Hinings, 1993). Archetype theory has, however, been criticized for its functionalist bias and lack of attention to human agency (Kirkpatrick & Ackroyd, 2003). I find this critique largely justified. Typical studies of changing organizational archetypes discuss various structural and societal forces as factors that lead to transitions from one archetype to another; the practitioners with their efforts at making sense and shaping their own futures are largely neglected. The archetypes themselves are categorized in extremely broad and general terms, without the substantive, contextual, and historical specificity we witness when the concept formation and learning done by real, identifiable practitioners are taken as the focus of study.

In our studies of collective formation of culturally new functional concepts at work (Engeström, Nummijoki, & Sannino, 2012; Engeström, Pasanen, Toiviainen, & Haavisto, 2005), we have observed an interesting phenomenon that is partially captured by the story quoted as a motto at the beginning of this chapter, namely the story of Pippi Longstocking discovering the spink (Lindgren, 1997). Pippi had a name (the spink) but did not know what it represents. In some cases, collective concept formation seems indeed to move with the name of the concept in the lead, as if in search for contents for the name. In other cases, concept formation seems to move practically in the opposite order, with the embodied and enacted novel practice in the lead, but not having a name for it. The name may be attached to this novel practice only much later. In practically all cases we have encountered, there is some sort of a gap or discrepancy between the textual definition and the practical enactment of the emerging new concept.

In this chapter, I examine this curious discrepancy and the oddly opposite looking directions of concept formation, with the aim of constructing an explanatory framework for further analyses of the dynamics of collective concept formation as creation. I develop my argument with the help of data from concept formation efforts in two work organizations, namely the library of the University of Helsinki and home care service for the elderly in the city of Helsinki.

In the next section, I sketch a set of theoretical tools for examining concept formation as movement in space. I then introduce the two cases and the data I build on. After that, I examine dynamics of concept formation in each case in turn. Finally, I discuss the relationship between the two cases as well as the implications of my analysis for our understanding of creativity and learning at work.

CONCEPT FORMATION AS MOVEMENT IN SPACE

There are at least two important theories that treat concept formation as continuous movement. These are the dialectical theory of ascending from the abstract to the concrete (Davydov, 1990; Il'enkov, 1982) and the theory of cognitive trails formulated by Cussins (1992, 1993). Both of these theories are foundational for the analysis presented in this chapter.

For Il'enkov and Davydov, a fully developed theoretical concept, or a genuine theoretical generalization, is based on a "cell" that represents a complex system in a simple, "pure" form. Such a cell retains all the basic characteristics and relationships of the whole system. It is also an ever-present, common part of the whole. Davydov (1990) developed these insights into a fully elaborated theory of generalization and concept formation. His view of the process of theoretical generalization may be summarized with the help of Figure 12.2.

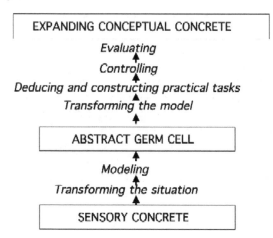

Figure 12.2 Summary of Davydov's view of theoretical generalization (Engeström, 2009, p. 326).

In Davydov's analysis, theoretical concept formation is a multistep process in which an abstract germ cell is first constructed by means of transforming the initial situation experimentally and analytically, and then modeling the emerging idea. The cell is studied by testing and transforming the model. Subsequently, the cell is used to construct increasingly complex extensions and applications, as well as to reflect on and control the very process of generalization. The process leads to rich, continuously expanding living systems, the conceptually mastered concrete. This process of ascending from the abstract to the concrete is also the core of the model of expansive learning (Engeström, 1987).

Cussins's theory of cognitive trails is a philosophical theory of embodied cognition where the basic metaphor is that of a person moving in a territory. The key concepts are perspective-dependence and stabilization.

Imagine a person standing somewhere in the middle of a city. The person's ability to find his or her way to any desired location regardless of the person's initial position is called perspective-independence. In such case, the perspective-dependence ratio is high—close to 1. The perspective-dependence ratio is close to zero when the person is completely unable to find his or her way to any desired location in the territory. People learn to move around in a territory by moving around in the territory. In so doing, they make cognitive trails.

> Trails are both person-made and world-made, and what makes persons and worlds. Trails are in the environment, certainly, but they are also *cognitive* objects. A trail isn't just an indentation in a physical surface, but a *marking* of the environment; a signposting for coordinating sensation and movement, an experiential line of force. Hence the marking is both experiential and environmental. . . . Each trail occurs over time, and is a manipulation or a trial or an avoidance or capture or simply a

movement. It is entirely context-dependent . . . Yet a trail is not transitory (although a tracking of a trail is): the environmental marking persists and thereby the ability to navigate through the feature-domain is enhanced. (Cussins, 1992, p. 673–674)

As multiple trails are marked, some trails intersect. Intersections are landmarks. A territory is structured by means of a network of landmarks. Such structuring means increasing the perspective-dependence ratio.

Along with the perspective-dependence ratio, there is another dimension that characterizes the development of cognitive trails, namely stabilization. Stabilization may also be characterized as blackboxing:

Stabilization is a process which takes some phenomenon that is in flux, and draws a line (or builds a box) around the phenomenon, so that the phenomenon can enter cognition (and the world) in a single act of reference. (Cussins, 1992, p. 677)

There comes a time when it is best to stabilize a network of trails so that the space is treated cognitively (functions) as a given unit (an object!), and then build higher-order feature-spaces . . . One familiar and important way in which stabilization is achieved is by drawing a linguistic blackbox around a feature-space: the imposition of linguistic structure on experiential structure. . . . A region of feature-space starts to function as an object as it is dominated by a network of trails and stabilized by a name. (Cussins, 1992, p. 679–680)

In Figure 12.3, the point of maximum generality is depicted with the help of an oval. This is where objects, concepts, and explicit propositions emerge.

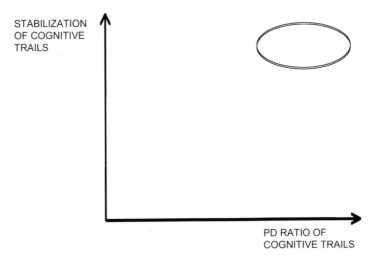

Figure 12.3   Generality as high perspective-dependence ratio and high stabilization (Cussins, 1992, p. 683).

Cussins depicts cognition as *appropriate spiraling* in the two-dimensional terrain depicted above. He calls this movement "virtuous representational activity."

> The course of a cognitive phenomenon (a dynamic, representational activity) may be plotted on a graph whose axes are the PD [for perspective-dependence] ratio of the cognitive trails and the degree of stabilization of the cognitive trails. Let us suppose that an activity starts out with low PD ratio and low stabilization. As the field starts to become structured—the creatures start to find their way around a landscape (as the theorist would say)—PD ratio will increase. A network of cognitive trails is temporarily established, and this provides for the possibility of stabilization. Both stabilization and PD ratio continue to increase, until the work concentrates almost entirely on the stabilization of trails that are in place. However, once a network of trails is tightly stabilized it becomes less flexible, and as the nature of the field of activity changes over time, PD ratio will start to decrease as stabilization increases. Further improvement in way-finding will then require that a stabilized region of cognitive trails be established for a period of time in order to allow PD ratio to increase again. In other words, *virtuous* representational activity is the effective trade-off of the relative merits and demerits of PD ratio and stabilization. Virtuous activity may itself be represented as a figure, a shape, in the two-dimensional space of the PD ratio/stabilization graph. It is not hard to see that the virtuous form of representational activity has the shape of a spiral. (Cussins, 1993, p. 249–250)

In workplaces engaged in transformation efforts, cognitive trails are typically made in multiparty encounters, discussions, and debates. The trails become manifest when there are attempts at stabilization and generalization. In other words, collectively and discursively produced cognitive trails are identifiable by attempts at articulation of explicit ideas or concepts, typically in the form of proposals or definitions.

Davydov's theory regards concept formation primarily as a vertical process. It may be criticized for its lack of attention to the horizontal dimension of debate and hybridization between multiple perspectives and traditions. On the other hand, Cussins's theory says little about the quality of different concepts and about the specific actions or steps that need to be taken in order to create a theoretical concept that goes beyond mere description and classification of superficial features of the terrain. Both Davydov and Cussins pay little attention to the existence of historically earlier concepts and trails, made and defended by often powerful institutions and ideologies that have to be confronted and sometimes forcefully rejected and reshaped in the process of creating a new, expansive concept.

However, these two theories brought together provide a powerful foundation for further work. Both Davydov and Cussins emphasize two characteristics that are crucial for the purposes of this chapter. First, both of these authors see concept formation as a lengthy, indeed practically unending, process of stepwise stabilization (and subsequent destabilization) of an emerging concept. Second, both Davydov and Cussins see concept formation as a process that transcends the divides between mental and material, between mind and body. For these authors, concept formation operates not only with symbols, words, and language; it is grounded in embodied action and artifact-mediated enactment in the material world.

These observations lead me to propose a general theoretical hypothesis about the creative dynamics of collective concept formation within and between complex activities. According to this working hypothesis, such concept formation may be regarded as movement in a space defined by means of two dimensions, namely the dimension of stabilization (the vertical dimension in Figure 12.4) and the dimension of representational modality (the horizontal dimension in Figure 12.4).

Any frozen sample of or moment in the process of collective concept formation may be placed in the appropriate quadrant of Figure 12.4. However, the true potential of the diagram should be found by using it to analyze and depict movement—progression of collective concept formation from one quadrant to another. I try to accomplish this in the rest of this chapter.

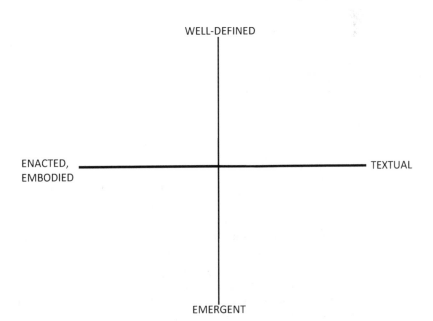

Figure 12.4   Formation of functional concepts as movement along two dimensions.

TWO CASES: SETTINGS AND DATA

My first case stems from a project conducted between 2009 and 2012 in the library of University of Helsinki. In 2009, the library management asked my research group to conduct an intervention study that would help the library professionals and managers in their efforts to redefine the services, ways of working, and organization of the library. We conducted a Change Laboratory intervention first in the campus library of biosciences, then in the central campus library that serves humanities, social sciences, and behavioral sciences. This chapter focuses on the Change Laboratory intervention conducted in the central campus library.

The Change Laboratory is a formative intervention method aimed at triggering and fostering an expansive learning process in which the participants analyze the contradictions of their activity system and develop a new model for it (Engeström, 2007). An activity system refers to the relatively durable formation of people focused on shaping a shared object with particular instruments, rules, and division of labor. The dynamic internal relations of activity systems are often modeled with the help of the triangular diagrams used in Figures 12.5 and 12.6 (Engeström, 1987).

The digitization of information and the emergence of powerful web-based tools of information storing and searching have led to a radical decrease in researchers' physical visits to the library and also in their use of physical books and journals. A gap has emerged between researchers and academic libraries. This contradictory situation is schematically depicted in Figure 12.5.

Within a period of two months, we held eight Change Laboratory sessions. To discuss experiences of implementation of solutions designed in the Change Laboratory, we held two follow-up sessions several months later. The first as well as the two last sessions and the follow-up sessions were held with the library staff only. The other sessions were held with both the library staff and various combinations of representatives of the four pilot research groups—Cognitive Science, Communication Law, Finnish Language, and Gender Studies. Our raw data consists of videotapes of the eight Change Laboratory sessions and two subsequent follow-up sessions. The videotapes were transcribed. In this chapter, I build on earlier analyses of this data (Engeström et al., 2012; Engeström, Rantavuori, & Kerosuo, 2013).

My second case stems from three successive intervention research projects on the Helsinki City municipal home care, initiated in 2006 and still continuing. Helsinki home care supports elderly people who live at home with various kinds of medical problems. The task is complicated by the fact that the population of Finland is aging very rapidly, and it is increasingly difficult to recruit and retain competent home care workers. When the home care worker encounters his or her elderly client, time is spent mainly to help the client in bathing and/or toileting,

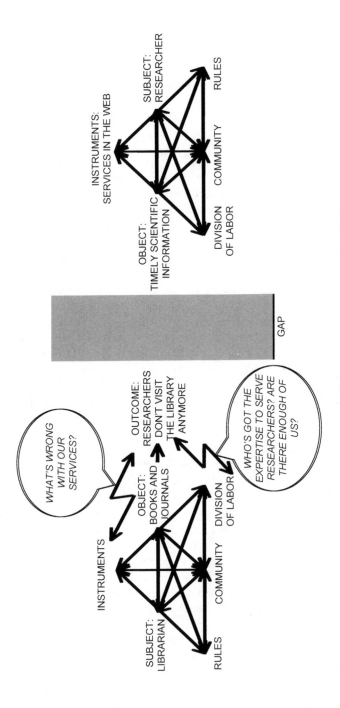

Figure 12.5 Contradictions of the activity system of the library.

feeding, giving medications to the client, and informing the client about other possible services. Fulfilling these tasks usually takes up all the time of the home care worker, leaving little opportunity for him or her to focus on the clients' broader needs and risks. The big problems of loneliness, immobility, and dementia are typically left in the shadow of the necessary minimum tasks. Thus, there is a growing tension between the fragmented services delivered and the holistic needs of the clients (Nummijoki & Engeström, 2010). This contradictory situation is schematically depicted in Figure 12.6.

A paradox of home care practice is that home care workers perform daily chores *for* the clients although they know that getting up from the chair and doing these daily chores *with* the worker would support the elderly clients' mobility and functional capacity. In our projects, the facilitation of the client's *physical mobility* emerged as the most advanced attempt at constructing and implementing a new concept to transcend the contradictions of home care. The transformation attempt is built on practical introduction of a new tool kit, the mobility agreement and systematic mobility exercises, in regular home care visits. In these encounters, both the worker and the client face the challenge of conducting new actions. The home care worker presents to the client the simple idea of agreeing to do regularly certain physical exercises, embedded in normal household chores, with the support of the home care worker and a visual booklet. The exercises are initiated right away. The embedding and anchoring of these exercise actions into the daily routines takes time and needs to be persistently pursued.

The core data consists of videotaped home care visits, recorded while or after the mobility agreement was introduced. These visits represent the home care workers' and clients' early efforts to include mobility exercises in their daily routines. We have scrutinized in detail a sample of 13 such videotaped home care visits conducted in 2008 and 2009. To get access to the longitudinal process of concept formation, we recorded a follow-up home care visit to a 87-year old client. During this visit, besides the regular services and mobility exercises, the emphasis was on joint reconstruction of the client's and the home care workers' experiences of implementing the mobility agreement over the past two years. These reconstructions are backed up and enriched with the help of the patient records and nurses' notes of this client. In this chapter, I build on earlier analyses of this data (Engeström et al., 2012; Engeström & Sannino, 2011; Nummijoki & Engeström, 2010).

The detailed procedures of data analysis are explained in the original studies on which this chapter builds. In the library case, the original analyses were focused on the longitudinal dynamics of learning actions and construction of the object over the course of the successive Change Laboratory sessions. In the home care case, the original analyses were focused on the discursive dynamics of concept formation within singular home care visits.

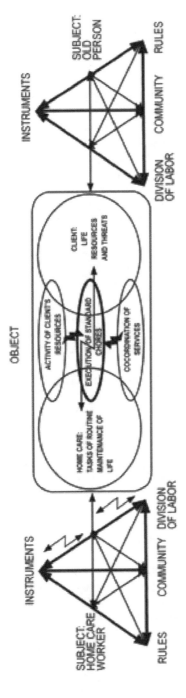

Figure 12.6   Contradictions in the activity system of the home care (Engeström & Sannino, 2011, p. 383).

THE LIBRARY CASE: CONCEPT FORMATION
WITH THE NAME IN THE LEAD

In the library case, the working hypothesis of our project was that research groups do in fact need new kinds of library services to master large and complex sets of data as well as the demands of information search, electronic publishing, evaluation of one's own research, and visibility in the scientific community. Our preparatory analysis led us to assume that the present object of the library's work with researchers was an individual researcher's discrete request for publications or publication-related information. The needed new object would be a long-term partnership with a research group needing support in the management of data, publishing, and following the global flow of publications. This new object would require a new division of labor, new competences, and a new organization model for the library—a new concept was needed for the library services aimed at researchers.

We researchers suggested *knotworking* as the name of this new concept. "The notion of knot refers to rapidly pulsating, distributed and partially improvised orchestration of collaborative performance between otherwise loosely connected actors and activity systems" (Engeström, Engeström, & Vähäaho, 1999, p. 346; see also Engeström, 2008) In knotworking, services would be coconstructed and continuously reconfigured in flexibly changing collaborative formations or partnerships between librarians and research groups. In recent discussions of the future of libraries, a related concept has been suggested, namely *embedded librarianship* (Kvenild & Calkins, 2011; Shumaker, 2012).

The notion of knotworking resembles to some extent the idea of "adhocracy" (Mintzberg, 1979; Toffler, 1970; see also Dolan, 2010), commonly defined as an organizational philosophy or style characterized by adaptive, creative, and integrative behavior which, in contrast to a bureaucratic style, is flexible and nonpermanent. However, the notion of knotworking is less romantic and more specific, defined by the characteristics of (1) pulsating movement of tying, untying, and retying together otherwise separate threads of activity and expertise needed for a task, typically between service providers and their key clients, (2) being not reducible to any specific individual or organizational entity as the center of control—the center does not hold, there is change in the locus of initiative from moment to moment, (3) requiring both rapid problem-driven improvisation and a shared long-term commitment, perspective, or plan, and (4) operating by means of negotiation and flexible agreements.

Key managers and staff members of the library quickly adopted the idea of knotworking as a starting point for the change effort, and the entire project was named Knotworking in the Library. Yet, besides a brief introduction to the idea at the beginning of the Change Laboratory process, we did not attempt to define or fix the exact contents of the concept. The name knotworking became somewhat like the spink of Pippi Longstocking.

Table 12.1 Frequency of Use of the Terms "Knot" and "Knotworking" in the Change Laboratory Sessions

Session 1	1
Session 2	0
Session 3	1
Session 4	1
Session 5	3
Session 6	6
Session 7	13
Session 8	13

The frequencies of the use of the terms knot and knotworking in the eight Change Laboratory sessions (excluding use of the name of the project) are shown in Table 12.1.

The table shows a marked increase in the use of the key notions knot and knotworking, starting in session 5 and culminating in sessions 7 and 8. Perhaps more interesting, in the early sessions these terms were practically exclusively used to refer to collaboration *with external clients*, the research groups. But starting in session 6, the term began to be increasingly used to actually envision the way the librarians wanted to learn to work and interact *within the library and across the boundaries of the different university campus libraries*. This shift was something the interventionists did not expect or plan. The shift is manifested in key excerpts from a follow-up session of the Change Laboratory.

Librarian 4: Now we have founded in the spring a joint editorial team, with the approval of P [director of the Central Campus Library] and A [director of the Viikki Science Campus Library]. At the moment it has members from the Central Campus and from Viikki, but of course we hope to get members from other campuses as well. We have met once and interacted a lot in other forms. So far we have done fine-tuning [in the web pages] and added information concerning the Central Campus, so that it is not anymore just a service for Viikki. [. . .] Our dream is to make it a good tool that we can genuinely offer to researchers. . . .

Interventionist: Who is the leader of the editorial team?

Librarian 4: [laughing] I don't know if we actually have a leader. . . .

Library director: It is a self-organizing editorial team. . . .

Librarian 4: We wanted to make it. We have these different levels, the level of the whole university library and the campus level. Sometimes this causes rigidity. So we thought that we will make a somewhat unofficial, grassroots level [. . .] Actually we put together a knot here, around this problem. We thought that if we get something very official, it will not make progress, and we wanted it to go forward.

A similar shift in the notion of knotworking appears also in the talk of the library director in the following excerpt.

Library director: What we have learned from this knotworking with research groups (the clients), and I actually hope it will happen, is that we will get similar thinking rooted inside our own organization. . . . We wouldn't demand anymore a hierarchical administrative approach always when there is a new problem to solve . . . Instead, we have clear development responsibilities and within those people have the possibility to quite freely form such knot-like small groups across the responsibility boundaries. We aim at a certain kind of self-organizing capability . . . And in some areas this is already becoming visible. Such ad-hoc groups have emerged.

These excerpts illustrate how the concept of knotworking had to some extent been appropriated by the librarians as a mediating means in their expansive learning effort. When the concept was first introduced to the librarians, it was just an abstract idea. Later on in the excerpts presented above, they adopted the concept as mediating means serving a practical agentive effort of their own. At the same time, the meaning of the concept has been expanded. It is no more just a call for collaboration and coproduction with research groups. Such externally oriented effort has now been grounded and founded on a new perspective of working closer to home, within the library organization. One might say that a somewhat idealistic notion of knotworking has been expanded downward, so that it has its feet on the ground. The elusive, skeletal name has begun to gather flesh and blood around it.

In the follow-up session of the Change Laboratory, the library director asked the participants whether they should continue using the term knotworking or change the name. The decision was made to keep this term as it was working for them. By questioning her personnel whether to continue using this word knot or to find some other word, the director acknowledged that the term was brought to them; it did not fully belong to them, and it came from somewhere else. Yet the term was by now to a large extent perceived as *their own*. This indicates that there has been literally an appropriation of the notion of knotworking by the participants, appropriation understood as making something one's own. The knot for them is still a concept in the making, rather than a fully formed concrete concept. But the excerpts of the librarian and the director indicate that the knot is progressively filled with both theoretical contours and empirical contents.

The story of Pippi Longstocking discovering spink is not unique. The search for an unknown or poorly grasped object that has a name but not a very clear shape is an important theme in literature. Melville's (1949) *Moby Dick* is a classic example. The white whale is mythical, yet also all too real and material. Carroll's (2011) *The Hunting of the Snark* is a humorous version of the theme. The national epic of Finnish folklore, the *Kalevala*, contains a core story of the search for mythical Sampo (see Engeström, 2005). In all these cases, the elusive object has a well-established name. To become a concept, the name cries for material, social, and discursive embodiment. The library case demonstrates that this can be a workable path also in the collective creation of a new concept for a work activity facing serious contradictions. Those who initially introduce the name should just be aware that the concept will most likely take shape in ways that do not fully correspond to their initial expectations. Such deviations and shifts are exactly what is needed to make it a concrete, expanding concept rather than merely an administratively sanctioned shell.

The library case may now be examined in the framework of the two dimensions of movement depicted in Figure 12.4. The idea of knotworking initially suggested by the researchers and adopted by representatives of the library was an emergent textual notion. It was available as a preexisting abstract idea, explained in publications. On the other hand, for the participants, it was an emergent notion in that its general contours were not easily transfered and concretized in the context of practical work in the library. Thus, the initial notion of knotworking is placed in the lower right-hand quadrant in Figure 12.7.

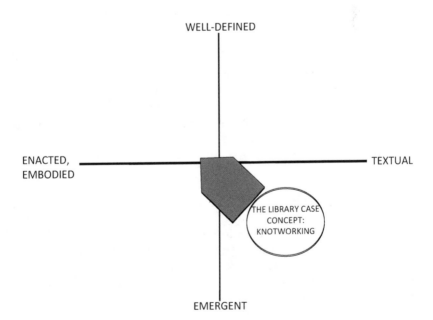

Figure 12.7 The movement of the concept of knotworking in the library case.

The notion of knotworking was gradually concretized and reshaped by the library practitioners. The initially abstract textual notion became materially enacted and embodied in the practical initiatives of the practitioners and the director. In this process, the idea of knotworking began also to gain a sharper and more stable shape. The stabilization of the concept was in its fairly early stages when we concluded our project. The core idea of knot as the potential germ cell of the new concept was still mainly specified by means of examples rather than modeled as a general principle. Thus, the arrow in Figure 12.7 shows the concept moving toward the lower and, at least tendentially, also the upper left-hand quadrants of the diagram.

THE HOME CARE CASE: CONCEPT FORMATION
WITH PRACTICE IN THE LEAD

In the home care case, our observations of interactions between nurses and clients led us to suggest a possible germ cell of a new concept of physical mobility of the elderly.

> We suggest that getting up from the chair, or sit-to-stand, may be such a germ cell for the emerging conceptualization of mobility and functional capacity within home care for the elderly. This means that the transformation effort in home care may be analyzed as a process of expansive concept formation at work. (Nummijoki & Engeström, 2010, p. 68)

In home care encounters, standing up from the chair (or sit-to-stand) emerges as a germ cell because in practice one has to get up to reach the upright position in order to move. It is foundational for any other kind of physical movement. In other words, it can be seen as the smallest and simplest initial unit of a complex totality, as something ubiquitous, so commonplace that it is often taken for granted and goes unnoticed and as opening up a perspective for multiple applications, extensions, and future developments.

Perhaps the most demanding criterion of a germ cell is that it must carry in itself the foundational contradiction of the complex whole. In standing up from the chair, this is the contradiction between the motives of safety and autonomy. For the subject, the contradiction typically manifests itself as a critical conflict between fear of falling and the need to move. The safety motive leads one to use furniture as support to make standing up from the chair easier and safer—which also means that one becomes increasingly dependent on external support. The autonomy motive leads one to rely on one's own muscles when standing up from the chair, which is harder and riskier but also fosters one's independence. From the home care worker's time-pressured point of view, this contradiction appears as tension between getting the job done quickly and safely versus investing in additional, perhaps risky efforts that may subsequently pay off in the form of improved autonomy of the client. Neither component of the contradiction can be eliminated. Safety and autonomy both repel and require one another.

In our in-depth analysis of the follow-up home care visit to an 87-year old client (Engeström et al., 2012), we used the actions involved in ascending from the abstract to the concrete as an analytical grid with the help of which we identified passages of talk and physical interaction during the visit relevant to this type of concept formation. In the video and transcript of the home care visit, we identified passages that represent the actions of questioning, modeling, examining the model, implementing, and reflecting on the process. We named these five types of actions as (1) articulating a conflict of motives, (2) forming a germ cell, (3) examining the germ cell model, (4) implementing the model by ascending to the concrete, and (5) reflecting on the process and its outcomes. Because of the retrospective nature of the conversation in this visit, the transcript did not contain here-and-now questioning and analysis of the existing practice. Instead, it contained important segments in which the original experiencing of the conflict of motives was recollected, both emotionally and analytically.

An aggravated conflict of motives—remaining in bed versus remaining autonomous—made standing up a vital focus of joint efforts at the beginning of this particular client's case. After that, standing up from the chair has remained a solid core and object of reflection in the client's expanding mobility.

The germ cell was formed through repeated collaborative physical enactment. The bodily action schemas and associated physical artifacts (chairs, tables, stairs, utensils, mirrors) served as a rich reservoir for mediation and material anchoring. This does not mean that the concept formation process was nonverbal or unarticulated. Physical enactments were regularly accompanied by verbal exchanges between the client and the nurse, and the reflective verbal reconstruction of events and experiences of the past two years was a crucial component of the process.

In our analysis of the home care visit, we identified segments that represent six trails of expanding from the abstract germ cell of standing up from the chair toward the concrete concept of mobility. The outcomes of our analysis are summarized in Figure 12.8.

Figure 12.8 depicts ascending from the abstract to the concrete not simply as a vertical progression. Movement from the abstract germ cell toward the concrete is depicted as multidirectional, star-like expansion by means of trails in space. This view connects the dialectical theory of concept formation with the ideas of cognitive trails (Cussins, 1992).

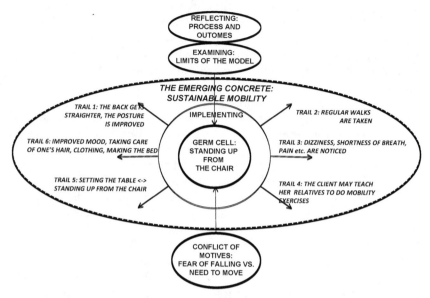

Figure 12.8   Ascending from the abstract to the concrete in the home care case (Engeström et al., 2012, p. 304).

The new concept of mobility still does not have a fixed verbal label or an authorized description. However, several facts indicate that we are actually dealing with a genuinely expansive new concept, taking shape and having an impact in the multiorganizational field of home care in the City of Helsinki and beyond. The Helsinki Health Centre's mobility agreement effort was awarded with the Mayor's Prize for Achievement in 2010. The Helsinki Health Centre Strategy and Balanced Score Card document for 2011–2013 states: "Home care clients have a care-plan which includes the mobility agreement. Measure for monitoring this is sit-to-stand test as part of the mobility agreement: First measurement in first quarter and the final measuring in fourth quarter of the year, and the results will be recorded in electronic health database." The Finnish National Audit Office's Report (2010, p. 97) mentions the Helsinki home care model and the regular sit-to-stand exercises as recommended advances. All this means that the efforts of individual clients and their nurses are spearheads of much broader conceptual change.

What is new and creative in the concept being developed in the daily encounters between old people and their home care workers? First of all, the emerging new concept is a way to transcend and overcome the contradiction between safety and autonomy, or between fear of falling and the need to move. Smart movement overcomes the fear for movement. Second, the new concept embeds and integrates mobility into necessary everyday chores and actions, into the flow of the life activity of the old person. It is not movement and exercise as separate actions aimed at improvement of physical condition; it is movement necessarily needed to get by. Third, the new concept sees mobility as accomplished and largely performed together, jointly between the client and the home care worker (or some significant other). It is not mobility of an isolated individual. This social distribution is also material distribution, relying on often innovative uses of everyday household artifacts such as chairs, tables, stairs, mirrors, and utensils. Finally and perhaps most important, the new concept frames physical mobility in terms of sustainability rather than in terms of achievement and competition. We might actually call the new concept *sustainable mobility*.

Knowledge and good intentions alone seldom lead to significant change in routine behavior, especially when the change seems to require increased work and effort. As Leont'ev (1978, p. 65) emphasized, the formation of effective intentions and goals is "not an instantaneous act but a relatively long process of approbation of the goals by action and by their objective filling." Citing Hegel, Leont'ev pointed out that a person "cannot determine the goal of his acting as long as he has not acted" (p. 65). He concluded that "the realized activity is richer and truer than the consciousness that precedes it" (p. 78). The home care case shows that collective concept formation may well proceed with practical actions first, and the naming and textualization following only later.

The home care case may now be examined in the framework of the two dimensions of movement depicted in Figure 12.4. The starting point in this case was in enacted physical mobility exercises, centered around the crucial initial step of standing up from the chair. The new notion of mobility was initially very emergent and diffuse. This starting point is located in the lower left-hand quadrant in Figure 12.9.

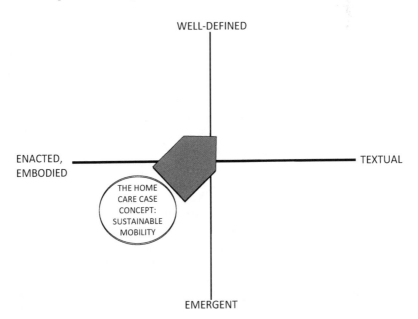

Figure 12.9   The movement of the concept of sustainable mobility in the home care case.

As practitioners and researchers reflected on the experiences and evidence gained in these embodied practical encounters, standing up from the chair began to take shape as the initial abstraction or germ cell of the new concept. The articulation of this germ cell is depicted in Figure 12.9 with the help of the arrow moving from the lower left-hand quadrant into the upper left-hand quadrant of the diagram. The reaching of the arrow toward the upper right-hand quadrant expresses the ongoing attempts at naming and textually stabilizing the new concept.

CONCLUSION: COLLECTIVE CONCEPT FORMATION AS CREATION

Figures 12.7 and 12.9 represent two patterns of movement in collective concept formation at work. In the first case, the formation of the concept of knotworking in the library of the University of Helsinki moved with the name in the lead, toward concretization and expansion in practical actions. In the second case, the formation of the concept of sustainable mobility for the elderly in the home care of Helsinki moved with practical embodied actions in the lead, toward a well-defined germ-cell core and eventually also toward textual stabilization.

These patterns may indicate that the movement does not seem to have to happen in a particular order or direction. It may be that the most important challenge of collective concept formation is to ensure in the long-run movement across all the quadrants. This may eventually lead to something like a combination of a high persepective-dependence ratio and high degree of stabilization in Cussins's (1992, 1993) terminology (see Figure 12.3).

On the other hand, even if the starting point may be in any of the four quadrants, there may still be a dominant directionality in the process of concept formation. Both cases discussed in this chapter seem to move clockwise around the intersection of the two dimensions. This might be seen as corresponding to the basic logic of ascending from the abstract to the concrete (Davydov, 1990), or expansive learning (Engeström, 1987).

Both cases, the first one proceeding with the name in the lead, the second one with practice in the lead, led to significant accomplishments of creation that have changed the patterns of activity in the respective settings. This indicates that both routes of collective concept formation can serve expansive learning and creation of culturally novel practices. The process of creation is not restricted to a single path.

In recent discussions of creativity, the distinction between the Big-C creativity of prominent individuals and the little-c everyday creativity has played an important role. Kaufman and Beghetto (2009) suggest that there are more variations than these two. Their notion of professional expertise as an intermediate "Pro-c" creativity is of particular interest. Unfortunately, these authors still subscribe to the linear notion of gradual individual transition from a novice to an expert: "The concept of Pro-c is consistent with the expertise acquisition approach of creativity . . . This approach suggests that prominent creators require 10 years of preparation in a domain of expertise to reach world-class expert-level status" (Kaufman & Beghetto, 2009, p. 5).

If we abandon the individual as a privileged unit of analysis and redirect our analytical gaze to real transformations in work and organizations, we gain a very different angle on work-related creativity. Creativity appears as practititoners' and their clients' collective efforts and struggles to redefine the idea of their activities—to construct and implement qualitatively new concepts to guide and organize the work practice. This kind of creativity cannot be neatly located in a standard scale from Big C to small c, simply because the individualist unit of analysis of that very scale is inadeaquate. Collective concept formation at work is creation in the sense of forging the future, building new worlds of work while dwelling in those worlds.

In this chapter, I have argued that concept formation, collective learning, and creation may be regarded as aspects of one and the same process of expansive transformation of work activities from the ground up, by practitioners and their clients or partners. This does not give us a license to ignore critical distinctions. What exactly is creative about concept formation within processes of expansive learning needs to be demonstrated by means of evidence on the cultural novelty and practical transformative power of the concept formed. Much work needs to be done on the sustainablity, spread, and consequences of new functional concepts created in ways similar to the processes described above.

ACKNOWLEDGMENTS

The research on which this chapter is based has been financially supported by the University of Helsinki Center for Properties and Facilities (project Knotworking in the Library, PI Yrjö Engeström), by the Finnish Funding Agency for Technology and Innovation Tekes (project Implementation Conditions of Integration Innovations in Health Care: Organizational Volition and the Voice of the Client, PI Yrjö Engeström), and by the Academy of Finland (project Concept Formation and Volition in Collaborative Work, PI Yrjö Engeström).

REFERENCES

Carey, S. (2009). *The origin of concepts*. Oxford, England: Oxford University Press.
Carroll, L. (2011). *The hunting of the snark*. London, England: Tate Publishing.
Cussins, A. (1992). Content, embodiment and objectivity: The theory of cognitive trails. *Mind, 101*, 651–688.

Cussins, A. (1993). Nonconceptual content and the elimination of misconceived composites. *Mind & Language, 8*, 234–252.

Davydov, V. V. (1990). *Types of generalization in instruction: Logical and psychological problems in the structuring of school curricula.* Reston, VA: National Council of Teachers of Mathematics.

Dolan, T. E. (2010). Revisiting adhocracy: From rhetorical revisionism to smart mobs. *Journal of Futures Studies, 15*(2), 33–50.

Edsall, L. (2003). *Concept cars: From the 1930s to the present.* Lyndhurst, NJ: Barnes & Noble.

Engeström, Y. (1987). *Learning by expanding: An activity-theoretical approach to developmental research.* Helsinki, Finland: Orienta-Konsultit.

Engeström, Y. (2005). Introduction: In search of the Sampo. In Y. Engeström (Ed.), *Developmental work research: Expanding activity theory in practice* (pp. 9–14). Berlin, Germany: Lehmanns Media.

Engeström, Y. (2007). Putting Vygotsky to work: The change laboratory as an application of double stimulation. In H. Daniels, M. Cole, & J. V. Wertsch (Eds.), *The Cambridge companion to Vygotsky* (pp. 363–382). Cambridge, England: Cambridge University Press.

Engeström, Y. (2008). *From teams to knots: Activity-theoretical studies of collaboration and learning at work.* Cambridge, England: Cambridge University Press.

Engeström, Y. (2009). The future of activity theory: A rough draft. In A. Sannino, H. Daniels, & K. D. Gutiérrez (Eds.), *Learning and expanding with activity theory* (pp. 197–211). Cambridge, England: Cambridge University Press.

Engeström, Y., Engeström, R., & Vähäaho, T. (1999). When the center does not hold: The importance of knotworking. In S. Chaiklin, M. Hedegaard, & U. J. Jensen (Eds.), *Activity theory and social practice: Cultural-historical approaches* (pp. 345–375). Aarhus, Denmark: Aarhus University Press.

Engeström, Y., Kaatrakoski, H., Kaiponen, P., Lahikainen, J., Laitinen, A., Myllys, H., . . . Sinikara, K. (2012). Knotworking in academic libraries: Two case studies from the University of Helsinki. *Liber Quarterly, 21*(3/4), 387–405.

Engeström, Y., Nummijoki, J., & Sannino, A. (2012). Embodied germ cell at work: Building an expansive concept of physical mobility in home care. *Mind, Culture, and Activity, 19*(3), 287–309.

Engeström, Y., Pasanen, A., Toiviainen, H., & Haavisto, V. (2005). Expansive learning as collaborative concept formation at work. In K. Yamazumi, Y. Engeström, & H. Daniels (Eds.), *New learning challenges: Going beyond the industrial age system of school and work* (pp. 1–43). Kansai, Japan: Kansai University Press.

Engeström, Y., Rantavuori, J., & Kerosuo, H. (2013). Expansive learning in a library: Actions, cycles and deviations from instructional intentions. *Vocations and Learning, 6*(1), 81–106.

Engeström, Y., & Sannino, A. (2011). Discursive manifestations of contradictions in organizational change efforts: A methodological framework. *Journal of Organizational Change Management, 24*(3), 368–387.

Engeström, Y., & Sannino, A. (2012). Concept formation in the wild. *Mind, Culture, and Activity, 19*(3), 201–206.

Fauconnier, G., & Turner, M. (2002). *The way we think: Conceptual blending and the mind's hidden complexities.* New York, NY: Basic Books.

Greeno, J. G. (2012). Concepts in activities and discourses. *Mind, Culture, and Activity, 19*(3), 310–313.

Greenwood, R., & Hinings, C. R. (1993). Understanding strategic change: The contribution of archetypes. *Academy of Management Journal, 36*(5), 1052–1081.

Il'enkov, E. V. (1982). *The dialectics of the abstract and the concrete in Marx's Capital.* Moscow, Russia: Progress Publishers.

Kaufman, J. C., & Beghetto, C. A. (2009). Beyond big and little: The four C model of creativity. *Review of General Psychology, 13*(1), 1–12.

Kirkpatrick, I., & Ackroyd, S. (2003). Archetype theory and the changing professional organization: A critique and alternative. *Organization, 10*(4), 731–750.

Kvenild, C., & Calkins, K. (Eds.). (2011). *Embedded librarians: Moving beyond one-shot instruction.* Chicago, IL: Association of College and Research Libraries.

Leont'ev, A. N. (1978). *Activity, consciousness, and personality.* Englewood Cliffs, NJ: Prentice-Hall.

Lindgren, A. (1997). *The adventures of Pippi Longstocking.* New York, NY: Viking.

Mareschal, D., Quinn, P. C., & Lea, S. E. G. (Eds.). (2010). *The making of human concepts.* Oxford, England: Oxford University Press.

Melville, H. (1949). *Moby Dick.* New York, NY: Simon & Schuster.

Mintzberg, H. (1979). *The structuring of organizations: A synthesis of the research.* Englewood Cliffs, NJ: Prentice-Hall.

Murphy, G. L. (2004). *The big book of concepts.* Cambridge, England: The MIT Press.

National Audit Office's Report. (2010). *Vanhuspalvelut. Säännöllinen kotihoito [Services for older citizens: Regular home care].* Helsinki, Finland: Valtiontalouden tarkastusvirasto [National Audit Office].

Nersessian, N. J. (2012). Engineering concepts: The interplay between concept formation and modeling practices in bioengineering sciences. *Mind, Culture, and Activity, 19*(3), 222–239.

Nummijoki, J., & Engeström, Y. (2010). Towards co-configuration in home care of the elderly: Cultivating agency by designing and implementing the mobility agreement. In H. Daniels, A. Edwards, Y. Engeström, T. Gallagher, & S. Ludvigsen (Eds.), *Activity theory in practice: Promoting learning across boundaries and agencies* (pp. 47–71). London, England: Routledge.

Sawyer, R. K. (2012). *Explaining creativity: The science of human innovation* (2nd ed.). Oxford, England: Oxford University Press.

Scott, R. A. (2011). *The Gothic enterprise: A guide to understanding the medieval cathedral.* Berkeley: University of California Press.

Shumaker, D. (2012). *The embedded librarian: Innovative strategies for taking knowledge where it's needed.* Medford, NJ: Information Today.

Toffler, A. (1970). *Future shock.* New York, NY: Random House.

Contributors

Harry Daniels is professor of education in the Department of Education at the University of Oxford and a fellow of Green Templeton College. Professor Daniels' chief research interests are: sociocultural and activity theory; innovatory learning in the workplace; special needs and social exclusion; and social, emotional, and behavioral difficulty, including exclusion from school.

Anne Edwards is professor of educational studies in the Oxford University Department of Education where she co-convenes the Oxford Centre for Socio-cultural and Activity Theory Research. She has written extensively on professional learning in schools and in interprofessional settings, drawing primarily on cultural historical accounts of learning and practices. Her most recent work has focused on the nature of relational expertise and how common knowledge is built and employed by professionals who are able to collaborate on complex problems.

Viv Ellis is professor and head of education at Brunel University in London, UK and was until recently co-convener of the Oxford Centre for Sociocultural and Activity Theory Research. He is also a visiting professor at Bergen University College in Norway. His current research interests focus on teacher learning with particular reference to broader understandings of professionalism and the relationships between higher education and schools. His new book *Transforming Teacher Education: Reconfiguring the Academic Work* will be published by Bloomsbury in 2014.

Yrjö Engeström is professor of adult education at University of Helsinki, Finland and professor emeritus of communication at University of California, San Diego. Engeström was awarded an honorary professorship by University of Birmingham, UK, in 2000 and an honorary doctorate by University of Oslo, Norway, in 2005. He is known for his theory of expansive learning and for the methodology of developmental work research. His current research is focused on learning and development in transformations of work, particularly in collaborative relations between multiple activity systems.

Gerhard Fischer is professor in the department of computer science, fellow of the Institute of Cognitive Science, and director of the Center for Life-Long Learning & Design at the University of Colorado, Boulder. He is a member of the Computer Human Interaction Academy and a fellow of the Association for Computing Machinery. His research interests include: lifelong learning, design, meta-design, software design, creativity, social creativity, distributed intelligence, human-computer interaction, and design-for-all.

Silke Geithner is a postdoctoral research fellow at Dresden University of Technology, Department of Organization Studies, Germany (since 2009). She studied adult education and business administration. Her research mainly focuses on the transformation of work and the impact on learning and development, the integration of individual and collective learning at work from an activity-theoretical approach, and participatory learning methods (e.g., serious playing); she has several years of experience in research and supervision of change projects in medium-sized companies and public administration.

Kai Hakkarainen is a professor of education at the University of Turku, Department of Education. Hakkarainen has carried out research on knowledge-creating learning from elementary to higher education and professional networks. His and collaborators' many investigations have addressed how learning and human intellectual resources can be expanded by sharing of cognitive efforts and using cognitive "prostheses" based on skilled use of information and communication technologies.

Kaisa Hytönen is a PhD student at the University of Turku, Department of Education. She works as a researcher in a project that examines higher and further education and professional expertise in emerging knowledge-intensive fields. Her dissertation focuses on examining horizontal and vertical transitions during expert careers. Her research interests involve networked expertise and professional learning and development.

Karin Johansson is a postdoctoral research fellow and the director of artistic research at the Department of Music Education and Performance, Malmö Academy of Music, Lund University, Sweden. Following her PhD thesis "Organ Improvisation—Activity, Action and Rhetorical Practice" (2008), she now works with the project "(Re)thinking Improvisation," funded by the Swedish Research Council and the international research network Choir in Focus. She is a performing organist with special interests in early and contemporary music.

Peter Johnson is professor of computing science at the University of Bath. He is a distinguished visiting scientist at the UK Defence Science and Technology Laboratory and holds an appointment as a member of the Defence Scientific Advisory Council of the Minister of Defence. His research interests are: collective capability, human computer systems, autonomous systems, social media in emergency response, shared knowledge and energy reduction, and predicting disruption in complex manufacturing processes through the analysis of informal communications.

Sten Ludvigsen is professor at InterMedia, University of Oslo. He has specialized in sociocultural perspectives on learning, cognition, and development. He undertakes research about how to use digital learning resources in and between colocated and distributed settings, in the educational sector and workplace settings. He is former director of InterMedia (2004–2009), and he has led the National Research School in Educational Science (2008–2012). Currently, he leads the research group CHANGE at the Faculty of Education, University of Oslo.

Juho Makkonen is a student of education at the University of Helsinki. He is currently pursuing a longitudinal investigation of doctoral students' experiences of pursuing monograph versus article theses in the field of education.

Reijo Miettinen is professor of adult education in the Institute of Behaviourial Sciences of the University of Helsinki and works in the Center for the Research on Activity, Development and Learning. His research group has studied network collaboration, producer-user relationships, and learning in innovation processes. His recent publications include *Dialogue and Creativity: Activity Theory in the Study of Science, Technology and Innovations* (Lehmanns, 2009) and *Innovation, Human Capabilities and Democracy: Towards an Enabling Welfare State* (Oxford University Press, 2013).

Monika Nerland is professor of the department of educational research, University of Oslo, where she currently leads the research group for workplace learning. She specializes in research on knowledge cultures and learning in professional education and work, and has recently been the leader for the project Learning Trajectories in Knowledge Economies (LiKE, 2008–2011), funded by the Research Council of Norway. This project conducted comparative studies of knowledge practices and learning in four professions: nursing, teaching, computer engineering, and accountancy.

Annalisa Sannino is academy research fellow at the Centre for Research on Activity, Development, and Learning in the Institute of Behavioural

Sciences at University of Helsinki. In her recent work, she focuses on the emergence of agency and on the dynamics through which discourse leads to envisioning and implementing material changes in educational and work activities. She is the leading editor of the volume *Learning and Expanding with Activity Theory* (coedited with Harry Daniels and Kris Gutierrez), published in 2009 by Cambridge University Press.

Klaus-Peter Schulz is associate professor of strategy and innovation at ICN Business School in Nancy and Metz, France. His research is related to workplace education and organizational learning. He particularly focuses on learning and development processes and methodologies in different types of enterprises and nonprofit organizations. Prior to his university career, he was program manager for innovation and organizational development at an international pharmaceutical company.

Pirita Seitamaa-Hakkarainen is professor of craft studies in the Department of Teacher Education, University of Helsinki. She is also a docent at Aalto University. Her research interests focus on expert-novice differences in designing, as well as the facilitation of collaborative design through technology-enhanced learning environments.

Marc Thompson is academic director of the MSc Consulting and Coaching for Change at the Said Business School, Oxford University. He is a fellow and academic tutor at Green Templeton College where he codirects the Future of Work research program. Marc teaches on and directs a range of innovative customized programs, mainly for science and technology organizations.

Hal White is an independent scholar who has specialized in preparing manuscripts, PhD theses, academic articles, and books for publication since the early 1990s. His efforts are concentrated in his degree area, the field of educational psychology.

Katsuhiro Yamazumi is professor of education at Kansai University in Osaka, Japan. Drawing on a framework of cultural-historical activity theory and its interventionist methodology, he studies historically new forms of pedagogical practice and also explores interventions in a hybrid educational project called "New School," which attempts to transform traditional school learning. Additionally, his intervention research investigates teachers' expansive learning and professional development, moving beyond an encapsulated concept of traditional school learning and the institutional boundaries of school organizations.

Author Index

Subject Index